THE
ELECTIONS

OF

2000

Series on Law, Politics, and Society
Christopher P. Banks, Editor

THE
ELECTIONS
OF
2000

*Politics, Culture, and Economics
in North America*

EDITED BY
MARY K. KIRTZ,
MARK J. KASOFF,
RICK FARMER, AND
JOHN C. GREEN

The University of Akron Press
Akron, Ohio

Manufactured in the United States of America
First edition 2006

09 08 07 06 05 5 4 3 2 1

Library of Congress Cataloging-in-Publication Data

The elections of 2000 : politics, culture, and economics in North America / edited by
Mary Kirtz ... [et al].— 1st ed.
    p. cm. — (Series on law, politics, and society)
  Summary: "Collection of original essays on the year 2000 elections in Mexico, the
United States, and Canada"—Provided by publisher.
  Includes bibliographical references and index.
  ISBN 1-931968-19-5 (cloth : alk. paper)
  ISBN 1-931968-30-6 (paperback : alk. paper)
  1. Elections—North America. 2. North America—Economic integration.
3. Regionalism—North America. 4. Elections—Canada. 5. Elections—United States.
6. Elections—Mexico. I. Kirtz, Mary, 1943– II. Series.
  JJ1018.E44 2004
  324.97'0054—dc22   2004021380

The paper used in this publication meets the minimum requirements of American
National Standard for Information Sciences—Permanence of Paper for Printed Library
Materials, ansi z39.48—1984. ∞

CONTENTS

FIGURES

TABLES

Preface

THE ESSAYS IN THIS COLLECTION are the product of a conversation among scholars, spanning national borders and disciplinary boundaries, about the increasing integration of Canada, Mexico, and the United States and the development of a "continental perspective." This conversation has been underway for some time, reflecting the causes, challenges, and consequences of economic, cultural, and political integration in North America. The conjunction of national elections in all three of the great North American democracies in 2000 offered us the opportunity to deepen this conversation and engage in scholarly discourse from a "continental perspective."

A teleconference entitled *"The Political, Economic, and Cultural Impacts of the Recent Elections in Canada, Mexico, and the United States: Perspectives from Three Nations,"* held April 12, 2002, embodied this new approach. The event was coordinated at the University of Akron, in the United States, with teleconference links to University of Windsor, Canada, and Universidad de las Americas-Puebla, Mexico. The video transcript of this unusual conference is available on CD-ROM from the Ray C. Bliss Institute of Applied Politics at the University of Akron. Earlier drafts of some of the chapters in this collection were delivered at the teleconference, but other materials appear only in the transcript or in this book. Thus, these two sources are separate and complementary products of our conversation.

This project was co-sponsored by the Ray C. Bliss Institute of Applied Politics at the University of Akron and the Ohio Canadian Studies Roundtable, a joint project of the Canadian Studies Programs at the University of Akron and Bowling Green State University, Ohio. At the University of Akron, Kim Haverkamp, Tom Kemp, and Michelle Daley made important contributions. The Ohio Canadian Studies Roundtable provided invaluable assistance with the able efforts of Sonia Dial. We also owe a special thanks to our colleagues at the University of Windsor, Stephen Brooks, and at the Universidad de las Americas–Puebla, José Garcia Aguilar.

The project was partially funded with grants awarded by the Department of Foreign Affairs and International Trade of the Government of Canada. Special thanks go to M. Jean Labrie, Head of the Canadian Studies International Academic Relations Division, Ottawa; Dr. Daniel Abele, Academic Relations Officer, Canadian Embassy, Washington, D.C.; and Mr. Dennis Moore, Public Affairs Officer, Consulate General of Canada, Detroit, Michigan.

Janet Bolois of the Bliss Institute and Waubgeshig Rice, a Canadian intern, who came to the University of Akron through the auspices of the International Council of Canadian Studies, deserve recognition for their work on the manuscript, and we are deeply appreciative of the efforts of Michael J. Carley and his colleagues at the University of Akron Press.

We were privileged to participate in this conversation, and we hope our modest efforts will encourage its extension and deepening in the future.

Mary K. Kirtz
Mark J. Kasoff
Rick Farmer
John C. Green

Part I

Prologue

Toward a Continental Perspective

Mary K. Kirtz, Mark J. Kasoff, Rick Farmer,
and John C. Green

E ACH OF THE THREE MAJOR COUNTRIES on the North American continent—Mexico, Canada, and United States—held a national election in the year 2000, providing a rare opportunity to consider the possible emergence of a "continental perspective." Such a perspective has been widely discussed since the 1994 enactment of the North American Free Trade Agreement (NAFTA). What were the commonalities and differences underlying the politics, cultures, and economies of the three great North American democracies? How might these patterns be revealed in the elections of 2000? What were their implications for the future of North Americans? These questions were posed to a group of interdisciplinary colleagues in all three countries, and this collection of essays represents some of their answers.

Anthony DePalma provides an introduction to these issues in his essay "Reluctant Trinity." The elections of 2000 revealed the growth of common interests among Mexico, Canada, and the United States, and the prospects for greater cultural and economic integration. At the same time, the elections also revealed the individuality of each political system, the rivalries among national leaders, and the limits of cooperative policies. The Mexican election had the largest impact on these continental relationships, partly because the election suggested that Mexican democracy was perhaps moving closer to that of its neighbors. Also intriguing is the prospect that Mexico will develop a "special relationship" with the United States, much like the "special relationship" that has long existed between Canada and the United States.

More importantly, each of these elections was about the legitimacy of the government. On the one hand, the Mexican election produced a historic change in power: the victory of Vicente Fox and the National Action Party (PAN) represented the first defeat for the ruling Institutional Revolutionary Party (PRI) since the establishment of the present Mexican government in 1929. This election was about the very nature of the Mexican regime.

On the other hand, the Canadian national election produced routine results: the sitting prime minister, Jean Chrétien, dissolved parliament at a propitious time and won a large victory to stay in power. This election was not primarily about the nature of the Canadian regime, but rather about the choice of leaders. The victory strengthened the Liberal Party's hold on power and increased national unity in Canada.

The 2000 American election fell somewhere between the Mexican and Canadian elections, raising some questions about the legitimacy of the regime while changing the party in power. The unanticipated closeness of the election and the disputed ballots in Florida made the election of Republican George W. Bush highly suspect in the minds of many Americans, and yet the transition of power caused no disruption of the government.

Alejandro Moreno describes the "coalition for change" that elected Vicente Fox and allowed the first opposition party in modern Mexican history to occupy power. The "coalition for change" was surprisingly diverse, dominated by strong demands for democratization. Diverse coalitions were also a theme in the American election, dubbed "a contest of surprises" by Rick Farmer and John Green. In defiance of pre-election expectations, George Bush and Al Gore fought to a tie—one that was only broken by a controversial Supreme Court decision. In contrast, the Canadian election was a more typical affair. Lydia Miljan finds that the Canadian media distracted voters by emphasizing trivial rather than substantive issues in the campaign, while Brian Tanguay reports on the unexpected success of the Liberals in Quebec and its consequences for the sovereignty movement. This result may have further legitimized the Canadian regime.

Despite the different contexts, some common themes emerged. In all three elections, cultural factors played a prominent role, often to a greater extent than expected. For example, religion played an important role in all three campaigns. Economic issues were also a key feature in these elections, especially the role of government in maintaining prosperity. These common themes sketch the outlines for the development of a continental perspective in the future.

In terms of culture, Mary Kirtz and Carol Beran take an in-depth look at one aspect of this development: the presence of Canadian and Mexican culture in the United States. They find considerable evidence that American popular culture is deeply influenced by its neighbors through immigration and language. Steve Brooks describes a similar phenomenon: a convergence of the political style between Canada and the United States. Based on election rhetoric, Brooks argues a convergence of U.S.–Canadian values, a trend that may extend to Mexican leaders as well.

Mark Kasoff reviews the impact of economic factors on the politics of the three nations. He offers a detailed picture of the economic forces, especially trade, that are slowly and steadily integrating North American markets. However, he concludes that such economic integration is unlikely to lead to political integration in the future. Isidro Morales provides a deeper exploration of these issues in post-2000 Mexico. He examines NAFTA and plans for its expansion, concluding that it may be difficult for the new administration to deliver on its promises, given the politicization of trade and new foreign policy initiatives.

Manuel Orozco offers an epilogue to this discussion with a reminder that North America includes more than the three largest democracies. In "Beyond Trinity," he explores elections and parties in Central America. Democratization is also underway in these nations, many with a history of authoritarian regimes. Within each national context, elected leaders seek to cope with the forces of cultural and economic integration.

Of course, this collective raises as many questions as it answers. For example, will democratization further expand or retard the development of a continental perspective? Or will the march of cultural and economic integration overcome the uniqueness of each of the North American democracies? And how are these two issues related? These essays are intended to provide the basis for future exploration of these crucial matters.

CHAPTER 1

Reluctant Trinity:
The North American Elections of 2000

Anthony DePalma

The United States is destined to have a 'special relationship' with Mexico, as clear and strong as we have with Canada.

—*George W. Bush,* August 25, 2000

THE STRING OF EXTRAORDINARY EVENTS that took place in 2000 seemed both to affirm the mounting awareness of a North American consciousness and neatly bring to a close the painful first years of the new American continent. The most visible and portentous manifestation of that continental conversion was the series of three almost concurrent national elections in 2000. The first was held in Mexico in July. Then, in November, both Canada and the United States elected leaders, although it wouldn't be until almost the end of the year that Americans knew George W. Bush would become their next president.

The last time the electoral processes of all three nations of North America had been so finely synchronized was in 1988. The national leaders elected that year—George H. W. Bush, Brian

Mulroney, and Carlos Salinas de Gortari—shared a vision of a more integrated North America. Their awareness of the opportunities offered by working together rather than standing apart eventually led to the signing of the North American Free Trade Agreement (NAFTA) in 1994. Twelve years later, the electoral calendars again coincided, and the leaders selected by voters this time—George W. Bush, Jean Chrétien, and Vicente Fox Quesada—each recognized that a strong North American identity was a vital national interest in their respective countries. Each made plans to strengthen and deepen relations across the continent, while protecting the sovereignty of their own nations. Each also faced other challenges, of course, starting with the domestic divisions that had prevented them from receiving a majority of the popular vote in their countries and developing a clear mandate to govern. Bush and Fox had to work with deeply divided congresses, while Chrétien faced a parliament that was badly splintered along regional lines, as well as continued fragmentation of the Canadian political landscape. The key words for all three were "unite" and "compromise."

Their simultaneous starts generated a certain synergy within North America. The words and actions of these three men over the course of the year harmonized the continent in a way that hadn't been possible before. United in an encompassing vision and unafraid to exploit the advantages of the new North American relationship, each laid out plans and took initial steps that could come to be seen as a significant turning point in the history of continental America.

Someday, the first few days of July may very well be observed as a continental holiday; the communal celebration of North America's rediscovery. July 4 is, of course, U.S. Independence Day, and in Canada, July 1 is Canada Day: the commemoration of the founding of the Dominion of Canada. From now on, Mexicans may be tempted to view July 2 as their own "independence day" and the founding of a democratic Mexico. On that date in the year 2000, the land of Zapata had its first peaceful revolution, ending the Institutional Revolutionary Party's (PRI) seventy-one-year grip on power and setting the stage for a true democracy with the election of Fox's National Action Party (PAN).

Fox's own myth had already grown large enough to become fairly well known across North America in 2000. A larger-than-life rancher and business executive who once headed the Mexican division of that most American of consumer products, Coca-Cola, Fox entered Mexican politics on the side of the fiscally conservative, Catholic-leaning National Action Party, the perennial runner-up during the last half century of Mexican politics. He had caught the attention of journalists and their editors early on, and no American or Canadian article about Fox failed to mention his cowboy boots or the trucker-sized belt buckle with FOX carved into it that he wore constantly. From his earliest days in politics, Fox made clear that he was not afraid to go toe-to-toe with the PRI, and the indomitable PRI was just as clearly frightened by the combination of *pantalones* and popular appeal that Fox embodied. Fox ran for governor of his home state of Guanajuato in 1991, but the election was marred by fraud, and President Salinas appointed a substitute governor, Carlos Medina, also from the PAN. This kept Fox from governing a small state, but it didn't derail his ambitions or his party's certainty that he was the man who could defeat the PRI. When President Salinas wanted to overhaul the land redistribution provisions of Article 27, he needed the PAN's support to get the necessary two-thirds vote in Congress. PAN leaders saw this as an opportunity to remove a remnant of Mexican xenophobia that prohibited a candidate without pure Mexican heritage from running for president. That included Fox, whose grandfather was an Irish-American immigrant from Ohio and whose mother was born in Spain. Salinas was forced to accept that amendment in order to get his land reform passed. But he insisted that the new requirements for candidates not take effect until the elections of 2000. Having waited so long, the PAN could afford to be patient a while longer.

Even though he couldn't form an opposition alliance with Cuauhté-moc Cárdenas, Fox overcame PRI candidate Francisco Labastida's early lead. His surge in popularity wasn't due to the unique appeal of his platform; very little light showed between the positions of Fox and Labastida on economic management, social spending, and Mexico's links with the rest of North America. Fox ran a smart American-style campaign, while Labastida seemed stuck in the past. Mexico had already changed substantially, and a great deal of that political, economic, and social transformation had taken place since 1993. Many factors contributed to Fox's historic win, but the primary reason was that Mexicans had finally made up their minds that it was time for a change. On July 2, they gave Fox the victory he—and many parts of Mexico—had sought for so long.

Traditional PRI leaders were left licking their wounds after July 2. Many blamed Ernesto Zedillo, the accidental president, for losing control of the system that had served the party so well for so long—a system attacked by President Fox in January when his government accused the oil workers' union and Pemex of siphoning money from the government-owned oil monopoly to help finance Labastida's campaign. With his popularity plummeting, Fox needed something like an anti-corruption campaign to rally the people again. Immediately after the election, he had been hailed as a hero: the strong man Mexicans wanted to lead their country into democracy and prosperity. But few observers were willing to express any caution or to remember that Mexico had been in a similar position in 1993, when Carlos Salinas was praised for having brought Mexico to the threshold of the First World. Fox had made so many promises during the campaign that to complete them would take sixty years, not the single six-year term to which he was limited by the constitution.

He had style and charisma, but Fox was also so wrapped up in his own personality that at times he could resemble the *caudillos* with whom Mexico has had such a troubling relationship for so long. When he took the oath of office on December 1 he offended Congress—where the PRI was still powerful enough to obstruct his plans—by changing the official oath and including the pledge to work "for the poor and marginalized of this country," words not included in the constitutional version of the oath that he was required to recite. While many Mexicans agreed with the sentiment, they worried about Fox's obvious comfort with doing things his own way. The controversy also marked the beginning of a stalemate between Fox and Congress that continues today.

What Fox had accomplished by winning was so significant that most Mexicans, along with foreign observers watching his early moves, were willing to overlook some of his more glaring inconsistencies. What he lacked in discipline, he more than made up for in courage and vision—for Mexico and for the whole of North America. With the help of President Zedillo, he managed a smooth transition that broke the thirty-year cycle of economic disasters accompanying new presidents. But having escaped that spell, Fox and Mexico rushed headlong into a steep economic slowdown. Mexico, now hitched to the bumper of the U.S. economy, was being dragged along behind as its neighbor's economy skidded off track. What helped Mexico survive that rough first year was the confidence investors had in the country's institutions and structures, and the relative stability of the peso, which set it apart from most other emerging markets.

During the five months between the election in July 2000 and his December inauguration, Fox visited Washington and Ottawa. He declared that Mexico saw itself as a legitimate and full member of the North American community: "There is no doubt that NAFTA is not only a commitment for us; it is a partnership."[1] He said he not only supported NAFTA 100 percent, he also declared that it was time to deepen and strengthen the agreement so that the benefits of free trade were more equitably shared across the continent. During his stopover in Washington he surprised Mexico's own diplomatic staff at the embassy in Washington by telling U.S. President Bill Clinton that he was already looking beyond NAFTA toward the European Union, or something like it: "Really what we are proposing is an economic convergence, a holistic view of the problems and the opportunities, and pursue at the end a narrowing of the gap in development between Mexico and the two great nations of the United States and Canada."[2] He tried to sweep away the old shibboleths of Mexican sovereignty and anti-Americanism in one stroke. Perhaps not immediately, he said, but in forty years it would make sense for Mexico, Canada, and the United States to have open borders, like those in Europe, which allow for the free passage of both goods and people from one country to the other. Perhaps, he suggested, North America could be seen as a continent with common interests and shared resources benefiting all North Americans from the Yukon to the Yucatan.

Fox was also blunt about the new reality of North America. The United States and Canada needed Mexican labor, he stated, and Mexicans needed more economic opportunity than Mexico could provide. Fox wanted Washington and Ottawa to fund a development bank that would help Mexican industry grow. In essence, he was asking the U.S. and Canada to take some responsibility for Mexico. His underlying message was that the nations of North America weren't just neighbors anymore. Unless Mexico prospered, the rest of the continent could not prosper: "The elections of July second give us a window of opportunity to press forward a new vision of our place in the world. First and foremost, that vision is founded on a new partnership with the United States and Canada that builds on existing institutions and creates the foundation for a shared North American area of peace and prosperity."[3]

This was the essence of a message Fox would deliver again in Washington, this time during the first week of September when he captivated the White House during an official state visit. Fox stood as an equal with President Bush and boldly called for an immigration agreement by the end of the year.

Five days after he left Washington, the World Trade Center collapsed. Among the casualties in the rubble were Fox's initiatives, and, some thought, the new relationship between the United States and Mexico promised by George W. Bush.

During the summer of 2000, George W. Bush also started to outline his notion of North America. He made no bones about the fact that foreign affairs were not his strong point but that as governor of Texas he was quite familiar with the country south of the Texas border and had visited Mexico several times. During the campaign he said he considered Mexico a front door to all of Latin America and, while he may not have known how to pronounce the names of the leaders of Uzbekistan or Tajikistan, he did consider Mexico and the rest of the Western Hemisphere to be part of "the neighborhood."

Bush promised that if elected, he would meet with Fox before either of them was inaugurated to demonstrate their shared interests and common commitment to solving the problems facing both countries. He had heard Fox outline his ideas about the border, and while he saw some positive signs, the borders were there and they needed to be protected. The issue was not whether to go ahead with integration, but to what degree. The vision of common interest seemed to have so captivated Bush that at one point in the campaign he mentally erased the border between the United States and Mexico. During one of the presidential debates with Al Gore, Bush combined the U.S. and Mexico into an ersatz unified body when he spoke about the surging price of oil and said he had talked to Fox about "how best to be able to expedite the exploration of natural gas in Mexico and transport it up to the United

States, so we become less dependent on foreign sources of crude oil."[4] Mexican commentators chided Bush for considering Mexico something other than a foreign source of oil, although they did not doubt that he meant to import more of Mexico's prized national resource. The slip of the tongue irked some Mexicans but generally they saw Bush as a friend whose experience on the border helped him understand their needs. "Should I become president," Bush had said during the campaign, "I will look south, not as an afterthought but as a fundamental commitment of my presidency."[5]

Combined, the imperfect statements of Bush and Fox had carried North American identity from theory to political reality, but reality rarely arrives without complications. The promised meeting between the presidents-elect never took place. The post-election dispute in the United States prevented Bush from being declared president-elect until after Fox was sworn in. Bush, congratulating him, reiterated his promise to work closely together. Clearly, Bush thought Fox was a man he could work with, and North America was a concept he felt comfortable thinking about. In a policy speech during the campaign, Bush had predicted that the United States would be able to enter into a "special relationship" with a democratic Mexico that would be as strong as the relationship that had existed with Canada for years. "Historically, we have no closer friends and allies," Bush had said. "With Canada, our partner in NATO and NAFTA, we share not just a border but a bond of good will. Our ties of history and heritage with Mexico are just as deep."[6]

There was no way to tell how Bush's conservative views and pro-business attitudes would influence his decisions about relations with Mexico, Canada, and the rest of the world. Nor could anyone have guessed how much the world would change during Bush's first year in office, or what impact world events would have on the North American relationship.

The legal maneuvering to count ballots in Florida and close the 2000 election in the United States took thirty-six days—exactly the same length of time as the entire federal campaign and election that Prime Minister Jean Chrétien had called for November 27. But it was an election that nobody else in Canada seemed to want. Chrétien was in the third year of his second five-year term when he decided the time was right to hold another election. Chrétien gambled that by calling an election early, he could stave off an attack from the newly constituted Canadian Alliance Party and its right-leaning leader, Stockwell Day. Chrétien's intuition was on target, but the sharpest political minds in Canada doubted his wisdom right up to the time the polls closed.

The brief Canadian campaign had little to do with major issues, and produced few dramatic moments. Under Chrétien, the Liberals had become free trade converts and unabashed supporters of closer ties to the United States. Day, the leader of the Alliance, was a fiscal conservative with a buzz cut and an easy smile who hailed from Alberta, the western province most aligned with American ways, from tax policy to health care. Unlike the 1988 election in which John Turner had accused Brian Mulroney of selling out Canada by signing the free trade agreement, continental integration was not an issue in 2000. It was a given. The campaign was mostly about personalities and turned particularly dirty by Canadian standards. Newspapers criticized the candidates for resorting to "U.S.-style advertising," implying that this was a lamentable development.[7] At one debate, the Alliance and the Liberals traded barbs over which party was more in favor of establishing a two-tier, Americanized health care system that permitted private clinics to operate.

Chrétien won big, increasing the Liberal majority to match roughly its level after the 1993 election, stopping the Alliance dead in its tracks west of Ontario, and most surprisingly, stealing several seats from the already staggered separatists in Quebec.[8] A few days after his victory, Chrétien was playing golf in the United States with President Clinton. It was a symbolic outing for two reasons: it proved how much Chrétien had overcome his earlier reluctance to appear too cozy with the American president and it tipped off observers to a changing dynamic in Canada's sense of the North American balance of power. The Canadian Ministry of Foreign Affairs tried mightily to persuade Chrétien to use a speech that weekend at Duke University to regain some of the ground Canada had lost to Mexico after Fox's dramatic statements about North American integration in August. But Chrétien had reacted strongly against some of Fox's most radical ideas about the border and was cool to the Mexican's overall message. His reasons became clearer after the Duke speech. In the end, according to one diplomat, Chrétien removed "the heart and a lot of the message" from the prepared text and instead of discussing a trilateral view of North America, the prime minister reverted to praising the special relationship between Canada and the United States.

A defensive speech, it unwittingly underscored Ottawa's preoccupation with Mexico and that country's growing impact on the consciousness of the United States. Whereas Mulroney had originally seen Mexico as a potential ally with the potential to correct some of the imbalance existing in North America, Ottawa increasingly looked at Mexico as a rival and a competitor—not only for American business but also for its special relationship with the United States. The election of George W. Bush intensified those feelings because he was so clearly comfortable with Mexico. "We have enjoyed a special relationship with the United States but we no longer have it," former Foreign Affairs Minister Lloyd Axworthy said. "It's gone."[9]

Axworthy made those comments at a policy conference in Ottawa that gathered Canada's best thinkers to highlight critical issues facing the country in the new millennium. Their meeting took place during a decisive week in North America. It began with the Canadian elections and ended with Vicente Fox's swearing-in as the first opposition president in Mexico in seventy-one years. In between, Al Gore contested the election results in Florida, a manual recount of the votes in that state was delayed, and the U.S. Supreme Court heard arguments on George W. Bush's appeal of a Florida Supreme Court ruling extending the date for certifying the election results.

The convergence of events in all three nations made it easier to think about a North American approach like the one Fox had outlined. At the policy conference, concern about Bush's plan for a continental missile defense system revived the old conflict between security and sovereignty for Canada. The growing productivity gap between Canada and the United States, along with the threat posed by an economically sound Mexico that was becoming a powerful exporter and a favored locale for corporate investment, were raised continually as worrisome themes. Renée St-Jacques, Director General of Micro-Economic Policy Analysis for Industry Canada, the government's commerce ministry, demonstrated the challenge clearly: Canada's share of American imports had held steady at about 20 percent during the 1990s, but Mexico's had doubled during that time and by 1999 was about half the size of Canada's and gaining fast. During Chrétien's third term, Canadian diplomats had also focused on the rivalry with Mexico. In some cases, they had decided that it was to Canada's advantage to continue to pursue its special bilateral relationship with the United States without trying to incorporate a Mexico that is gaining in economic and political strength.

The elections of 2000 provided a synchronized opportunity for a fresh start in the relationship between North America's three major nations. The inescapable differences among the three ensure that they will remain individual countries whose unique perspectives sometimes do not coincide. The borders will continue to be protected, against one another and against those outside the continent who are hellbent on doing harm. Economic competition and painful inequalities across borders will continue. The real test of these continental bonds will not come over decisions in the common interest but in confrontations over deep differences. There will always be issues on which the United States, Canada, and Mexico disagree. As September 11 demonstrated, the bonds of community and common interest that tie Canada, Mexico, and the United States together make them a reluctant trinity, always together, though not always in agreement.

PART II

The Electoral Politics of 2000

CHAPTER 2

The Coalition for Change: Voters and Parties in the 2000 Mexican Election

Alejandro Moreno

THE PRESIDENTIAL ELECTION OF 2000 is a crucial point in Mexico's long democratic transition. Vicente Fox, the Alliance for Change candidate, won the presidency thanks to the support of a broad-based electoral coalition, a modern-day melting pot of different ideologies and sociodemographic features. The governing party's defeat was its first after seventy years of uninterrupted rule. The "coalition for change," as I will call the electoral coalition that voted for Fox, was a sociopolitical phenomenon that evolved during the twelve to fifteen years prior to the 2000 election. During the 2000 campaigns and the election itself, the alliance achieved its more recent shape and meaning.

At least since the mid-1980s, Mexicans have been split into two political camps. One of them is younger, more educated, urban, and holds pro-democratic and liberal points of view. The other is older, less educated, more rural, authoritarian, and fundamentalist in its views. The former tends to vote for the opposition and electorally supported the rise of the National Action Party

(PAN) over the Democratic Revolutionary Party (PRD). The latter tends to vote for the Institutional Revolutionary Party (PRI) and constitutes the core support of a party with a long tradition in government. In 2000, the desire for change was stronger than ever, and Vicente Fox benefited from it, as well as from the support of an ideologically and regionally diverse electoral coalition. Turnout differentials also broadened Fox's electoral base and reduced the PRI's prospects of keeping the presidency for six more years.

According to exit poll data, about two-thirds of those voters who supported Fox in 2000 said they had voted for a change, rather than for a specific party, candidate, or policy program. Certainly, many of the voters for change identified with the PAN, and some others found a very attractive candidate in Fox. But the main motivation behind their votes was the desire to make change a reality. In a country where the PRI had controlled the presidency for seven decades, change was about alteration of leadership rather than a shift in policy orientation. Thus, a political campaign with a charismatic candidate emphasizing change offered a potent message that activated the main divisions in Mexican society.

What was the nature of the electoral coalition for change? What was its underlying meaning? What kind of Mexicans formed part of it? Where are its origins? How likely is it to last beyond 2000? In this chapter I address these questions by analyzing different types of survey data gathered in the 1990s and in 2000.

THE MEXICAN ELECTORAL SYSTEM ON THE EVE OF THE 2000 ELECTIONS

Despite the predominantly authoritarian nature of its political system, elections have been held regularly in Mexico since the 1930s, following the end of the revolutionary period: presidential elections every six years and congressional elections every three years since 1934. At least until the late 1980s, the PRI dominated every election and ran almost uncontested. The coalition for change was not an accident of the 2000 elections; it was an evolving sociopolitical phenomenon that had had its first major electoral impact in the 1988 presidential election, when the PRI candidate faced a real challenge for the first time since the party's creation in 1929.

Before the 1980s, there were two electoral episodes where the PRI faced some challenge. One was in 1940, when Juan Andrew Almazán, significantly supported by middle-class voters, ran for president against Manuel Ávila Camacho, President Lázaro Cárdenas's appointee. As some historians have noted, the election's violence and bloodshed far oustripped any fair political competition.[1] Bullets were more important than ballots once again in 1952, when General Miguel Henríquez significantly challenged Adolfo Ruíz Cortines in the race to succeed President Miguel Alemán. "Henriquismo" became synonymous with opposition.

Despite these incidents, the PRI's hegemony characterized Mexican national elections. The PRI obtained three-quarters of the vote share in every national election from 1964 to 1979. In 1976, José López Portillo ran unopposed; the PAN decided not to nominate a candidate to protest the lack of fair conditions, and Portillo received about 94 percent of the votes cast. In that year's congressional races, the PRI got 86 percent of the votes. The first major political reform came in 1977 as a consequence of the legitimacy crisis produced by the 1976 one-candidate contest, and more political parties were allowed to register for national elections. Support for the PRI in legislative elections dropped from 74 percent in 1979 to 69 percent in 1985, to 68 percent in 1985, and to 51 percent in 1988. After bouncing back to 62 percent in 1991, support for the PRI fell again to 50 percent in 1994 and then to 39 and 38 percent in 1997 and 2000 respectively.[2] In other words, support for the PRI dropped by almost one-half in the last three decades of the twentieth century.

The challenges to the PRI in 1940 and 1952 were products of party splits, a phenomenon which reoccurred in 1987, when Cuauhtémoc Cárdenas, the son of one of Mexico's most beloved presidents, broke from the PRI and ran for president in the 1988 election. The National Democratic Front, a coalition of several small socialist and leftist parties, as well as PRI defectors, backed his candidacy. Cárdenas obtained 31 percent of the national vote; the election was regarded as highly fraudulent, since the counting system shut down when the election returns seemed to favor the opposition against the PRI candidate, Carlos Salinas de Gortari. Salinas officially won the election with 51 percent of the national vote, the lowest percentage that the PRI had ever received in a presidential election until then.

Mexicans voted for president again in 1994, a year of strong political and economic turmoil. The North American Free Trade Agreement (NAFTA) had gone into effect on January 1, the same day Mexicans learned about an indigenous uprising and masked guerrillas—known as Zapatistas—in the southern state of Chiapas. A major political assassination took place in March, just three and a half months before the election. The PRI candidate, Luis Donaldo Colosio, was shot in the head at a campaign rally in the Baja California state. Ernesto Zedillo, who replaced Colosio as PRI candidate, won the election with just 50 percent of the vote. The opposition vote was split mainly between the PAN's Diego Fernández de Cevallos (27 percent) and PRD's Cuauhtémoc Cárdenas (17 percent).

In December 1994, shortly after the Zedillo administration took office, significant peso devaluation triggered the deepest economic crisis of the 1990s. The peso depreciated value against the U.S. dollar over 100 percent in just a few days, and the exchange rate went from slightly under three pesos per dollar before the devaluation to just over nine pesos per dollar over the next two years. Having received most of the blame, former president Salinas went on a hunger strike and quickly went from being a highly popular president to a highly unpopular former president. His misfortunes with Mexican public opinion increased during the Zedillo administration, after his brother, Raúl Salinas, was accused of corruption, drug trafficking, and the plotting of another major political assassination. A top PRI official, José Francisco Ruíz Massieu, who had also been married to Salinas's sister, was fatally shot in Mexico City. The economic crisis, scandals, and the Zapatista uprising would pave the way for the 2000 presidential race.

Political Parties

Although there have been several parties in modern Mexico, three deserve attention for their political relevance and electoral performances in the present electoral arena: PRI, PAN, and PRD.[3] The PRI was founded in 1929 under the label PRN, or National Revolutionary Party, by President Plutarco Elías Calles (1924–1928), head of the winning camp in the Mexican Revolution. In a speech, Calles said that the age of *caudillos* had ended and the age of institutions had begun. President Lázaro Cárdenas (1934–1940) gave the party a corporatist structure, incorporating unionized workers and peasants and making its relationship to the state almost symbiotic for many years thereafter. Under Cárdenas, the party's name changed to the Mexican Revolutionary Party, or PRM, and changed again to its current name of the Institutional Revolutionary Party, or PRI, under President Miguel Alemán (1946–1952), when the new urban middle class was incorporated into it. An entrepreneur, Alemán was also the first civilian to become president after the 1929 revolution.

The PRI was able to incorporate dissent into its regime. Also, the one-party system was legitimized with significant economic growth in the 1950s, when import-substitution industrialization delivered what many call the "Mexican Miracle." Its success was questioned in the political arena by members of the student movement of 1968. The use of force, including the "Massacre of Tlatelolco" where a number of students were shot during a demonstration, deepened the authoritarian image of Mexican politics and increased resentment among the Mexican middle class. The PRI's ideological stands and policy directions changed from one president to the next. For example, during the 1980s, economic policies switched from nationalization to privatization. Also, government officials and party leaders, often one and the same, were increasingly involved in corruption scandals in the 1970s and 1980s. Corruption and economic crises were, thereby, some of the most common issues associated with the long-ruling party. The PRI lost a great deal of its electoral support in the 1990s, but still remains one of the two strongest political parties in Mexico.

The National Action Party (PAN) was founded in 1939, partly as a reaction to the corporatist and leftist policies of President Lázaro Cárdenas, and also as a protest against the anti-clerical orientation of the Mexican state that had started in the 1920s. The party had Catholic and entrepreneurial bases, and served as the real opposition to the PRI from the 1940s to the 1980s. Despite its Catholic, middle-class origins, the PAN has clearly become a catchall party in recent years, which has helped boost its success in national and local elections. The party joined the international Christian Democratic movement in 1998.[4] The PAN obtained only 5 percent of the national vote in the 1942 midterm elections, when it participated for the first time. Its support had increased to 27 percent of the national vote by the 1997 legislative elections, and then to 38 percent in the congressional races of 2000. In 2000, the PAN presidential candidate, Vicente Fox, won the presidency with 43 percent of the national vote.

The Democratic Revolution Party, PRD, was the result of the 1988 electoral coalition that backed Cuauhtémoc Cárdenas in his first presidential quest. Founded in 1989, the PRD gathered members of small socialist, communist, and workers' parties that had represented the Mexican left in previous years, as well as PRI defectors. Although many of its members supported economically leftist policies, the main issue behind the party label was that of Mexico's democratization. The PRD had its best performance in the 1997 legislative election, receiving about 26 percent of the national vote. In other national elections the PRD has not reached 20 percent. Under the campaign slogan "It's time for the sun to rise" (the PRD's logo is an Aztec sun), the PRD attracted many voters who wanted a change and who later supported Fox in 2000.

Voting Cleavages

It is likely that the coalition for change has its origins in Mexico's modernization process, since it draws its main support from the more educated and urban electorate that started to vote against the PRI in local elections long before 2000.[5] But its scope and reach go beyond an explanation merely based on a modernization theory. It involves an understanding of the patterns of partisan identification, an assessment of political cleavages, and an appraisal of voter coordination.

The Mexican electorate is a sophisticated one, but a relatively simple and parsimonious explanation best accounts for Mexican voting behavior: Mexicans have been politically split into two sides, those who support the one-party regime that embraced the revolutionary label, and those who oppose it. This split has not been about the specifics of governance, but about the nature of the regime itself.

As Mexican elections became more competitive, due to a long process of political liberalization and reforms, the regime-based political split became stronger and more evident. It crystallized in the electoral arena in a way that even shaped the meaning of "left" and "right" ideologies. The left was supportive of a more open society, stood for more competitive elections, and demanded wider political and civil rights. The right supported established authority and sought to keep the ruling party in power. A first look at the characteristics of this divide was developed in a classification of the Mexican political parties in the late 1980s. Such classification was based on interpretations of the parties' strategic positions along a pro-system/anti-system axis of political conflict and their ideological positions along the traditional left-right axis.[6]

The advent of professional and academic survey research in Mexico brought this division into focus. Using survey data gathered around the 1988 and 1991 national elections, Jorge I. Domínguez and James A. McCann argue that voters decided first whether to vote for the PRI or not, and, if not, they would then choose between the other options.[7] Thus, voting was viewed as a two-step decision process in which the first step was some plebiscitary consideration on the PRI. Based on further evidence, Moreno shows that in the 1990s, Mexicans were split over several relevant dimensions of political competition, the most significant being a democratic-authoritarian cleavage that overshadowed the socioeconomic concerns that defined left and right.[8] The parties' average positions were scattered along the different dimensions of competition: political views, social and moral stands, and socioeconomic preferences. Comparative survey data showed that the dimensions of political conflict in Mexico were also relevant, to a higher or lesser degree, in other young Latin American democracies.[9]

The nature of the coalition for change in 2000 reflects the politically relevant split that had already been observed in the 1990s, with an important difference: the winning coalition in 2000 was wider and more ideologically heterogeneous than it had ever been. Support for Vicente Fox was higher than any other candidate among voters from the left, center-left, center, and center-right, and across all the country's regions, especially in the more indus-

trialized northern states. The average Fox voter was more educated, urban, younger, and as we will see presently, more liberal
than the average PRD or PRI voters. The average Fox voter was
also centrist in his economic views and as pro-democratic as the
PRD's.

From this analysis, I draw the following conclusions about the
coalition for change. The average PAN voter has held a centrist
view about several relevant dimensions of political conflict in
Mexico and, more importantly, on all of them combined. Rather
than being a compact, Christian Democratic party electorate, the
PAN has developed a catchall nature that combines middle- and
working-class voters from left to right.[10] The 2000 coalition that
supported the PAN was even wider and more ideologically heterogeneous than the 1997 PAN coalition; and the coalition that
supported Fox was even wider and more heterogeneous than the
PAN's.

This pattern is explained by several facts. First, the proportion
of leftist voters decreased during the 1990s, and the consequent
shift to the right benefited the PAN, not the PRI, mostly at the
expense of the PRD. Second, a significant number of PRD supporters from the left and center in 1997 became PAN supporters
in 2000; and a significant number of PRI supporters from the right
in 1997 also supported the PAN in 2000. Consequently, the PAN
support increased across the entire political spectrum, especially in
the center, the most populated region of all. Third, some voters
from the left who supported PRD congressional candidates in
2000 did not support Cuauhtémoc Cárdenas for president, but Vicente Fox. This shift gave Fox an even higher and more ideologically heterogeneous share of the vote in his presidential quest than
that of the PAN in the congressional races.

Fifth, participation made a difference: the voter for change
was more likely to vote in 2000 than the PRI voter, which had
negative consequences for a ruling party that was used to mass

electoral mobilization. Across the entire political spectrum, support for the PRI presidential candidate, Francisco Labastida, was about the same as the support received by PRI congressional candidates, with no observable differences between the votes for either office. Additionally, support for Labastida was lower among likely and actual voters than among the general population. Fox benefited from a comparatively low turnout, as compared to the official turnout figures registered in previous presidential elections. The official turnout figures were 77 percent in 1994, and 64 percent in 2000.

The analysis developed in this chapter relies on national surveys that represent both the Mexican electorate as a whole—and also screened for likely voters—and actual voters.[11] In order to prove my points, I will first analyze the distribution of left and right in Mexico and discuss its significance in Mexican elections. Secondly, I will discuss the mean placements of the party electorates on the three most relevant dimensions of political conflict that result from a factor analysis and how they have changed in the last few years, thereby affecting the nature of party support. I will then move on to analyze individual vote choices by developing a multinomial logit model applied to exit poll data from 1997 and 2000, and focus on the differences of the presidential and the congressional vote in 2000. Finally, I will apply the vote model to pre-election polls and look at the differences in support among the entire surveyed population and among the sub-sample of likely voters. The model proves to be a good fit across different types of survey data and attains statistical significance using variables that have proved their relevance in previous studies. In my analyses, I discuss the estimated probabilities of the vote derived from the models and also develop the main argument about the coalition for change with more detail.

THE LEFT-RIGHT DISTRIBUTION IN MEXICO, 1990–2000

One of the key variables used in this chapter is the individuals' self-placement on a left-right scale. This variable helps show the Mexican parties' and candidates' sources of support in the 1990s and in 2000. But before delving into partisan features, it is important to make a few remarks on the stability and change of the left-right distribution in Mexico. According to the Mexican component of the World Values Survey, the great majority of Mexicans are consistently located in the center and center-right sections of the left-right continuum, creating a bell-shaped distribution of left and right positions.[12]

However, when we focus more sharply on the differences from one survey to the next, a clear pattern emerges in the 1990s. The category farthest to the right gained more individuals at the expense of the center and, mainly, the center-left. Mexican society moved slightly to the right from 1990 to 1997, but much more dramatically from 1997 to 2000. The mean placement for all respondents in a collapsed five-point measure increased from 3.14 to 3.16 between 1990 and 1997, and then to 3.45 in 2000.[13] The bell-shaped distribution seems to be very stable in non-electoral periods, but it tends to polarize and takes on a three-modal pattern during periods of political campaigns. This phenomenon was observed for the first time in the 1997 legislative election, when there was an "evidently dramatic increase of the extreme categories (of the left-right continuum) and a decrease in the centrist positions."[14] Some observers argue that the three-modal pattern showed up again in surveys conducted right before the PRI primary held on November 7, 1999, and that left-right orientations had a significant impact on vote choices.[15]

The meaning of this shift to the right will be elaborated in more detail below. For now it is sufficient to say that it had significant implications for the dynamics of party support in Mexico in 2000.

The leftist PRD received the major damage. The PRD's share of the national vote in the 1997 midterm election was about 26 percent, but it dropped to 19 and 17 percent in the 2000 congressional and presidential races, respectively. The shift to the right also raises an interesting paradox: the party farthest to the right during this period, the PRI, did not grow stronger during the 1990s, but weakened.

During the 1990s, the major underlying meaning of left and right reflected a democratic-authoritarian dimension of political conflict based on concerns about the nature of the Mexican regime.[16] The left was associated with support for political reform and a democratic government, while the right was associated with support for the status quo, which meant keeping the PRI in power. As political competition increased and opposition parties defeated the PRI in local elections, this left-right divide mirrored the liberal and fundamentalist split. The left aligned with the liberals on many issues, whereas fundamentalists were religious and nationalist and more likely to reject abortion and homosexuality.[17] The left-right axis also continued a socioeconomic line of conflict, which has proven to be less relevant than the former two dimensions but still significant.[18]

Using previous research, I constructed two-dimensional party axes using the three dimensions just described.[19] In the first dimension, labeled as "democratic-authoritarian," attitudes pointed toward a military government, democracy's ability to keep order, perform economically well, and its problems of indecisiveness. The second dimension, labeled "liberal-fundamentalist," includes attitudes toward abortion, homosexuality, single mothers, gender roles, and religiosity. The third dimension, defined as "social redistribution versus capitalist incentives," includes attitudes on the role of the state vis-à-vis the individual and preferences for equality versus individual incentives. The three factors explain a cumulative variance of 43 percent. This type of analysis has been used

to map average party electorates,[20] and average societal placements.[21]

This analysis shows that both the PAN and the PRD have more
pro-democratic supporters than the PRI, and they are, on average,
more liberal as well.[22] The main difference between PAN and
PRD supporters is observed along the socioeconomic axis, with
the PRD more to the left and the PAN more toward the center-
right. From 1997 to 2000, the PRD electorate became slightly
more pro-democratic, slightly more fundamentalist, and also more
economically leftist.

Perhaps the PRD electorate was influenced by the 2000 Cárdenas campaign, which had a predominantly nationalist tone and
criticized the privatization policies implemented by the PRI. Cárdenas's slogan on a number of television spots reflects the economic nationalism of his messages: "No privatization of the
electric industry. Let's say it out loud, Mexico is ours." If true, this
probably explains the movement toward a less liberal position and
more economically leftist position. Unlike the PRD, the PAN remained at almost the same position on the democratic-authoritarian
axis but appeared much more liberal in 2000 than it was in 1997.
This increasing liberalism of PAN supporters reflects the attrac-
tion of liberal segments of the Mexican electorate to the PAN
candidate, Vicente Fox, mostly at the expense of the PRD, although he received support from independent voters as well.
Clearly, the PAN drew most of its supporters from the most liberal
and pro-democratic segment choosing between the three main
parties in 2000.

The PRI voters, on average, hold the most authoritarian and
fundamentalist views of the mainstream party supporters. Moreover, from 1997 to 2000 the average PRI supporter became even
more authoritarian and more fundamentalist. The struggle to
maintain the "official" party and its "official" candidate in power
started during the 1999 primary process, when Francisco Labastida

was continuously attacked as the candidate of the status quo. However, the most significant movement of the PRI electorate was not along the sociopolitical axis, but along the socioeconomic continuum. Having been predominantly on the right, and nearest to the pole of capitalist incentives that characterized much of the Salinas and Zedillo administrations, the average PRI supporter became much more centrist on economic matters from 1988 to 2000.

This difference is significant, and it is worth an explanation. Much of the negative tone of the PRI primary campaign focused on the problems created by the "neoliberal," free-market-oriented policies implemented during the last three PRI administrations. Being close to Carlos Salinas, a symbol of economic and structural reform in Mexico, was a handicap for the two main political contenders for the PRI presidential nomination, Francisco Labastida and Roberto Madrazo. Both of them changed the clearly promarket discourse that had prevailed among the PRI leaders in recent years to messages favoring more social and economic redistribution policies. The result points to a more economically leftist and more fundamentalist average PRI supporter.

Despite this shift to the left on the socioeconomic axis, the PRI was, on average, to the right of the PAN and the PRD. These latter parties also moved slightly to the left on the socioeconomic continuum. Along this line, the PRI is on the right, the PRD on the left, and the PAN in the middle, as had been the case throughout the 1990s.[23] Also, as in the 1990s, the PAN benefited from its central position, attracting defectors from the PRI and the PRD, as well as independent voters. The PRD moved away from the center on every axis, thereby losing chances to benefit from the numerous available centrist voters. It seems that much of what the PRD lost, the PAN won, especially among liberals.

A MODEL OF VOTE CHOICE

What explains voters' decisions in the 2000 election? A model of vote choice based on survey data may offer some answers.[24]

As explanatory variables, the model employs measures of regional and demographic characteristics of the respondents, party identification, ideological self-classification, religiosity, opinions about the candidates, presidential approval ratings, retrospective economic evaluations, and an indicator of those who said they voted for a change in 2000. After dropping some variables with relatively weak explanatory power, the model also is a good fit across the different surveys. This makes it possible to draw conclusions from three different perspectives: changes in voting behavior from the 1997 to the 2000 election; differences between congressional and presidential vote choices; and the impact of turnout, observing the differences between likely voters and the general population.

Voting for Congress

Let us focus first on the congressional voting model in table 2.1, which uses data from a national exit poll conducted among actual voters in 2000. The reason to start with the congressional vote is that its comparison with the 1997 vote (in the midterm legislative election) will give us a first hint about the nature of the coalition for change in 2000. How different was support for the political parties in each election, not just in its magnitude but also in its composition and meaning? According to the results of the model, there are significant differences in support for the PAN, as compared to both the PRD and the PRI.

Support for the PAN, as opposed to the PRD, was higher in the more industrialized north and the mostly Catholic central-western regions of the country but lower in the more rural, less developed south. Unlike other previous indicators of confessional voting in

TABLE 2.1.

A Model of Vote Choice for Congress and President in 2000: Multinomial Logit Estimates from a National Exit Poll

	CONGRESS				PRESIDENT			
	PRD/PAN*		PRI/PAN*		Cárdenas/Fox		Labastida/Fox	
	Coefficient	Significance	Coefficient	Significance	Coefficient	Significance	Coefficient	Significance
Intercept	.414	.459	-1.496	.005	-.173	.749	-2.329	.000
Gender (Female=1)	.188	.195	.344	.010	.349	.048	.314	.047
Age	.008	.800	.030	.288	.089	.018	.073	.032
Education	-.091	.177	-.135	.030	-.136	.097	-.136	.066
Income	-.049	.279	.002	.961	-.130	.026	-.019	.706
North	-.408	.037	-.036	.839	-.443	.067	-.520	.015
Center-West	-.688	.003	-.251	.199	-.379	.150	-.258	.262
South	.318	.072	.315	.074	.027	.900	-.050	.809
Rural	.003	.988	.623	.000	.340	.134	.564	.006
Church attendance	.110	.066	.156	.007	.110	.128	.186	.006
Labastida opinion thermometer	-.042	.126	.260	.000	-.036	.286	.423	.000
Fox opinion thermometer	-.323	.000	-.273	.000	-.510	.000	-.441	.000
Cárdenas opinion thermometer	.353	.000	.067	.015	.435	.000	.007	.826

	B	Sig.	B	Sig.	B	Sig.	B	Sig.
President Zedillo's job approval	**-.117**	.046	.050	.411	-.028	.649	**.197**	.007
Personal economic situation	.041	.644	.375	.372	.156	.150	**.230**	.023
National economic situation	.023	.786	.023	.776	.064	.534	.012	.906
Vote for change	-.087	.547	**-.648**	.000	**-.434**	.012	**-1.223**	.000
Left-right self-placement	**-.123**	.027	.037	.900	-.042	.524	.106	.114
PRI strong partisan	-.228	.452	**1.943**	.000	-.831	.052	**2.112**	.000
PRI weak partisan	-.057	.844	**1.809**	.000	-.742	.066	**1.963**	.000
PAN strong partisan	**-1.273**	.000	**-1.415**	.000	**-1.724**	.000	**-2.021**	.000
PAN weak partisan	**-1.732**	.000	**-1.224**	.000	**-2.330**	.000	**-1.556**	.000
PRD strong partisan	**2.354**	.000	.736	.246	**2.316**	.000	-.814	.210
PRD weak partisan	**2.074**	.000	-.124	.770	**2.172**	.000	-.040	.927
-2 Log likelihood	3057.584				2153.214			
Chi-Square	3540.618				4448.082			
Significance	.000				.000			
Pseudo R-Square (Cox and Snell)	.679				.751			
Cases included in analysis	2,891				2,955			

*PRD includes the Alliance for Mexico; PAN includes the Alliance for Change. Coefficients in boldface are statistically significant at 0.05 level or less.

Mexico, frequent churchgoers were significantly more likely to vote for the PRD than for the PAN in 2000, and voters with a leftist orientation were also more likely to support the PRD.[25] This provides another piece of evidence about the orientation of PAN supporters in 2000.

Support for the PAN, as opposed to the PRD, was also higher among those who held a favorable opinion of Vicente Fox but significantly lower among those who had a positive image of Cuauhtémoc Cárdenas, the PRD's presidential candidate. Presidential approval is also important: those who approved of President Zedillo's job were more likely to support the PAN over the PRD. As expected, party identification played an important role in affecting people's choices: PAN identifiers were significantly more likely to support their party in the election, and strong PAN identifiers were much more likely to do so than weak PAN identifiers. The same applies to PRD identifiers.

Gender and education are significant variables in explaining support for the PAN, as opposed to the PRI. While women were less likely to vote for the PAN, educated voters were more likely to support the PAN. Rural voters tended to vote for the PRI, and regional differences of support are only significant in the south, where voting for the PRI was more common than voting for the PAN. Demographically, then, support for the PAN was higher among more educated Mexicans and lower in rural Mexico. Voting for the PAN, as opposed to the PRI, was less likely among frequent churchgoers, just as in the PAN-PRD comparison. Again, this reflects the difference in the PAN's 2000 electoral coalition in comparison with the past: these findings from exit poll data are consistent with the increase of liberal PAN supporters shown earlier with World Values Survey data.

Opinion thermometers for Fox and Labastida explain the vote choice in the expected ways for the PAN and the PRI: a favorable image of Fox increased an individual's probability of voting PAN, while favorable opinions of Labastida increased the probability of voting PRI. Additionally, the Cárdenas opinion thermometer is also significant: voters with a favorable opinion of Cárdenas were less likely to vote for PAN congressional candidates and more likely to support the PRI ones. Contrary to expectations, PRI candidates for Congress did not benefit from President Zedillo's high approval ratings in 2000. Presidential approval does not explain the difference of vote between PAN and PRI, suggesting that the message for change and criticism directed at the PRI regime was not targeting the Zedillo government. The *priista* president enjoyed approval ratings higher than 60 percent at the time of the election, and he was highly popular even among *panistas*. Still, the desire for change accounts for the significant variation in support for the PAN versus the PRI. Those who voted for a change were much more likely to support PAN candidates. In this case, left-right orientations do not make a major difference, but party identification plays a role that confirms all expectations: PRI and PAN identifiers were significantly more likely to vote for the PRI and PAN, respectively, with strong identifiers even more likely to do so than weak identifiers.

Compared to the 1997 congressional elections, the PRI's share of the vote remained relatively stable, dropping only from 39 percent in 1997 to 38 percent in 2000. The PRD's share fell dramatically, from 26 percent to 19 percent (together with other minor parties that formed the Alliance for Mexico in 2000). And the PAN increased its share from 28 percent alone in 1997 to 40 percent, together with the Green Party, under the Alliance for Change in 2000.[26] The estimated probabilities of vote choice for the two elections do indeed reflect these trends and offer a look at where the respective losses and gains came from. The PRD lost significant ground on the left and the PAN won a great deal there, especially among educated and liberal segments of the left. The PRI lost ground on the right, giving the PAN a wide coalition across most of the political spectrum. The coalition for change in 2000 was even more ideologically heterogeneous than the congressional coalition in 1997, when some observers noticed the PAN's catchall character.[27]

Voting for President

The nature of the coalition for change is clearly depicted by the type of support that the PAN obtained in the 1997 and 2000 elections. However, voting for Vicente Fox demonstrated an even stronger desire for change than voting for the PAN. The Fox vote was larger and more heterogeneous than the PAN vote. In order to explain this, let us return to table 2.1 and focus on the model of presidential vote.

Voting for Fox, as opposed to Cárdenas, is explained by several demographic variables, as well as by candidate image, party identification, and by the desire for change. Women were more likely to vote for Cárdenas, but Fox attracted a younger, better educated, and more well-off electorate, as indicated by the variables for age, education, and income. The probabilities of voting for Fox were also higher in the country's northern region, and, unlike the PAN, Fox did not find significantly strong opposition in the south. Support for Fox was more evenly distributed across the country than was support for the PAN. Opinion thermometers and party identification provide the expected results, with favorable opinions about each candidate increasing the chances of voting for that respective candidate, and strong and weak partisans significantly supporting their party's candidate. In this case, PRI identifiers were significantly more likely to vote for Fox than for Cárdenas. According to research based on panel data gathered during the presidential campaigns, negative messages and mudslinging between Fox and Labastida brought serious consequences to the PRI candidate, influencing some PRI voters to turn their backs on

Labastida.[28] Also, some PRI primary-thwarted voters who supported the losing candidate, Roberto Madrazo, were likely to cast their votes away from the PRI in the presidential election.[29] It seems that disillusioned *priistas* opted to vote for Fox before they did so for Cárdenas. Most notably, voters motivated by a desire for change were more likely to support Fox, not Cárdenas.

The main influences behind the Fox vote, as opposed to the Labastida vote, reflected sociodemographic and regional characteristics, religiosity, candidate images, retrospective evaluations, party identification, and, of course, the change factor. Support for Labastida was more likely among women, older voters, and less educated Mexicans. Rural voters were a significant source of support for the PRI candidate, while the northern region was much more likely to vote for Fox. Income, however, was not significant in this case. Candidate image, represented by the opinion thermometers, influenced vote choices in the expected ways, and presidential approval worked in favor of Labastida. Interestingly, pocketbook evaluations, measured with retrospective judgments of personal economic situations, were important determinants of the vote for president. Those who considered themselves better off than in the previous year were more likely to vote for Labastida, while those who thought they were worse off were more likely to support Fox.

As usual, party identification influenced the vote in the expected ways, with partisans supporting their respective party candidate. However, left-right self placement was not significant in accounting for the Labastida vote, as opposed to Fox's. Although Labastida's main support came from the right, and very little from the left, Fox was able to draw significant rightist support, and even greater support from the center and left, as will be illustrated later. The desire for change was simply one of the most significant variables accounting for the Fox vote, as opposed to Labastida's. After all, the main point of change was a profound desire to vote the

PRI out of office. As many observers noticed during the campaigns, the presidential election had become a plebiscite on the PRI regime. Francisco Labastida was just the candidate that represented it.

In summary, bringing about a change was one of the most significant influences behind the vote for Vicente Fox, and against the PRI, in 2000. The model shown in table 2.1 indicates that there were other important influences too. The Fox coalition received significant support from young and educated Mexicans from different regions of Mexico, especially the north. According to the regression coefficients, the 2000 election did carry some expression of economic dissatisfaction, especially from pocketbook concerns. In contrast, national economic retrospective evaluations were not that important. The Peso Crisis of 1995 seems to have brought important electoral consequences based on pocketbook evaluations, rather than sociotropic concerns.

These results suggest three conclusions. First, there is an almost indistinct pattern of voting for Labastida and the PRI congressional candidates along the left-right continuum. Supporting Labastida for president was basically the same as voting for the PRI for Congress, and the more right-wing the voter, the more likely he or she would vote for them. Second, Cuauhtémoc Cárdenas and the PRD-led Alliance for Mexico drew higher support from the left, but the probabilities of voting for Cárdenas were lower than the probabilities of voting for his party's congressional candidates in every category of the left-right continuum. The more leftist voters gave the PRD/Alliance for Mexico congressional candidates as many as five percentage points more than their presidential candidate. The same difference is observed among center-left voters. Toward the end of the campaign, one of Fox's messages focused on getting *Cardenistas* to vote for what the PAN candidate called the real option for change and asked them to make a vote that mattered. The so-called *voto útil* (or strategic vote) is reflected in the lower support drawn by Cárdenas in comparison to the PRD/Alliance for Mexico, especially among left and center-left voters. In the election, that alliance obtained 19 percent of the official vote, while Cárdenas got 17 percent.

Unlike Cárdenas, Vicente Fox got more votes than the PAN-led Alliance for Change. The vote share for the presidential candidate was 43 percent, whereas PAN and the Green congressional candidates got 39 percent altogether. According to opinion polls, support for the Greens at the national level was between 2 to 4 percent. The difference in support for Fox and the congressional candidates came from all over the political spectrum, except on the right, where the probabilities of voting for Fox and the PAN were similar, but much lower than in the rest of the political spectrum. Support for Fox was as much as eight percentage points higher than that of PAN congressional candidates among leftist voters. Also, the PAN alliance performed best among center voters, declining toward the left and right sides, whereas support for Fox was evenly distributed from the left to the center-right. The coalition for change that translated into presidential votes was wide flung in ideological terms, which can probably be explained by strategic voting as well. Based on panel data, Beatriz Magaloni and Alejandro Poiré argue that although Fox's victory in 2000 cannot be attributed only to strategic coordination, strategic voting played an important role in increasing Fox's share of the vote. According to their findings, some *Cardenistas* who considered their candidate a sure loser voted for Fox. The results presented in this chapter confirm that there was an important segment of leftist voters who supported the PRD congressional candidates but voted for Fox for president.

The Role of Turnout

The outcome of the 2000 presidential election was determined not only by the magnitude of political preferences behind each candidate, but also by turnout. The official turnout in the 1994 presidential election was about 77 percent. Turnout in 2000 was about 64 percent, thirteen percentage points less than six years earlier. This significant difference in turnout decreased the PRI's chances to keep the presidency, and, consequently, increased Fox's to win it. Pre-election polls widely published a few days before the election showed a slight advantage in voting intentions favorable to the PRI candidate, but these polls did not screen their results by likely voters; doing so would have shown a slight Fox advantage over Labastida. Turnout was particularly low in the countryside, where the PRI usually performs better. We should turn next to analyzing the differences in vote choice between those who were likely to vote as opposed to the whole surveyed population.

Table 2.2 shows the statistical model, but this time using pre-election survey data gathered between April and June 2000 in independent national samples. The analysis used a pooled data set and screening of likely voters was done using the following variables: likelihood of voting on a ten-point scale, interest in the campaigns, and, of course, whether the respondent was a registered voter or not. These screening filters of likely voters provided a very accurate estimation of the election outcome in the pre-election polls, and seem the best way to observe, with the data at hand, the differences in support between voters and nonvoters.[30] The main assumption is that the coalition for change was not only about ideological orientations and demographic characteristics, but also about participation. Those who supported Fox were more likely to turn out on election day than those who supported Labastida.

The results of this analysis for the general population show that the significant variables explaining presidential preferences were education, candidate image, and party identification for all candidates. Additionally, the southern region and church attendance were significant in the Cárdenas-Fox comparison, and gender, in-come, the northern region, the rural context, presidential ap-proval, left-right orientations, and the desire for change in the Labastida-Fox comparison.

The analysis of likely voters brings some additional differences: in the Cárdenas-Fox comparison some variables that were not sig-nificant in the analysis of the total sample gained significance among likely voters. That is the case for age, income, the Labastida opinion thermometer, and national retrospective evalu-ations. (Favorable evaluations of the economy were linked to the Fox vote.) Education and church attendance lost significance. In the Labastida-Fox comparison age also gains significance, and the rural variable loses it. In this case, retrospective economic evalua-tions did not influence the choice between Fox and Labastida. A first conclusion from the analysis of likely voters is that age made a significant difference. Younger voters were much more likely to vote for Fox than for Labastida.

In summary, Fox benefited from an unexpectedly low turnout in 2000, as compared to the 1994 presidential election. His perfor-mance was higher among likely voters than among the general population. Labastida's story is the opposite: his performance would have been apparently better had more Mexicans turned out on election day. Cárdenas did get a higher support among leftist likely voters, but a lower one among those in the center. The coalition for change was a configuration of voters that were very likely to be pro-democratic, liberal, young, educated, urban, from all regions of the country but especially the north, from all over the left-right continuum except the right, and, on top of that, they were more likely to vote on July 2, 2000. Beyond these factors, the most significant explanatory variables behind the support for Fox, as opposed to Labastida, were the identification with PAN—although Fox drew the highest support among independents vot-ers as well—and a clear desire for change.

TABLE 2.2.

A Model of Vote Choice for President in 2000: General Population and Likely Voters: Multinomial Logit Estimates from National Pre-Election Polls

| | GENERAL POPULATION | | | | LIKELY VOTERS | | | |
| | Cárdenas/Fox | | Labastida/Fox | | Cárdenas/Fox | | Labastida/Fox | |
	Coefficient	Significance	Coefficient	Significance	Coefficient	Significance	Coefficient	Significance
Intercept	1.900	.002	.379	.465	2.141	.047	.627	.493
Gender (Female=1)	.089	.548	.219	.067	.154	.543	.135	.490
Age	.007	.209	.007	.128	.021	.021	.013	.082
Education	-.301	.000	-.231	.000	-.165	.181	-.212	.034
Income	-.083	.108	-.072	.087	-.181	.023	-.105	.090
North	.028	.886	.453	.003	.267	.420	.530	.029
Center-West	.065	.768	.112	.515	.502	.171	-.020	.942
South	.368	.056	.248	.131	.474	.162	.324	.230
Rural	.057	.743	.282	.041	-.359	.237	-.036	.874
Church attendance	-.161	.008	-.054	.283	-.124	.215	.013	.872
Fox opinion thermometer	-.597	.000	-.614	.000	-.815	.000	-.739	.000
Labastida opinion thermometer	-.030	.348	.421	.000	-.099	.068	.418	.000
Cárdenas opinion thermometer	.572	.000	.041	.131	.674	.000	.040	.390

	B	Sig.	B	Sig.	B	Sig.	B	Sig.
President Zedillo's job approval	-.083	.149	**.100**	.047	-.076	.437	**.145**	.076
Personal economic situation	-.006	.965	-.07	.308	.123	.560	.154	.362
National economic situation	-.183	.141	.021	.832	**-.336**	.097	-.020	.901
Vote for change	-.124	.412	**-1.236**	.000	-.404	.114	**-1.194**	.000
Left-right self-placement	-.035	.250	**.054**	.017	-.015	.761	**.104**	.017
PRI strong partisan	**-1.003**	.041	**2.546**	.000	-.959	.230	**2.400**	.000
PRI weak partisan	.151	.553	**2.256**	.000	-.068	.873	**2.018**	.000
PAN strong partisan	**-2.663**	.000	**-2.272**	.000	**-2.104**	.003	**-2.169**	.000
PAN weak partisan	**-2.394**	.000	**-2.110**	.000	**-2.193**	.000	**-2.680**	.000
PRD strong partisan	**3.249**	.000	-.633	.384	**4.498**	.000	-.038	.977
PRD weak partisan	**2.176**	.000	-.203	.502	**2.413**	.000	-.373	.434
-2 Log likelihood	3469.545				1309.998			
Chi-Square	6551.945				3509.304			
Significance	.000				.000			
Pseudo R-Square (Cox and Snell)	.734				.769			
Cases included in analysis	4,946				2,398			

Coefficients in boldface are statistically significant at 0.05 level or less.

CONCLUSION

The Mexican democratic transition through sharpened party competition has been an excellent natural laboratory for political scientists interested in understanding the dynamics of party support and the configuration of new party systems. The outcome of the 2000 presidential election has been explained from different perspectives, including the impact of a divisive open primary, the effects of campaign messages and contents, the role of strategic voter coordination, the confirmation of the importance of party identifications, the role of turnout, and so on.

Following my previous research in Mexico and Latin America, I have argued that the winning electoral coalition in 2000 was an evolving phenomenon in evidence since at least 1988. The split of two politically relevant camps shows an older, less educated, more rural, more authoritarian, and fundamentalist electorate that predominantly supported the PRI versus a younger, more educated, urban, and pro-democratic electorate that sought a change and supported opposition parties. In 2000, the desire for change was stronger than ever, and it translated mainly into votes for Vicente Fox.

The coalition for change was ideologically and regionally widespread, confirming the catchall character of the PAN. In comparison to 1997, when the PRI lost control of Congress for the first time, the PAN drew higher support in 2000 from the entire political spectrum, gaining from the PRD's losses on the left, and the PRI's losses on the right. In 2000, the PAN coalition was more heterogeneous than ever. Still, support for Vicente Fox was even broader than the PAN's. The PAN electorate confirmed its pivotal position in 2000, becoming generally the centrist party that nonetheless draws support from left and right as no other party in Mexico, stretching even the broad boundaries of a catchall party. The PRD has its niche on the left, but has lost self-identified voters in recent years, given an observable shift to the right in the distribution of the Mexican electorate. However, all party electorates moved to the left on socioeconomic concerns, after more than one decade of predominantly market-oriented policies in Mexico. The PRI's movement to the left on this axis is the most noticeable and significant and probably reflects the change in discourse among its current leaders.

"Change" was a powerful message that activated the major political opposition in Mexican society. For most people, change was about alternation, not a shift in policy orientations. The coalition for change has no ultimate meaning once change has occurred, but its ideological and demographic features make it likely that the PAN will continue to draw significant support in coming elections, independently of Fox's performance in office. Moreover, the balance of party support, which in current polls shows a slight PAN advantage over the PRI among the general population, is likely to lean more toward the PAN if the PRI is not able to mobilize supporters as it once did. Given their sociodemographic characteristics, PAN supporters are more likely to turn out voluntarily on election day. The midterm election in 2003 will provide further evidence about this question.

CHAPTER 3

A Contest of Surprises: The 2000 Election in the United States

Rick Farmer and John C. Green

THE 2000 ELECTION IN THE UNITED STATES can be fairly described as a "contest of surprises," in two senses of the phrase. First, the closeness of the vote (and disputes over counting the ballots) might have been surprising in any event, but they were stunning in light of pre-election expectations. For instance, it was widely believed that the strong economy would allow Vice President Al Gore to extend the Democratic Party's hold on the White House. Furthermore, it was also believed that both moral and foreign policy issues would work to the advantage of the Democrats, giving the Republicans little leverage against President Clinton's popular record. Behind these expectations was a series of assumptions about the political and demographic factors at work in the electorate.

Because few of these pre-election expectations were borne out, many observers believed that the election would undermine citizens' faith in the government. This fear points to the second sense in which the election was a "contest of surprises": it is a contest as to which of the unanticipated results was *most* surprising. While we will leave it to the readers to make their own judgments, we conclude that the results were not so surprising as to endanger the legitimacy of the American regime. Indeed, the following catalogue of surprises suggests that the 2000 results are well accounted for by three things: a high degree of partisan unity among voters; the offsetting impact of economic, moral, and foreign policy issues; and the great demographic diversity of the American electorate.

THE FIRST SURPRISE: A VERY CLOSE VOTE

The 2000 election has been fittingly described as the "perfect tie" and it is worth reviewing just how close the election was.[1] In formal terms, George W. Bush became the forty-third president because he obtained 271 votes in the Electoral College, one more than required by the U.S. Constitution; Al Gore received 267, for a difference of four electoral votes. Bush's total included the electoral votes from Florida, where he had a 537-vote margin out of 5.8 million ballots cast. The U.S. Supreme Court allowed this thin margin to stand when it decided *Bush v. Gore* by a five to four vote.

Bush did not win a popular vote plurality, obtaining just 47.9 percent of the total vote, while Gore obtained 48.4 percent, for a margin of about 500,000 of 105 million cast. Gore's small plurality was a two-fold surprise. Pre-election predictions assumed a much larger margin for Gore, and in the last days of the campaign, most observers concluded that Gore might well lose the popular vote, but win the Electoral College.[2] The small level of support for minor parties was sufficient to deny anyone a majority, including Ralph Nader's 2.9 percent for the Green Party and the one percent of all other minor parties combined (principally Pat Buchanan of the Reform Party, Harry Browne of the Libertarians, and John Hagelin of the Natural Law Party).

All told, Bush's 47.9 percent exceeded his father's losing 37.7 percent of the popular vote in 1992—but did not match his father's winning of 53.8 percent in 1988. Gore's 48.4 percent was slightly lower than the Clinton-Gore 49.2 percent in 1996, but higher than the Clinton-Gore winning margin of 43.3 percent in 1992 and the Dukakis losing vote of 46.2 percent in 1988. It is worth noting that the minor party vote of about four percent was small compared to recent elections, especially Ross Perot's 1992 (19 percent) and 1996 (8 percent) performances. Voter turnout in 2000 was low, with just 51.2 percent of the eligible voters casting a ballot. This figure was slightly higher than in 1996 (48.9 percent) and 1988 (50.3 percent), but far lower than the 55.2 percent in 1992, when Perot first appeared on the ballot.

The close 2000 vote extended to other contests as well. The Republicans held on to control of the House of Representatives by just five seats out of 435. Meanwhile, the Democrats gained five seats in the Senate, producing an unprecedented 50-50 tie. Vice President Dick Cheney's tie-breaking vote allowed the Republicans to organize the body—until Jim Jeffords of Vermont became an independent in 2001, giving control to the Democrats. Similarly slim margins were recorded in numerous state and local elections.

One reason for the close vote is that the major parties nominated well-known, centrist candidates, who united their respective partisans and competed effectively for independents. Table 3.1 reports the degree to which each party's voters were united, based on the Voter News Service Exit Poll. (For purposes of reference, the percentage of the reported vote is listed across the top of the table; it differs slightly from the official vote tallies reported above.)

TABLE 3.1.

The 2000 Presidential Vote and Political Factors

	Gore	Bush	Nader	Other	ALL
ALL	**48.4**	**48.0**	**2.5**	**1.1 =100%**	**100%**
Party Identification					
Democrat	86	11	2	1 =100%	39
Independent, other	45	47	6	2	26
Republican	8	91	1	*	35
					100%
1996 Presidential Vote					
Clinton	82	15	2	1 =100%	44
Dole	13	85	1	1	35
Perot, others	27	60	10	4	9
New 2000 voter	44	52	3	1	12
					100%

% rounded to nearest whole number
* less than 1 percent
Source: 2000 VNS National Exit Poll (N=13,259)

As the first entry in table 3.1 shows, Gore received some 86 percent of self-identified Democratic voters, which make up 39 percent of the electorate. Bush received 91 percent of the 35 percent of the electorate that self-identified as Republicans. Although few partisans defected to either side, Bush fared slightly better in this regard. Also, Bush won a slim plurality of the 26 percent of the electorate who claimed to be independents or identified with a minor party. Nader did especially well with the latter and drew twice as many votes from self-identified Democrats as Republicans. Nader might well have cost Gore several key states, including Florida and New Hampshire. But other minor party candidates, such as Pat Buchanan, might have cost Bush states as well, such as New Mexico, Iowa, and Wisconsin.

Thus, Bush was able to pull nearly even with Gore in the popular vote by uniting Republicans, attracting independents, and minimizing minor party defections. Evidence of this success can be seen in the relationship of the reported 1996 vote and the 2000 choice (the second entry on table 3.1). Gore obtained 82 percent of those who said they voted for Clinton (and Gore) in 1996. Likewise, Bush obtained 85 percent of the reported Dole voters. However, Bush also received three-fifths of the 1996 minor party voters, mostly Perot's backers, while Gore got just a little more than one-quarter. Bush also received a majority of the new presidential voters (those who claimed not to have cast a ballot in 1996).

By itself, this high degree of party unity should not have been all that surprising, but many analysts failed to anticipate it, assuming that the issue mix would allow Gore to win strong support beyond core Democratic constituencies.

THE BIG SURPRISE: ECONOMIC ISSUES

Many observers believed that Al Gore would win the 2000 election handily because of the strong economy. Certainly, there were potent examples from past campaigns, including the first President Bush's come-from-behind victory in the 1988 election. Academics contributed to this expectation with a series of well-publicized press reports of mathematical models that predicted a significant Gore win.[3] Although Gore did indeed win the two-party vote, the strong economy did not generate the kind of widespread support for the incumbent party most observers anticipated.

Table 3.2 looks at economic matters and the 2000 presidential vote. The first entry is a powerful predictor of election outcomes: overall, is the country on the "right track" or the "wrong track"? In line with the strong economy, two-thirds of the electorate chose the "right track" option, and Gore won three-fifths of these voters. In contrast, Bush won almost three-quarters of the one-third of the electorate that chose the "wrong track" option. Here is one place where the minor party candidates may have hurt Bush in the close contest, siphoning off some economic discontent.

TABLE 3.2.

The 2000 Presidential Vote and Economic Issues

	Gore	Bush	Nader	Other	ALL
ALL	**48.4**	**48.0**	**2.5**	**1.1 =100%**	**100%**
Overall, the country is:					
On the right track	61	36	2	1 =100%	**67**
On the wrong track	20	74	4	2	**33**
					100%
Economic conditions:					
Excellent	70	26	2	1 = 100%	**20**
Good	45	52	3	1	**66**
Not so good/poor	33	62	3	2	**14**
					100%
The government should:					
Do more	74	23	3	1 =100%	**45**
Do less	25	71	2	2	**55**
					100%
Issue priorities:					
Health care	64	33	3	*	**8**
Economy, jobs	60	39	1	1	**18**
Medicare	60	39	1	*	**7**
Social Security	58	40	1	1	**14**
Education	52	44	3	1	**15**
Other issues	43	51	4	2	**13**
World affairs	40	54	4	2	**13**
Taxes	17	80	2	1	**14**
					100%

% rounded to nearest whole number
* less than 1 percent
Source: 2000 VNS National Exit Poll (N=13,259)

Historically, "right track" responses are closely connected to the performance of the economy. The next entry in table 3.2 addressed the state of the economy directly. One-fifth of the electorate rated the economy as "excellent," and it strongly backed Gore. In contrast, the one-sixth of the electorate who thought the economy was poor or very poor strongly backed Bush. However, the two-thirds of voters who regarded the economy as "good" voted for Bush and not Gore. Taken together, these figures suggest two conclusions: the strong economy helped Gore, but the anticipated level of voter support did not materialize.

Economic concerns extend beyond the performance of the economy to government policies designed to enhance economic well-being. The next entry in table 3.2 summarizes this matter by asking if the government should "do more" or "do less" in domestic policy. The results present a stark pattern: almost three-quarters of those who wanted the government to "do more" supported Gore and nearly as many of those who wanted the government to "do less" backed Bush. Note, however, that a majority of the electorate preferred the latter. Thus, on the question of government activism, Bush edged out Gore.

The final entry in table 3.2 lists issues that voters reported as salient when they cast their ballots. This list must be viewed with some caution because the options were preselected, and thus may not capture the voters' most pressing concerns. Indeed, the "other issues" entry reflects individuals who did not pick one of the options offered, presumably because other matters had higher priority.

Gore did quite well among voters who were concerned with traditional social welfare policies, receiving nearly two-thirds of those who stressed health care, and about three-fifths of those who focused on the economy (and jobs) and programs for the elderly (Medicare and Social Security). However, one-third and two-fifths of these citizens voted for Bush. An even better example of

Bush's success in this regard was education, a traditional Democratic issue where Gore received only a slim majority. Although Bush won a slight majority of the "other" responses, and a majority of voters concerned with world affairs (a point we will return to presently), the only issue he won decisively was taxes, receiving eight of ten ballots from the one-sixth of the electorate who chose this priority. On balance, then, Gore benefited from economic and social welfare issues, but Bush did well enough on these issues and other matters to break even at the polls.

THE CONTINUING SURPRISE: MORAL ISSUES

Many analysts also expected that moral issues would not play a significant role in the 2000 campaign. For one thing, the Monica Lewinsky scandal did not lead to the removal of President Clinton from office, to the great dismay of social conservatives. And some of the chief advocates of moral conservatism, such as the Christian Coalition, were in disarray. However, pundits regularly underestimate the impact of moral questions on politics and 2000 was no exception.[4] Although the impact of moral issues on elections should surprise no one, it continues to upset the conventional wisdom.

Table 3.3 looks at moral issues and the 2000 presidential vote. The first entry is parallel to the first entry in table 3.2: in moral terms, is the country on the "right" or "wrong" track? Almost the opposite pattern appears, with only two-fifths believing that the country was on the "right track" morally and three-fifths claiming it was on the "wrong track." Almost two-thirds of the former backed Gore, and Bush won the latter by nearly two-to-one.

The scandals surrounding President Clinton were one reason for this dim view of the nation's morals, and the next entry reports the importance of scandal to the vote. Overall, a majority of the

TABLE 3.3.

The 2000 Presidential Vote and Moral Issues

	Gore	Bush	Nader	Other	ALL
ALL	**48.4**	**48.0**	**2.5**	**1.1 =100%**	**100%**
In terms of morals, the country is:					
On the right track	69	27	2	1 =100%	**40**
On the wrong track	33	62	3	2	**60**
					100%
Clinton scandal:					
Not at all important	75	19	4	2	**37**
Not too important	59	37	2	2	**17**
Somewhat important	28	70	2	*	**20**
Very important	18	80	1	1	**24**
					100%
Abortion should be:					
Always legal	70	25	4	1	**24**
Mostly legal	58	38	3	1	**35**
Mostly illegal	29	69	1	1	**28**
Always illegal	23	74	1	3	**13**
					100%
Candidate qualities:					
Experience	82	17	1	*	**15**
Handle complexity	75	19	4	1	**13**
Cares	63	31	5	2	**12**
Other qualities	49	46	2	3	**7**
Good judgment	48	50	1	1	**13**
Likeable	38	59	2	1	**2**
Strong leader	35	64	1	*	**14**
Honest	15	80	4	2	**24**
					100%

% rounded to nearest whole number
* less than 1 percent
Source: 2000 VNS National Exit Poll (N=13,259)

electorate claimed that scandal was "not at all" or "not too" important to their vote; Gore won three-quarters of the former group and almost three-fifths of the latter. However, the large minority of voters who claimed that the scandal was "somewhat" or "very important" voted decisively for Bush (70 and 80 percent, respectively). Clearly, the perception of moral problems helped Bush and hurt Gore. But it is worth noting that these perceptions were not strong enough to give Bush a majority of the popular vote. Instead, they just evened the score.

The next entry in table 3.3 reports attitudes on abortion, the quintessential moral controversy in recent times. Gore won large majorities of voters who believe abortion should be "always legal" (70 percent) and "mostly legal" (58 percent), while Bush had even larger majorities among those who wanted abortion to be "mostly illegal" (69 percent) and "always illegal" (74 percent). The patterns here are remarkably similar to the results on the Clinton scandals, except that pro-choice voters were a larger majority than voters who tolerated the scandals. It is likely, then, that moral issues benefited both major party candidates with key constituencies, but on balance favored Gore. When put together with the question on government activism in table 3.2, these data cast a new light on the 2000 election: the voters were on balance opposed to government action in the economic and moral spheres.

The final entry in table 3.3 reports voters' priorities with regard to a list of candidate qualities, factors often associated with moral character. As in table 3.2, this list was preselected, producing an "other qualities" category of respondents who did not choose one of the options. Gore did quite well among voters who were concerned with candidate "experience" and ability to "handle complexity," and a candidate that "cares." All told, 40 percent of the electorate focused on these qualities.

Interestingly, another 40 percent chose qualities on which Bush did very well: being "likeable," a "strong leader," and "honest."

The issue of honesty was especially important during the campaign, where exaggerations by the Gore campaign caused voters to question Gore's integrity—and perhaps connect him to President Clinton's failings. Of course, Bush suffered an "integrity" problem as well, when his past DUI conviction was disclosed just days before the election.

The major party candidates essentially broke even on the remaining qualities, with Bush edging Gore on "good judgment" and the reverse happening on the combination of "other" qualities. In sum, moral and character questions divided the electorate, undermining Gore's appeal but denying Bush a victory.

THE HIDDEN SURPRISE: FOREIGN POLICY

Foreign affairs played only a modest role in the 2000 campaign. As we saw in table 3.2, just 13 percent of the electorate gave "world affairs" priority in their vote. This pattern fit the pre-election expectations reasonably well, but it is surprising given the events that followed the campaign, including the terrorist attacks of 9/11 and the wars in Afghanistan and Iraq. This lack of attention to foreign policy reflects the fact that America was at peace and that the Clinton foreign policy was regarded as successful. Indeed, the principal debate of the campaign was whether George W. Bush had the necessary ability and experience to manage foreign affairs. However, despite the lack of attention, there were some important differences between the major candidates.

Table 3.4 reports attitudes on foreign policy and the 2000 vote, using data from the 2000 National Election Study.[5] The first entry concerns trade restrictions. Although a majority of the electorate opposed trade restrictions "to protect jobs," the issue divided both major political parties. For instance, Gore received 51 percent support from voters who supported trade limits, while Bush pre-

TABLE 3.4.

The 2000 Presidential Vote and Foreign Policy Issues

	Gore	Bush	Nader	Other	ALL
ALL	**48.4**	**48.0**	**2.5**	**1.1** =100%	100%
Foreign Trade:					
Support import limits	51	46	2	1 =100%	46
Oppose import limits	47	48	4	1	54
					100%
Immigration:					
Increase	58	33	8	1 =100%	8
Keep the same	53	43	3	1	44
Decrease	44	52	3	2	48
					100%
Defense spending:					
Decrease	65	25	6	4 =100%	16
About the same	62	34	3	1	24
Increase	33	65	2	*	60
					100%

% rounded to nearest whole number
ᴵᴵ less than 1 percent
Source: 2000 National Election Study (N=1,807)

vailed by the slimmest of margins among voters who oppose such limitations. Other evidence reveals that attitudes on NAFTA resembled these overall results closely: in one pre-election poll, 47 percent of the public favored NAFTA and 39 percent opposed (with the remainder undecided).[6]

A similar pattern occurred on the question of immigration restrictions. Overall, a slim plurality of voters favored laws that would decrease immigration, but nearly as many wanted immigration policy to be unchanged. Bush received a slight majority among the former and Gore nearly an identical majority among the latter. (Gore won the small group who favored increased immigration by a substantial majority.)

The final entry is defense spending. Here a majority of the electorate favored increased defense spending. Bush won these voters—and Gore did well among those who favored the status quo and those who wanted a decrease in defense outlays. On balance, then, foreign policy probably helped Bush to tie Gore at the polls.

Each of these policies had implications for the "reluctant trinity" of the United States, Canada, and Mexico. Both Gore and Bush would have continued the policy of continental free trade embodied in NAFTA, but Bush had incentives to be sympathetic to immigration restrictions and a larger military role, policy directions reinforced by post-election events. However, relations with Canada and Mexico received only slight attention in the campaign, mostly in the form of Bush's greater interest in Mexico, symbolized by his personal relationship with Vicente Fox.

Nonetheless, it is worth noting the attitudes of the American public toward their continental neighbors circa the 2000 election, as reported in table 3.5. First, Americans had a positive view of Canada and Mexico, and second, the quality of the relationship with each country was different. Just before the 2000 election 63 percent of Americans regarded Canada as a "close ally" and another 23 percent as a "friend." In contrast, 28 percent of Americans saw Mexico as a "close ally" and 40 percent as a "friend." In neither case did many Americans have a negative view of the neighboring countries. These differences may reflect the longstanding military alliance between the United States and Canada, as well as the cultural similarities between the English-speaking majorities in both countries.

A separate set of questions adds some details to this picture. When asked about the relative "overall" importance of the two neighbors, almost one-half chose Canada, and a little over one-third Mexico. This result was consistent with the previous ques-

TABLE 3.5.

Attitudes toward Canada and Mexico circa the 2000 Election

Views of neighbors:

	Canada	Mexico
Close ally	63	28
Friend, not close ally	23	40
Not friend, not enemy	5	16
Unfriendly and enemy	2	4
Don't know/Refused	7	12
	100%	100%

Source: Harris Interactive, August 10–August 14, 2000 (N=1,010)

Which neighbor is more important to the United States:

	Overall	To American:		
		Politics	*Economics*	*Culture*
Canada	**45**	34	27	26
Not sure, the same	**20**	16	9	9
Mexico	**35**	50	64	65
	100%	100%	100%	100%

Source: *Time*, Cable News Network, Harris Interactive, May 23–May 24, 2001 (N=1,031)

tion. However, when the query focused on key aspects of the relationship, the pattern reversed itself. For example, one-half of Americans regarded Mexico as more important to American politics, compared to the one-third who named Canada. And the pattern becomes even more lopsided in economics and culture, where Mexico was chosen as more important by almost two-thirds and Canada by a bit more than one-fourth. These results may well reflect the growing prominence of the Hispanic population in the United States. Such evidence may well presage the creation of a "special relationship" between the U.S. and Mexico on a par—or perhaps greater—than the special relationship between the U.S. and Canada.

BEHIND THE SURPRISES:
DEMOGRAPHY AND THE 2000 VOTE

What lies behind the mixed and offsetting impact of the issues on the vote? One way to answer this question is to look at the voting behavior of key demographic groups, including those defined by socioeconomic status, and social and cultural characteristics. Some well-known patterns were evident, but the great demographic diversity the American electorate produced tended to offset them.

Socioeconomic Status

Table 3.6 looks at the presidential vote and three common measures of socioeconomic status: income, education, and self-identified social class. Since the days of the New Deal, socioeconomic status has been one of the pillars of the American party system. The Democrats have traditionally drawn strong support from lower status voters (the "have nots, have little, and have problems") and the Republicans have been strongly supported by upper status individuals (the "haves, have hope, and have help"). The 2000 election shows evidence of this pattern, but also some departures.

The first entry in table 3.6 is for 2000 household income. Voters who reported income of less than $30,000 voted 55 percent for Gore, while those who earned more than $50,000 voted 53 percent for Bush. Voters in the middle-range ($30,000 to $50,000) gave Bush a slight edge—and also supported the minor party candidates. So, the income gap between the highest and lowest categories in table 3.6 was about twelve percentage points. This gap

TABLE 3.6.

The 2000 Presidential Vote and Socioeconomic Status

	Gore	Bush	Nader	Other	ALL
ALL	**48.4**	**48.0**	**2.5**	**1.1 =100%**	**100%**
Income					
Under $30,000	55	40	4	1 =100%	23
$30,000 to $50,000	45	47	6	2	49
Over $50,000	44	53	2	1	28
					100%
Education					
High school or less	50	47	1	1 =100%	26
Some college, grad	45	51	3	1	56
Post-graduate	52	44	3	1	18
					100%
Social Class					
Working class	52	45	3	1 = 100%	21
Middle class	47	51	2	1	75
Upper class	56	39	3	1	4
					100%

% rounded to nearest whole number
Source: 2000 VNS National Exit Poll (N=13,259)

certainly fits with conventional wisdom, but it is worth noting another bit of conventional wisdom as well: due to differences in turnout, lower income groups were under-represented in the electorate compared to the population as a whole, and the higher income groups were over-represented.

A different pattern appears for education, the second entry in table 3.6. Voters with a high school diploma or less gave Gore a very slight advantage, with Bush doing nearly as well. In fact, Gore did much better among voters with post-graduate education, beating Bush 52 to 44 percent. Bush won the "some college and college graduate" category by a similar margin. These results are the product of a long-term trend: although high levels of education are associated with high income, many well-educated people vote Democratic rather than Republican.

A similar pattern can be seen in self-identified social class, the third entry in table 3.6. Of course, Americans overwhelmingly think of themselves as "middle class" regardless of their income, education, or occupation—as evidenced by the three-quarters of the electorate that claimed some kind of middle-class status in 2000. Bush won this large group by just four percentage points. However, Gore won decisively the small portion of the electorate who considered themselves "upper class," and also prevailed among the "working class" voters. So there was no significant "education" or "class" gap in the 2000 presidential vote.

These findings may help explain why economic issues did not help Gore as much as anticipated: the weakness of the socioeconomic underpinning of the vote opened the door for other factors.

Social Characteristics

Table 3.7 looks at three key social characteristics: gender, family status (marital status and the presence of at least one child at home), and age. The first entry in the table shows the much-discussed "gender gap": a majority of women voted for Gore and a majority of men for Bush. The size of the gender gap was about twelve percentage points, about the same as the income gap. Note, however, that the gender gap was almost symmetrical. Because women were more numerous in the electorate, Gore had a very slight advantage, but one almost offset by the fact that Bush did slightly better among women than Gore did among men.

Family status had a larger impact on the vote in 2000 than gender (second entry in table 3.7). Gore received some three-fifths of the vote of unmarried voters with children, a group especially concerned with government assistance. However, this group was almost four

TABLE 3.7.

The 2000 Presidential Vote and Social Characteristics

	Gore	Bush	Nader	Other	ALL
ALL	**48.4**	**48.0**	**2.5**	**1.1 =100%**	**100%**
Gender					
Female	54	43	2	1 =100%	52
Male	42	54	3	1	48
					100%
Family Status					
Unmarried, child	61	36	3	1 = 100%	8
Unmarried, no child	56	39	4	1	27
Married, no child	46	51	2	1	34
Married, child	41	56	2	1	31
					100%
Age					
Under 30 years	48	46	5	2 = 100%	17
30 to 50 years	47	49	2	1	45
Over 50 years	50	48	2	1	38
					100%

% rounded to nearest whole number
Source: 2000 VNS National Exit Poll (N=13,259)

times smaller than the opposite category, married voters with children (8 to 31 percent of the electorate, respectively), and the latter group voted strongly for Bush, by a margin of fifteen percentage points. Gore also did quite well among unmarried voters with no children, winning by seventeen percentage points, but lost to Bush by six points among the larger group of married people without children. Overall, the "family status gap" was twenty percentage points, nearly twice the size of the gender and income gaps.

The final entry in table 3.7 is age. Age often has an impact on politics, in large part because it represents the generational differences. But these effects were very muted in 2000: Gore edged out

Bush among voters under thirty and over fifty by the same slim margin, while Bush did slightly better with middle-aged voters. Older voters did not strongly support Gore, despite their special interest in Social Security and childhood connection to the New Deal. Indeed, among voters over 65, Gore's lead was just four percentage points. Similarly, the youngest voters did not strongly back Gore either, despite their special concern with education and other government programs. But here, the 5 percent of younger voters who backed Nader probably prevented a Gore majority. In any event, there was no "generation gap" in 2000.

These findings also help explain the surprising impact of economic issues on the vote: social factors that have tended to help the Democrats in past elections were offset by other factors that favored the Republicans.

Cultural Characteristics

Table 3.8 looks at three key cultural characteristics and the 2000 vote: place of residence, race, and religion. Many cultural differences are captured in the places where voters reside, with the cosmopolitan cultures of large cities contrasting with the middle-class values of suburbs and the traditional ethos of smaller cities and rural areas. As the first entry in table 3.8 reveals, these distinctions mattered in 2000: the large cities gave Gore three-fifths of their votes, while small cities and rural areas voted nearly as strongly for Bush. Interestingly, these two groups were about of equal size in the electorate (a little over one-quarter). The larger group of suburban voters gave Bush a very slight margin over Gore. Thus, Gore was competitive in the traditionally Republican suburbs.

Race is one of the most powerful factors in American politics, and the 2000 election was no exception (second entry in table 3.8). African Americans cast 90 percent of their ballots for Gore, a larger margin than usually occurs among this bedrock Demo-

TABLE 3.8.

The 2000 Presidential Vote and Cultural Characteristics

	Gore	Bush	Nader	Other	ALL
ALL	**48.4**	**48.0**	**2.5**	**1.1 =100%**	**100%**
Place of Residence					
Large City	61	35	3	1 =100%	29
Suburbs	47	49	3	1	43
Small City, Rural	38	59	2	1	28
					100%
Race					
Black	90	9	1	1 = 100%	10
Hispanic	62	35	2	1	7
Other Non-White	55	40	3	2	3
White	42	54	3	1	81
					100%
Religion					
Black Protestants	92	7	1	1 = 100%	8
Jews	78	20	1	1	4
Minority Catholics	67	30	2	2	5
Secular	61	32	6	2	11
Other Non-Christians	54	34	8	4	4
Hispanic Protestants	52	44	3	1	1
Infrequent Worship Attenders:					
White Other Christians	50	44	5	2	7
White Catholics	47	49	3	1	6
White Protestants	46	52	2	*	8
Frequent Worship Attenders:					
White Catholics	42	54	2	1	13
White Protestants	40	57	2	1	16
White Other Christians	34	63	3	1	6
"Religious Right"	14	84	1	1	11
					100%

% rounded to nearest whole number
* less than 1 percent
Source: 2000 VNS National Exit Poll (N=13,259)

cratic constituency. Indeed, George W. Bush's 9 percent was the worst performance of a Republican presidential candidate in many years. Gore also won smaller majorities among Hispanics (62 percent) and other non-whites (55 percent). One reason Bush did better with the last two groups was their internal diversity. For example, the Hispanic community varies according to country of origin, with, for example, voters of Mexican heritage being more Democratic and those of Cuban ancestry more Republican. Also, recent immigrants tended to prefer Gore more strongly and longer-term residents Bush.

Race and ethnicity strongly favored the Republicans in another respect: Bush won a solid majority of the white vote, which accounted for four-fifths of the electorate in 2000. Put another way, without support from minorities, Gore would have been defeated decisively. (In 2000, the small group of "Canadian-Americans" voted like other white Americans.) All told, there was a huge "racial gap" of 48 percentage points.

The final entry in table 3.8 is religion. Combining a number of exit poll questions produces a useful picture of the great diversity of American religious groups. The small size of these groups reveals the complexity of the major party coalitions in 2000.

The first five religious groups were solidly Democratic, as they have been for many years. Black Protestants voted even more strongly for Gore than African Americans as a whole, reflecting the central political role of the black church. Much the same can be said for minority Catholics, most of which were Hispanic. More than three-quarters of Jews voted for Gore, and so did three-fifths of the secular (non-religious) population, a newly emerged Democratic constituency.

In addition, Gore won a small majority of a polyglot category of "Other Non-Christians" (Muslims, Hindus, Buddhists, "New Age" adherents, and others) and Hispanic Protestants. It is worth noting that the minor party candidates also did well among the other non-Christians and secularists. Gore drew strong support from the one-third of the electorate that included the most obvious examples of religious diversity.

The remaining seven religious categories are varieties of white Christians. The first three are groups of voters who were infrequent churchgoers (less than once a week). Here, Gore received a bare majority of the "White Other Christians" and narrowly lost the white Catholics and white Protestants. Thus, Gore essentially broke even among the less traditional—and more liberal—white Christians.

Bush won a large majority of the four remaining groups, all of which reported frequent worship attendance (once a week or more). Bush did well among white Catholics (once a bastion of the Democratic Party), better among white Protestants (the largest portion of which are mainline Protestants, long a bedrock constituency of the GOP), and even better among these "Other White Christians" (which include conservative churches, such as the Latter Day Saints). But Bush's best group was the "Religious Right" (white, regularly attending Protestants who claimed to be members of the religious right), where he received 84 percent of the vote. This controversial constituency has become an integral part of the GOP coalition, having a role similar to African Americans among the Democrats.

Thus, there was a striking "religion gap" in 2000. The difference between black Protestants and the religious right was a whopping 78 percentage points (better than six times the size of the gender gap). Of course, this difference was partly based on race. But the difference between Jews and the religious right was 64 points (five times the size of the gender gap), and the comparable difference between seculars and the religious right was 47 percent (not quite four times the gender gap and equal to the racial gap). These patterns also help explain the impact of moral issues in 2000: the diverse cultural groups were deeply divided politically.

THE FINAL SURPRISE:
THE FLORIDA BALLOT DEBACLE

The 2000 election is most likely to be remembered for the disputed presidential ballots in Florida than the other surprises of the campaign. However, the ballot controversy arose directly from the closeness of the election. Indeed, the peculiar combination of politics, issues, and demography that produced the "perfect tie" nationally was most fully exemplified in the Sunshine State. Campaign strategy was a factor as well. Originally counted in the Bush column (in part because the candidate's brother was governor), Florida became a special target of the Gore campaign as election day approached. This effort very nearly paid off, but may have cost Gore the election elsewhere: the resources spent in Florida might have secured at least one of four Democratic-leaning states, any one of which would have given Gore an Electoral College win regardless of the Florida dispute. Gore lost New Hampshire by a nose and was also defeated in the Democratic bastion of West Virginia, in Bill Clinton's Arkansas, and in his home state of Tennessee.

The multiple failures of the Florida electoral machinery, both physical and institutional, certainly shocked most Americans. The weaknesses of punch-card ballots, ranging from "hanging chads" to "undervotes," revealed the lack of public investment in basic instruments of democracy, and raised serious questions about systemic neglect of poor and minority neighborhoods. Ballot design errors, such as the confusing "butterfly ballot" in Palm Beach County, showed even the well-intentioned efforts of local officials could deny citizens a voice. The lack of clear standards for judging disputed ballots and the intense partisanship of state and local election officials reduced further the legitimacy of the process. And the inability of many citizens to follow simple balloting instructions underscored the real-world limits of citizen participation.

It is worth noting, however, that such problems were not unique to Florida. In fact, many states had similar problems, and in at least three (New Mexico, Iowa, and Wisconsin) the margins were close enough that balloting failures might have made a difference in the outcome. These balloting failures were deeply embarrassing to the United States, which frequently criticizes other countries for poor election administration. Indeed, both Canada and Mexico had far fewer problems of this sort in 2000.

The combination of a close contest and balloting problems renders it unlikely that there will ever be a definitive answer to the Florida ballot dispute. Indeed, the intensive post-election review of the ballots by news organizations produced extensive grounds for debate. Such debate was encouraged by the unprecedented thirty-six-day post-election campaign waged by the Gore and Bush campaigns in the news media, canvassing boards, and courts. Americans were familiar (if often uncomfortable) with campaigning *before* the ballots are cast, but the rare spectacle of such campaigning *after* election day was especially unsettling. The major parties provided a steady stream of commentary and invective designed to influence public perceptions of both the election results and the post-election maneuvers. For more than a month, the nation watched the contenders criticize the legitimacy of the very process in which they were engaged. These efforts clearly hardened partisan lines, although it is unclear if either candidate prevailed.

The candidates' litigation strategies were at the center of these post-election campaigns. Gore focused on securing an expanded recount in four counties via the state courts, while Bush moved early into federal court, arguing the recount efforts violated the equal protection provisions of the U.S. Constitution. Both strategies produced some successes. After an extended legal tug-of-war, the Gore campaign eventually received a favorable ruling when the Florida state supreme court voted 4-3 to extend the recount.

The Bush campaign then appealed this decision to the U.S. Supreme Court, which, to the surprise of most observers, took the case. The result was two rulings in the precedent-setting case of *Bush v. Gore*, both of which favored Bush. The first ruling was decided by a 7-2 vote and found that the Florida balloting system did indeed violate the equal protection provisions due to the absence of a uniform standard for counting votes. The second ruling was decided by a 5-4 margin and ordered the end of the recount efforts in Florida. This second ruling was the most controversial, providing a storm of criticism in both political and legal circles.[7]

The short-term impact of the Florida ballot debacle was to intensify the political effects of the close contest, reducing the legitimacy of the winner—an effect that would have applied to Gore if he had prevailed, much as it affected Bush. An ironic result of the situation was that the Bush administration adopted a strategy of partisan confrontation in domestic and foreign policy, instead of the anticipated strategy of bipartisanship and cooperation.[8] In this sense, the surprises continued after the contest was resolved.

A CONTEST OF SURPRISES

In the end, which of the surprises in the 2000 contest were most important? In the short run, it might well have been the Florida ballot debacle, with its grand spectacle and partisan rancor. But from a longer perspective, the factors that created the close balloting may matter more. The high degree of unity among Democrats and Republicans was crucial. In this context, the weaker-than-anticipated impact of economic issues on the vote kept Gore from obtaining an overall majority, opening the way for other factors to matter. Meanwhile, the regularly neglected moral issues helped Bush pull even with Gore—as did the unnoticed influence of foreign policy. Although there was no way to know at the time, American attitudes on key issues tended to benefit Bush and provided a base for the Bush administration's approach to foreign affairs, especially after 9/11. These issues may well influence the future of the "reluctant trinity" among the North American democracies. The great demographic diversity of the American electorate lies behind these patterns.

What about the legitimacy of the American regime? There is no doubt that the "contest of surprises" sorely tested the patience of many Americans with the political process. The reputations of the major political parties, the new media, and even scholars were tarnished by the unanticipated results. Many election officials could hardly show their faces in public, President Bush entered office under a cloud of suspicion, and even the Supreme Court lost some of its luster. At a deeper level, the divisions among the citizenry over the future direction of the country were troubling to all manner of observers. But the legitimacy of the regime was not shaken, as illustrated by the national response to the crisis of 9/11. To some observers, this result may be the biggest surprise of all.

CHAPTER 4

Distracted Voters: Media Coverage of the 2000 Canadian Federal Election Campaign

Lydia Miljan

T HE 2000 CANADIAN CAMPAIGN appears at first glance to have had little impact on voter choice. The Liberal Party returned with its third consecutive majority government. The only major upset was that the governing Liberals gained ground in Quebec. The official opposition, the Canadian Alliance Party, finished the election with the same popular support it had when the campaign started: 26 percent. The New Democratic Party (NDP) and the Progressive Conservatives each showed small gains, with the NDP moving up from 6 percent to 9 percent popular support. The Conservatives had similar movement, going from 7 percent to 10 percent popular support.

These small advances, one could argue, illustrate how little campaign or media influences formed and changed public opinion in English Canada in 2000. That is not to say that the campaign or the media did not matter; they simply did not change opinions during the election period. In fact, this chapter will argue that the media mattered in two important ways: first, it reinforced already held views on the opposition parties with seemingly secondary issues; and second, its emphasis on another important election diffused interest and coverage on the Canadian contest. There are many assessments of the 2000 Canadian federal election. Most notably, the Canadian Election Study (CES) provides excellent statistical detail of voter dynamics, and in particular, the Liberal victory.[1] This discussion differs in that it concentrates on how media reports of issues outside the Canadian election also impacted the vote, and how the controversies of the campaign and influenced the official opposition's performance.

MEDIA AND ELECTIONS

The democracy literature argues that elections matter because they provide citizens with a direct say in the direction and tone of government. Media attention to elections makes a difference because the news media are the primary way in which citizens receive political and campaign information. As a consequence, what the news media say about candidates, campaigns, and parties can have a profound impact on the outcome of elections. Or so we are led to believe. But what if there were an election and no one paid attention? In a sense that is exactly what happened in the 2000 Canadian federal election campaign.

By several accounts, the 2000 election was unexciting. The CES addressed this issue when it examined the voter turnout. "A key question here is whether the low turnout simply reflected the fact that it was a 'boring' election or whether the low level turnout was attributable to deeper, structural factors."[2] Editorial writers discussed this view at some length at the time of the election. "Canadians showed their disgust," wrote Mordecai Richler in the *National Post*, "with a boring and ill-mannered campaign, and the inadequate choices available to them, only 63 percent of them going to the polls, a modern-day low."[3] Newspaper baron Conrad

Black lamented the Canadian political scene in the *Wall Street Journal:* "Americans who are concerned by their prolonged electoral controversy can take comfort from the fact we have just had one of the dreariest elections in the history of serious democratic countries. Five unbelievably unexciting political leaders, most of them heading parties that have no real reason to exist, avoided most serious issues and waged a campaign consisting largely of defamation."[4] Not only was the campaign considered lackluster, the election itself was deemed unnecessary by many. The election was called three years and four months into the Liberal government's mandate—a mandate that technically did not have to end for nearly two more years. Peter Gzowski complained in the *Globe and Mail*, "If health care is, as everyone keeps telling us, the defining issue of this unnecessary and frustrating election campaign, you'd think that four hours of debate among the leaders—counting the stilted session in French—would at least leave us clear about what each party is proposing."[5]

To understand media dynamics and coverage of the three elections held on the North American continent in 2000, we conducted a content analysis of national media news. The study is based on stories appearing in the two national Canadian newspapers, the *Globe and Mail* and the *National Post*. We also examine stories appearing on the flagship national television news programs of the publicly owned Canadian Broadcasting Corporation (CBC) as well as the privately owned CTV. Additional detailed analysis of television news is taken and compared with the CES content analysis of television news. These media were selected because they represent not only the major national media that exist in Canada, but also they have wide audience appeal and are tracked by politicians as well as political and business elites.

To be frank, the American campaign of 2000 was similarly denounced as being uninspired—at least until election night, when the whole world became enthralled with the contested outcome.

Neither the Canadian nor American election *campaigns* were as interesting or exciting as the Mexican election held that same year in which the seventy-one-year ruling Institutional Revolutionary Party (PRI) was ousted from office with the election of Vicente Fox of the National Action Party (PAN). Despite this historical event, major national Canadian media paid very little attention to the campaign in Mexico. The *Globe and Mail* supplied only 23 stories, while the *National Post* offered its readers 33 stories on the election. National television news gave it even less attention, with only 7 stories on CBC and 3 on CTV national newscasts for the July contest. In contrast, during the Canadian election campaign alone, the *Globe and Mail* provided 211, the *National Post* 257, CBC 36, and CTV 45 stories on the American choice.

The lack of interest or enthusiasm for an election is not a predictor for the amount of press attention paid to it. Nor, does it seem, is excitement in an election necessarily sufficient for coverage of a campaign. The Canadian election received the normal amount of attention and focus one would expect in a national race. Could, as the authors of the CES suggest, the excitement and interest of the public have an impact on the outcome of the race, or indeed, whether people voted at all? That is certainly the theme of previous election studies and partly explains why so many political scientists study not only the dynamics of the campaign but also pay special attention to the media messages delivered directly by the parties and candidates, as well as those mediated by the news media. Clearly, television has been the most influential element of the media. One of the reasons for this privileged position is its accessibility. No special skills are required to operate television technology. Audience literacy or education is no barrier to entry. As the price of television sets has fallen, income has ceased to prevent people watching. As a consequence, television has permeated most every home in the nation. Nearly 84 percent of the Canadian population had access to cable or satellite services in

2000.[6] While English-Canadian viewers tend to rely on American programming for entertainment, they prefer Canadian news and public affairs programming. Seventy-three percent of Anglophone news and public affairs viewing time is spent watching Canadian programming.[7] Over one-half of Canadians used television news as their primary source of information on the election campaign while 23 percent mentioned newspapers as their primary source.[8]

But how exactly does television, or any other medium, influence election outcomes? The answer lies in the "agenda-setting" theory. The argument is that even though the media might not have a direct effect on elections—telling audiences who to vote for—they nevertheless set the public agenda and influence what people talk about by giving primacy to some issues over others. This effect was said to be most pronounced on unsophisticated audiences or undecided voters. Yet, when what people actually learn from news was examined, it was found to have limited impact. The public often fails to recollect basic political facts, to recognize ideological leanings, or to recall candidate characteristics or names. As a result, the media have been blamed for having produced an uninformed citizenry, from which the conclusion was drawn that citizens were minimally influenced by media messages, or perhaps not at all.

Much of the literature on communication effects, especially TV, has been influenced by social psychological research. This research indicates that people use short cuts to form opinions on complex public policy issues. In a 1991 book, Samuel Popkin disputes the assertion that the citizenry is unshackled by arguing that members of the public do reason about candidates, parties, and issues.[9] While the voter may not recall every policy detail, the seemingly trivial aspects of electoral politics resonate with what he labeled "low-information rationality." Low-information rationality is a way to describe the public's intuitions and how they mesh detailed media information as well as political campaign advertising with their own experiences. Even though television and newspaper coverage of election campaigns may emphasize trivial components of the campaign, Popkin argued, they nevertheless influence the voter's decision.

A couple of Canadian examples from previous federal election campaigns illustrate Popkin's point. During the 1997 campaign, journalists covering his photo ops frequently ridiculed Gilles Duceppe, leader of the Bloc Québécois Party. In one case, a particularly unflattering picture of him wearing a plastic hygiene hat that looked like a shower cap was shown coast to coast when he visited a local cheese factory. The *Toronto Star*'s Robert McKenzie, in 1997, used that event to summarize the Bloc Québécois' election performance. The image was so powerful it was used to undermine the credibility of Mr. Duceppe for several years thereafter. In one sense, news clips and pictures showing Gilles Duceppe wearing a plastic cap at a cheese factory may be seen as detracting from the real issues of the campaign. Even so, it is as close to dogma as one ever finds in political campaigns: do not let the candidate be photographed in any kind of funny-looking hat. It happened to Michael Dukakis when he was photographed in a tanker's helmet during the presidential campaign against George H. W. Bush. Similarly, a photograph of Jean Chrétien wearing a UN infantry helmet *backwards* has been shown time and again to convey a powerful and critical image of his government's defense policy. In all these instances, the ridiculous image signalled to the public that the leader was unable to make prudent decisions.

A third and equally memorable example took place during the 2000 federal election when Stockwell Day stood by Niagara Falls and indicated that, like the water in the Niagara River, Canadians were heading south to the U.S. The river in fact flows north. Day's failure to grasp the direction the Niagara River flows was not just a mistake about Canadian geography. It indicated to Ontario voters that he knew little about what it means to live in Ontario, which carried the implication that he did not care much about the province either. The actual direction that the Niagara River flows was probably a surprise to most Canadians living outside the region, since the general direction of Great Lakes drainage flows from west to east. Indeed, to many Canadians living west of the Ontario border, criticizing Day on such a matter may simply have suggested that the "eastern" media was being unfair to Day, much as Bloquiste voters in Quebec may have detected an anti-separatist (and indeed anti-Quebec) attitude in the ridiculing of Duceppe. For Ontario voters, however, Day's mistake showed that he was not one of them and that any Alliance appeal to that province would take much more care and preparation. The rationality communicated by Duceppe's picture and Day's confusion over geography may have been low-level, but it was still rational, and it mattered a great deal.

THE ROLE OF RELIGION IN THE 2000 CAMPAIGN

As embarrassing and irritating as this kind of coverage might have been for Alliance supporters, it did not seem to have a profound impact on the ultimate vote for the Alliance Party. Rolling cross-section poll results from the CES illustrate that the "low information" gleaned from these events did not detract from their support. Nevertheless, it did not help it much either, and what is probably more accurate is that it reinforced already held beliefs about the Alliance Party and its leader as being a western protest party. When we examine the election campaign through this lens, we can see how the media coverage, rather than providing defining moments or critical events in which the vote changed, provided coverage that reinforced existing beliefs and patterns. The election campaign showed a remarkable consistency in voter support, but then the media coverage was also quite consistent in its tone and direction.

Shanto Iyengar and Donald Kinder, in *News That Matters*, argue that what they call the "priming" of issues shapes public understanding of what issues are important and how to judge them.[10] The term "priming" is used to describe the way a news item is emphasized at the expense of other issues or events. More recently, Thomas Nelson and Donald Kinder found that the "framing" of issues molded public understanding of the causes of problems and of the merits of alternative solutions.[11] The term "framing" describes the context in which an issue is placed and the image through which it is diffused. Doris Graber showed that very often TV audiences forget the factual basis for their conclusions about a candidate.[12] "Media facts," she said, are converted "into politically significant feelings and attitudes," but the facts themselves are forgotten. Others have argued that campaign events do not matter very much at all and that what counts is the *type* of information the public receives during a campaign,[13] particularly horse-race coverage—who is ahead, who is falling behind, who is about to make a stretch run—could influence the campaign contributions candidates receive for their electoral bid.[14] All of these considerations also look like low level rationality.

The assumption underlying most of the research dealing with media effects is that, by focusing attention on one thing rather than another, the media (and especially television) influence *what* audiences think about and also *how* they think about these issues. The assumption is reasonable enough insofar as events do not appear with an attached index number indicating their importance. In short, media selection of some events as being more important than others directs public attention and, one could argue, public resources, away from some problems and toward others. In other words, the importance of the media resides not just in the measurable and direct influence it has on the public but also in the influence politicians and groups believe it has.

Therefore, the way in which the leaders were portrayed may have had an impact on their vote share. What journalists do on a day-to-day basis is put stories in context, or frames. What parties try to do is ensure that the frame used for their candidate or policy benefits them. Often, to do this, they try to place "their" issues at the front of the agenda. According to Blais and his associates, part of the success of the parties is their ability to get the media to focus on the issues that "were on top of their own agendas."[15] As they note, the strong issue for the Liberals was health care, while it was a weak issue for the Alliance Party. For the Alliance, their strength lay in the issues of public finances. Television coverage focused primarily on health care, and secondarily on fiscal matters. However, the way in which the leaders were portrayed on the issues may have influenced how the public perceived them to stand on the issues.

It has been suggested that the way television spotlighted the religious beliefs of Stockwell Day had a deleterious effect on the party. In particular, the national broadcaster produced a documentary aired on November 15 that emphasized the religious beliefs of Stockwell Day, labeled *Fundamental Day*. This story examined his fundamentalist Christian beliefs and spotlighted his conviction of a literal reading of the Bible. One of the stories recounted in the documentary was a speech Stockwell gave to a group of students, ostensibly on evolution. Among other things, Day said in the speech that there is as much evidence "for creationism as there is for evolution." This story was then covered in newspapers across the country. When the CES team examined this question specifically, they found that it did not significantly affect the final outcome of the election. Immediately after the *Fundamental Day* report, ratings of Day did go down by "six points and Alliance vote intentions declined by five points." They note that the effect "seems to have been temporary. Day's ratings increased by five points in the last days of the campaign and vote intentions rose by two points."[16] Although his approval ratings did not seem to remain in decline as a result of this story, they did not improve much either.

To expect immediate as well as long-term effects of such a story might be overreaching. A number of other features of television news need to be emphasized to suggest its enhanced importance. The argument has often been made that television matters because it provides visual images as well as words. The issue is, unquestionably, complex, but in the view expressed here it is not so much the images as their accessibility that counts.[17] Audiences may well believe what they see, but they also see what they are told. Thus, when television stories are repeated in newspapers, magazines, and on radio, they become part of a widespread common stock of knowledge that is bound to influence the behavior of citizens. While the *Fundamental Day* story broke on television, it became a much bigger story in the subsequent days in newspaper editorials and open-line talk shows across the country.

Does that mean, as the researchers of the CES suggest, that the focus on religion had no impact on the Alliance vote? Probably not. When we examine the overall approval ratings of all the parties we find that very little happened during the campaign to change voters' views on the parties. What we can say, at least for this election, is that campaign coverage of "low-information rationality" reinforced existing beliefs, and sometimes concerns, about the various leaders and platforms. Let us examine the Alliance campaign in some more detail. According to the rolling cross-section poll of the Canadian Election Study, support for the Alliance was at 27 percent at the start of the campaign; by campaign's end it dropped to 25 percent, exactly what it had been in September, prior to the campaign's beginning. It should be noted that the 25 percent figure was the highest support the Alliance had since its inception up until the election writ was dropped. That is not to say that there was no movement for the Alliance during the campaign. There was; however, it was quite small and never rose above 31 percent. In fact, the Alliance reached that mark shortly after the campaign began, only to see it evaporate soon after. If anything, the CES shows that support for the Alliance hovered in a fairly narrow band of 6 percentage points ranging between 25 and 31 percent.

In this respect it can be argued that voters had pretty much made up their minds about what they thought of the Alliance and Stockwell Day *before* the election. In many regards, so too had the media. Their role in keeping that support consistent for the Alliance by running certain kinds of stories that kept already held beliefs, and sometimes, fears, reinforced those views.

The other issue that was linked very strongly to religion was that of abortion. The *Fundamental Day* story certainly linked it, as did other news accounts. When we examine television attention to the election in its entirety we see that the issue of abortion was the focus of only 3 percent of television news stories.[18] If, however, we treat the abortion issue as something subtler, as an issue that provides the public with a shortcut to process information, or as a frame for bigger issues, we can see that the issue could have far greater implications. The above statistics represented the amount of attention abortion received as a percentage of total issue mentions. In other words, any given story can mention a variety of issues and as such all those issues will compete for public attention. So a story ostensibly focusing on fiscal issues will have a high number of mentions of fiscal issues, but if in passing the journalist or commentator mentions abortion once, it will not have a high count. As a result, the overall attention to abortion will be considered quite low. But what if issues such as abortion are more salient to voters and simply count more in this "low-information rationality" way? In that instance we would like to know how many stories overall mentioned abortion. When we calculate coverage this way we find that stories that mentioned abortion comprised 11 percent of the *Globe and Mail*, 6 percent of the *National Post*, 8 percent of CBC, and 7 percent of CTV election coverage. Religion and racism—two issues that also made the Alliance controversial—did not warrant as much media attention as abortion. Religion alone comprised 2 percent of the *Globe*, 3 percent of the *Post*, and 5 percent each of CBC and CTV attention. Racism was mentioned in 2 percent of the *Globe*, 4 percent of the *Post*, less than 1 percent of CBC, and 4 percent of CTV stories. However, combined, these three controversial topics were mentioned by 15 percent of the *Globe*, 12 percent of the *Post*, 13 percent of CBC, and 16 percent of CTV stories. Considering that the top stories on television news for the campaign were health care at 22 percent and public finances at 16 percent, we can see that the issues that hurt the Alliance were at a constant ebb in the news coverage. True, not all these stories were mentioned all the time. The racism story really emerged around November 14 and subsided by November 20. The religion issue also emerged around that time and peaked around November 18. But religion was a story that never went away. The story was mentioned throughout the campaign. The abortion story had even more consistency and when we track the story over time we find that between the four major media outlets in the country, the abortion issue was mentioned every day of the campaign except November 12.

In contrast, the ethics issue, where the Liberals were vulnerable, comprised 12 percent of televisions' total attention to the election.[19] This coverage, however, was the dominant theme in those stories and did not fester throughout the campaign. So while it comprised 12 percent of overall television attention, only 3 percent of CBC and 4 percent of CTV stories on the election mentioned the issue. As for the newspapers, only 2 percent of the *Globe*'s and 4 percent of the *Post*'s stories on the Canadian election campaign addressed the Liberal scandals and controversies. As can be seen in figure 4.1, the volume of stories mentioning re-

Figure 4.1. Mentions of Issues That Were Harmful to the Alliance and Liberal Parties

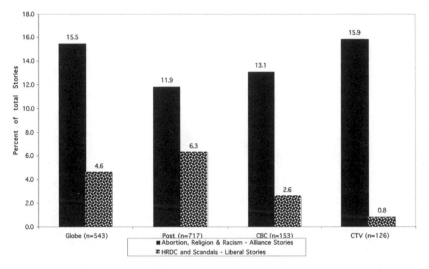

ligion, abortion, and racism—issues on which the Alliance was vulnerable—greatly exceeded the number of stories that mentioned the Grand-mère and HRDC scandals—issues that could harm the Liberals.

Abortion and religion provided a potent recipe for keeping the Alliance's low information messages always highlighted. In fact, the two were explicitly linked in seven *Globe and Mail,* five *National Post,* and four stories each in the national television news broadcasts. This combination then had a double impact. Stories that never mentioned abortion, but cued audiences about religious beliefs, could have had the frame of abortion in the background. The same held for religious stories. So even when abortion was not the main issue, it could have easily reinforced opinions on the issue as background low information that provided powerful reminders to judge the Alliance and Day.

The abortion story coupled with Stockwell Day's beliefs tied into the Alliance platform's pledge to put direct democracy in action. Critics charged that, according to the party, if 300,000 Canadians signed a petition calling for a direct vote on abortion, or any other issue, the Alliance would put the question to a vote. To illustrate how easy it would be to get 300,000 people to sign such a petition, the comedy satire program *This Hour Has 22 Minutes* asked Canadians to sign an Internet petition requiring Stockwell Day to change his name to Doris Day. The stunt ridiculed the Alliance leader, at the same time confirming Day's opponents' worst fears that it would be exceptionally easy to reach the 300,000 level on the abortion issue. Considering that the majority of Canadians support the right to have an abortion, this issue did not help the Alliance. According to the CES, 75 percent of Canadians think it should be "easy" or "very easy" to obtain an abortion. Other surveys worded somewhat differently put abortion proponents at the 84 percent level.[20] The CES authors note that abortion was an issue that could potentially have hurt the Alliance. They found that while "views on abortion did not have an independent effect on vote choice," pro-choice voters were less likely to vote Alliance. In English-speaking Canada, "only 26 percent of those who said it should be easy to get an abortion opted for the Alliance, compared with 45 percent of pro-life respondents."[21]

Again, according to the CES, abortion in and of itself does not explain the vote, but social conservatism does. Social conservatism is partly tied to religious beliefs. Those who are socially conservative tend to be less concerned about mixing religion and politics. The real story in this election was not how the Alliance failed to make progress into the Canadian heartland, or indeed, how the Liberals managed a third consecutive majority, but how the media used religion as a subtle way to reinforce Canadians' fears about Stockwell Day. The point about this issue is really how cleverly the media used "low-information rationality" to keep voters convinced of the danger of the Alliance Party. The CES argues, in contrast, that blaming the media might be misleading.[22]

The study's authors theorize that if the story had an impact, we would have seen Day's approval ratings decline over time. Since this did not happen, they conclude that we cannot blame the media. This assumption is false if we consider the pre-existing attitudes of the public and the role of low-information rationality. If, as we suggest, people already had set views about Stockwell Day and religion, media attention to it does not necessarily have to result in increased negativity. All that the media had to do was keep the issue in people's minds. The assumption that increased media attention to an issue results in a greater number of people feeling strongly toward the leader is not necessarily the case. What is important here is that opinions do not necessarily have to change. It is not as though journalists said that religion is bad. Stockwell Day was not attacked specifically for his religion, but circuitously through questions posed about whether he could ignore his religious convictions when governing.

Interestingly, no other leader's personal beliefs were framed in the same manner. No one made mention of Jean Chrétien's or Conservative leader Joe Clark's Catholicism. These two leaders were exempt from this type of scrutiny because they had secularized their political beliefs. A clue to the media's distrust of Day had more to do with their own religious creeds than that of the political leader. A 1996 survey of Canadian journalists found that 42 percent indicated that they belonged to a religious denomination. This was substantially fewer than the general population's religious membership of 61 percent. Similarly 32 percent of the journalists said they definitely believed in God, compared with 66 percent of the general population. Of the Catholic journalists, 62 percent did not attend mass on a regular basis.[23] This too was higher than Catholics in the general population, where 49 percent of Catholics in English-speaking Canada attended church two or more times a month, compared to 38 percent of the Catholic journalists.[24]

Given the fact that abortion and religion comprised such a relatively small proportion of the overall attention to the election, there is no reason to suspect that it would be a constant element in the campaign. This story really illustrates the role journalists play in keeping issues alive, and if not at the forefront of the news, at the back of people's minds. While the story itself does not appear to have affected the vote directly, its indirect effect at keeping the ratings of Day and the Alliance constant is clear.

Religion and abortion made the 2000 election campaign unique by Canadian standards. Canadians are used to talking about fiscal issues during elections, or even social programs and leadership. Moral and religious issues simply have not been as prominent in Canadian electoral politics as they have been in the United States.

THE ROLE OF THE AMERICAN ELECTION

The 2000 campaign also differed from previous elections in that there was no defining moment in which the media would frame subsequent election stories. For example, in 1993, Kim Campbell's infamous statement that an election was not the appropriate time to debate complex public policy issues such as health care set the frame for other statements made by Campbell and made her stories part of the "gaffe watch."

Ever since the Nixon/Kennedy debate, when Richard Nixon quipped that he lost the election because of his makeup man, journalists have looked to the debate to provide the defining moment. In Canadian history, the quintessential defining moment came in the 1984 debate when Brian Mulroney challenged then Prime Minister John Turner's acceptance of his predecessor's patronage appointments. In fact, these defining moments, or "knockout punches," are rare in election debates. The debate itself has become routine for politicians in that they prepare days in advance with coaches and advisors trying to ensure that they are not "scored" against. Nonetheless, the media as well as academics still place importance on the event and the analysis of campaign dynamics.

In the 2000 election, the leader judged as having the best performance was Joe Clark, the leader of the Progressive Conservative Party. While initial television reports declared no winner, several pundits, as well as the CES survey respondents, gave their nod to the Conservative leader. Forty-four percent of those interviewed after the English debate who had seen it thought that Clark had performed the best; 17 percent chose Day, 10 percent Chrétien, and 19 percent could not name a winner.[25] Joe Clark sustained a post-debate bounce of four percentage points, six percentage points among those who watched the English debate. The party's support also rose from 6 to 8 percent. The surge in support for Clark and the Conservatives lasted only a few days and did not sustain him through election night. Interestingly, only 36 percent of Canadians watched the English-language leaders' debate.[26]

One reason for the relatively small bounce and its short duration could lie in the fact that interest in the Canadian election waned at the time of the debates. No doubt this argument sounds farfetched. After all, the media were focused on the debates and primed audiences to tune into the debate and their analyses. CTV's anchor Lloyd Robertson urged Canadians to tune into their coverage throughout the week, culminating in his closing remarks on November 8: "And tomorrow night, here on CTV, the English-language debate, during which we'll be conducting an instant poll with your responses to the leaders' performances." How could attention and interest wane with such promotion? The answer lies in the fact that a far more compelling story was evolving that side-lined the debate. That story was, of course, the American election night results. As fate would have it, the French-language debates were held on November 8, 2000, the day after the U.S. election.

Figure 4.2. Canadian National Media Attention to Canada/U.S. Elections over the Length of the Canadian Election Campaign

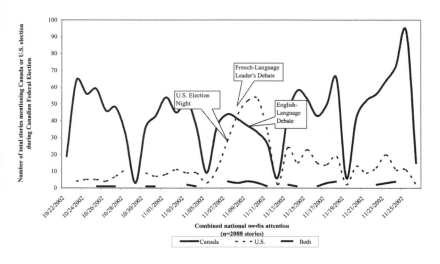

By the time of the English-language debate the next day, the entire world was captivated by the race for the White House. When we examine the debate week, we find there were more stories on the American election than the Canadian one in the *Globe and Mail* and on CTV News. The *National Post* provided twelve more stories on the Canadian election compared with the American, while the CBC gave the Canadian election three more stories than the U.S. election. When Canadian national media stories are tracked over time, U.S. election stories eclipsed Canadian stories.

Given these circumstances, it would be surprising for the leaders' debate to have a lasting impact. Coupled with the immediate explosion of stories and interest in the U.S. presidential results was the fact that the American election uncertainty continued well after the results of the Canadian election were known. Even outside of the week of the American election itself, the Canadian national media were quite diligent reporting on the U.S. campaign throughout October and November 2000. Hardly a day went by without at least one or two stories in the Canadian national media reporting on the U.S. race. This contrasts starkly with the Mexican campaign, held earlier in the year, to which the Canadian media gave only passing mention.

The Canadian media gave the U.S. election not only significant attention but prominent placement as well. During the Canadian election campaign period, stories about the U.S. election comprised 30 percent of the *Globe* and 30 percent of the *Post's* front-page election stories. On television, the U.S. election led off 18 percent of CBC and 21 percent of CTV news broadcasts during the Canadian election campaign.

At the height of the coverage, which coincided with the French-language debate, the U.S. election was featured even more prominently. On November 8, the top four stories of the CBC's *National* were devoted to the U.S. electoral ambiguity. Only after the first commercial break did the national broadcaster report on the French-language leaders' debates. The next day, the night of the English-language debate, CBC did lead with four stories on the event, but only after its host, Peter Mansbridge, promised coverage of the U.S. affair. "Good evening," began Mansbridge. "There's political drama on both sides of the border tonight as the elections in Canada and the United States continue to dominate the news. The U.S. presidential contest is still missing a winner. We'll bring you up to date on that story a little later. But first, of course, the campaign here and tonight's English-language debate."

CONCLUSION

Canadian elections do have significant events and these do influence voters. In some respects, the 2000 election was not significantly different from previous contests. Where this election differed was in the measurement of the effects. We often assume that for the media to have an impact, we need to measure change in opinion. What this election showed is that the media can be equally as powerful in reinforcing and maintaining existing ideas about the parties and their leaders. In 2000, the media focused on Stockwell Day and suggested questions about religion and politics; they focused less on the scandals and controversies surrounding the Liberal government's running of the HRDC.

This subtext tells only part of the story in the Canadian election in 2000. Apart from focusing on low-information cues, the media, like the public, were distracted from the Canadian election at a critical point in the campaign. While so often we expect leaders' debates to be pivotal points in the campaign, this simply did not materialize in 2000. Part of the problem lay in the fact that a far more interesting electoral event occurred in the United States. In many respects, the outcome of the U.S. election made for a more compelling story. Canadian attention to the American election campaign might have captivated Canadian interest to the extent that the 2000 Canadian campaign really did not matter, and that Canadians voted according to how they felt about the parties prior to the election.

CHAPTER 5

Quebec and the Canadian Federal Election of 2000: Putting the Sovereignty Movement on the Ropes?

A. Brian Tanguay

F OR THE INDEPENDENCE MOVEMENT IN QUEBEC, the outcome of the November 2000 Canadian federal election marked another bitterly disappointing setback on the road to sovereignty. Not only did Jean Chrétien—an object of intense loathing among the Quebec nationalist intelligentsia—succeed in winning his third consecutive majority, he did so while increasing the Liberal Party's share of both votes and seats in the province of Quebec.[1] For the second consecutive election, the Bloc Québécois (BQ) and its sovereignty option failed to generate much enthusiasm among Quebec's voters. Worse still, less than two months after the federal election, Premier Lucien Bouchard resigned as leader of the provincial Parti Québécois (PQ) and premier of Quebec, citing his inability to reinvigorate the independence movement as the principal reason for his departure from political life. Bouchard's successor, Bernard Landry, while more popular among the militant faction of the Parti Québécois (*les purs et durs*) than the erstwhile comrade-in-arms Brian Mulroney had ever been, has failed to breathe new life into the sovereignty project. He now finds himself at the helm of an increasingly unpopular governing party which risks being annihilated at the polls in the next provincial election.

What was the impact of the 2000 federal election on the Quebec "problem?" The central question posed in the analysis is whether the Liberals' 2000 "three-peat" foreshadows the inevitable collapse of the sovereignty project. Predictions about the future of Québécois nationalism are notoriously risky. Only fifteen years ago, in the mid-1980s, it appeared to many observers that Quebec's nationalist movement was on the ropes when a renascent Robert Bourassa and his Quebec Liberal Party defeated the Parti Québécois in the 1985 provincial election. In the span of five years, however, the independence movement in the province re-emerged stronger than ever, revitalized by the death of René Lévesque in 1987, the Supreme Court of Canada's decision on the language of commercial signs in Quebec in 1988, and the collapse of the Meech Lake Accord in 1990. It may well turn out that the PQ's current travails are merely temporary, and that the party and the movement need only find a dynamic new leader in order to recapture their former dynamism. As I argue here, however, a more plausible view is that the Quebec independence movement now faces a number of significant, and perhaps insuperable, social and political hurdles.

My analysis proceeds in three stages. In the next section, the backdrop to the 2000 federal election campaign is sketched, focusing in particular on the Chrétien government's two-pronged strategy for meeting the challenge of Québécois nationalism in the wake of the 1995 referendum on sovereignty. Plan A consisted of measures "to accommodate Quebec in the constitution and to meet some of the province's traditional demands," while Plan B involved an attempt to clarify "the process and the implications of

Quebec secession, and [to challenge] the sovereigntists' assumptions about these matters."[2] Simplifying somewhat, Plan A is the carrot and Plan B the stick in the federal government's strategic repertoire for responding to the challenge of the Quebec independence movement. The sovereigntists' inability to mobilize voters against Plan B, which they denounced as an anti-democratic assault on the right of the Québécois to self-determination, provided Jean Chrétien and the Liberals with a considerable strategic advantage during the election campaign. In the second section of the chapter, I examine the actual election results in 2000 to assess differing explanations of the outcome. Finally, I explore the obstacles now confronting the sovereignty movement in Quebec and the likelihood that they will be overcome. In conclusion, the current situation may be optimal for the Liberal Party of Canada, the "natural governing party" of the country, but it does not necessarily represent the ideal solution to the Quebec problem.[3]

BACKDROP TO THE 2000 FEDERAL ELECTION: THE SOVEREIGNTY MOVEMENT STALLS

Throughout its second mandate (1997–2000), the Chrétien government's political agenda was dominated by the need to formulate a response to the threat of Quebec secession. In the historic referendum on sovereignty-partnership held on October 30, 1995,[4] the NO side had emerged with a perilously narrow victory, winning 50.6 percent of the vote to the YES side's 49.4 percent.[5] Prime Minister Chrétien was personally vilified in the media and by many in the opposition parties for having failed to take the sovereigntist camp seriously at the outset of the referendum campaign, and for abandoning his "don't-worry-be-happy" strategy only when it was almost too late. Immediately after the referendum, therefore, the Chrétien government moved to mollify its critics by seeking to accommodate some of Quebec's historic demands. It passed legislation that committed the House of Commons to recognize Quebec as a distinct society; it also gave Quebec, along with four other regions, a veto over certain types of constitutional amendments. The Liberals transferred significant powers over job training to the province of Quebec, and they amended section 93 of the Constitution Act, 1867, at Quebec's request, to enable the province to create language-based school boards rather than confessional ones.[6] These measures, which together constituted the Chrétien government's Plan A, were designed to demonstrate the flexibility of the existing federal system and to prove to Québécois that their unique contribution to the development of Canada was appreciated by Ottawa—without, of course, giving the other provinces any hint that Quebec was somehow more special than they were.

At the same time that the Liberals were putting in place the elements of Plan A, they began to formulate a parallel strategy designed to deprive the sovereigntists of their exclusive control over the timing and mechanics of a future referendum. Partly the brainchild of the new minister of intergovernmental affairs in the Chrétien cabinet, Stéphane Dion,[7] and partly an echo of the hard line on Quebec that the Reform Party and Preston Manning had consistently advocated, Plan B was intended to "raise doubts among the Quebec electorate about the ease of secession by challenging the sovereigntists and putting them on the defensive."[8] In September 1996, the Chrétien government used its reference power to ask the Supreme Court of Canada to determine whether Quebec had the right to secede from Canada unilaterally under either the Canadian Constitution or international law.[9] This bold gesture was not without its critics in the media, in the opposition parties, and within the Liberal party itself; many feared that this legal strategy would inflame nationalist opinion in Quebec, provide the Parti Québécois with yet another example of the humiliation of the Quebec people, and thereby aid the sovereigntist cause.

The Supreme Court of Canada had not yet heard the legal arguments in the reference case by the time voters went to the polls in the 36th general election on June 2, 1997. Although the Liberals barely managed to hold onto their majority, winning just 155 seats in the 301-seat House of Commons, the results in Quebec were more encouraging, as they increased their share of the popular vote from 33 percent to 37 percent and their seats from 19 to 26 (see table 5.1). While national unity had been a dominant theme in the election campaign, the Bloc Québécois could credibly attribute its disappointing performance—it lost eleven percentage points in the popular vote and ten seats—to an inept campaign organization and the inexperienced leadership of Gilles Duceppe rather than to any popular rejection of its sovereignty option.[10]

TABLE 5.1.

Federal Election Results in Quebec, 1988–2000

| | | | | Election | | | | |
| | 1988 | | 1993 | | 1997 | | 2000 | |
Party	%	#	%	#	%	#	%	#
Lib	30	12	33	19	37	26	44	36
PC	53	63	14	1	22	5	6	1
BQ	—	—	49	54	38	44	40	38
Reform/CA	—	—	—	—	—	—	6	—
NDP	14	—	2	—	2	—	2	—
Other	3	—	3	1	1	—	2	—

% rounded to the nearest whole number
# : number of seats in the 75-seat National Assembly
Sources:
Tony Coulson, "Statistical Appendices: Canadian Federal Election Results, 1925–1993," in *Canadian Parties in Transition*, ed. A. Brian Tanguay and Alain-G. Gagnon, 2d ed. (Scarborough, ON: Nelson, 1996), tables B-20, B-21.

Chief Electoral Officer of Canada, *Official Voting Results*, Thirty-sixth General Election 1997, tables 7, 9; Thirty-seventh General Election 2000, table K.

The Chrétien government finalized Plan B after the 1997 federal election. In August 1998, the Supreme Court of Canada rendered its decision on the constitutionality of a unilateral declaration of independence by Quebec. In what was widely hailed as a masterful, politically astute judgment, the Court ruled that such a unilateral declaration of independence by Quebec would contravene both Canadian and international law.[11] Particularly damaging to the sovereigntists' legal case was the Court's finding that the right to self-determination under international law existed only:

> ... in situations of former colonies; where a people is oppressed, as for example under foreign military occupation; or where a definable group is denied meaningful access to government to pursue their political, economic, social and cultural development.... Such exceptional circumstances are manifestly inapplicable to Quebec under existing conditions.[12]

Sovereigntists could take solace in one aspect of the Court's decision, however. The justices argued that Canada would have a clear duty to negotiate with Quebec in the event of a "clear expression of a clear majority of Quebecers that they no longer wish to remain in Canada."[13] Here, the Court tacitly recognized that secessions are political as much as they are legal phenomena, something that many federalists, including Jean Chrétien and his close advisors, had been completely unwilling to acknowledge. Lobbing the ball deliberately back to the politicians, the Supreme Court justices wrote that "it will be for the political actors to determine what constitutes 'a clear majority on a clear question' in the circumstances under which a future referendum vote may be taken."[14]

Slightly more than a year after the Supreme Court handed down its decision on secession, the Chrétien government moved to meet the challenge posed by the justices. In December 1999,

Stéphane Dion, Minister of Intergovernmental Affairs, tabled in the House of Commons Bill C-20, An Act to Give Effect to the Requirement for Clarity as Set Out in the Opinion of the Supreme Court of Canada in the Quebec Secession Reference.[15] This piece of legislation stipulates that the House of Commons will scrutinize any future referendum question on the secession of a province within thirty days of being tabled in the provincial legislature, in order to determine its clarity. The bill excludes as unclear any question that focuses merely on a mandate to negotiate secession or that "envisages other possibilities in addition to the secession of the province from Canada, such as economic or political arrangements with Canada, that obscure a direct expression of the will of the population of that province on whether the province should cease to be part of Canada."[16] Thus both the 1980 and 1995 referendum questions in Quebec would have been rejected under the terms of the Clarity Act as unclear, since the first merely asked for a mandate to negotiate sovereignty-association, while the second referred to Quebec's formal offer of economic partnership to Canada.[17]

After lengthy debate in both the House of Commons and the Senate, the Clarity Act was finally passed and received royal assent on June 29, 2000, less than four months before Jean Chrétien issued his election call. Not surprisingly, sovereigntists were outraged by the Clarity Act and denounced it as a Soviet-style atrocity aimed at crushing not only the natural right of Québécois to self-determination but democracy itself. Some federal opposition party leaders were also openly critical of the law. Joe Clark of the Progressive Conservative Party, for instance, dismissed the legislation as Jean Chrétien's feeble attempt to compensate for his failings during the referendum campaign of 1995: "It is a classic case of a general fighting the last war." Clark anticipated some of the Senate's concerns about the bill, wondering why it conferred the power to vet referendum questions solely on the House of Commons, instead of sharing it with other key political actors—the Senate, Aboriginals, and the provinces, for example. He also attacked the rigidity of the legislation, which "limits dangerously the capacity of a future prime minister to protect our country against secession. It ties the hands of Canada and takes away the flexibility upon which Macdonald, Laurier, Mackenzie King and other prime ministers relied to keep this country together."[18]

Joe Clark paid a political price for his opposition to the Clarity Bill, as many members of his own party and a clear majority of English Canadians appeared to support the basic principles embodied in the legislation.[19] Nor were the sovereigntists able to mobilize public opinion in Quebec against what they viewed as Ottawa's anti-democratic assault on the province's right to determine its own fate. Within days of the introduction of the Clarity Act, the Quebec government responded with its own legislation, Bill 99, An Act Respecting the Exercise of the Fundamental Rights and Prerogatives of the Québec People and the Québec State.[20] This bill, which is currently the target of a legal challenge by the Equality Party in Quebec, affirmed that the "Québec people has the inalienable right to freely decide the political regime and legal status of Quebec" and that "the Québec people, acting through its own political institutions, shall determine *alone* the mode of exercise of [that] right."[21] However, the PQ and the Bloc failed utterly to generate anything resembling a groundswell of public opinion against the federal law or in support of the Quebec legislation. In fact, Bill 99 *and* Bill C-20 were greeted either by equanimity or indifference in Quebec. According to a survey conducted by Ekos Research Associates, Inc., the fears of Joe Clark, Jean Charest, and others that the federal government's Clarity Act would reinvigorate the sovereignty movement were unfounded: the short-term impact of the debate over the legislation (and its provincial counterpart, Bill 99) was "indiscernible" in Quebec, the authors of the study found. "Overall, the sovereignty movement remains mired in near record low levels of support . . . [T]here is no evidence of any rebound in sovereigntist fortunes [from the passage of the law]."[22]

Thus by the time Jean Chrétien called a general election for November 27, 2000, the federal government, for arguably the first time since the birth of the Quebec independence movement in the early 1960s, had wrested control over the political and constitutional agenda from the advocates of sovereignty.[23] Plan B and the Clarity Act played a key role in this reversal of fortunes. In addition, the proponents of Quebec independence were forced to cope with a number of internal problems after the 1995 referendum. As many observers had predicted, Lucien Bouchard's luster had dimmed somewhat after he left the federal political arena to assume the leadership of the Parti Québécois government in January 1996. Bouchard's search for the "winning conditions" that would guarantee a sovereigntist victory in a future referendum was sidetracked almost immediately by the day-to-day demands of provincial administration. Premier Bouchard alienated some of the most committed partisans of independence in his quest to balance the provincial budget (becoming one of the last provinces to do so) by slashing government spending after 1996. Labor unions, women's groups, and various community organizations, all strong supporters of the PQ's vision of an independent, *social democratic* Quebec, grew increasingly restive under Bouchard's leadership. Partly because of his policies of fiscal restraint, and partly because of doubts about the strength of his commitment to sovereignty, only 76.7 percent of the delegates to the biennial convention of the Parti Québécois in November 1996 endorsed Bouchard's leadership.[24]

In the 1998 provincial election, Bouchard was unable to improve on the performance of his predecessor, Jacques Parizeau. The PQ and the Liberals won about the same percentage of the popular vote (43 percent), but thanks to huge Liberal majorities in the predominantly Anglophone ridings of West Island Montreal, the PQ secured a comfortable majority in the National Assembly (seventy-six seats versus forty-eight for the Liberals). Opinion polls at the time of the PQ victory indicated that Quebec voters, like their counterparts in the rest of Canada, were suffering from severe constitutional fatigue. In a survey released in March 1999, Ekos Research Associates, Inc., asked voters whether they agreed or disagreed with the statement that "I am sick and tired of all this talk about the Quebec sovereignty issue." In Quebec, 62 percent of respondents agreed, while 76 percent in the rest of Canada did so.[25] An Angus Reid Group survey conducted in December 1998 found that 71 percent of respondents believed that the PQ should not hold another referendum on sovereignty during its mandate. This majority was constant across all age brackets and party affiliations (even 55 percent of PQ supporters felt that the Bouchard government ought not to hold another referendum in the next five years). The survey also showed that voters were pessimistic about Bouchard's intentions: 64 percent of those surveyed believed that Bouchard would start to work immediately after the election to establish the winning conditions necessary for a referendum on sovereignty, rather than attempting to work to improve Quebec's position within the Canadian federal system (which 73 percent of respondents wanted Bouchard to do).[26]

In summary, after nearly winning the referendum on sovereignty-partnership in October 1995, the sovereignty movement in Quebec stalled. By the time the federal election was called in October 2000, sovereigntists were divided and demoralized. Indeed, sovereignty is barely mentioned at all in the Bloc Québécois's election manifesto in 2000.[27] The timing of the election also favored the federal Liberal Party rather than the sovereigntists: the recent death (on September 28, 2000) of former prime minister Pierre Trudeau allowed Jean Chrétien to launch his re-election bid in the slipstream of nostalgia and euphoria generated by Trudeau's passing. The extraordinary outpouring of emotion for Pierre Trudeau prompted Chrétien to wrap himself in the mantle of defender of the "Trudeau vision" of compassionate liberalism, a legacy that was threatened by the extremism of Stockwell Day and the Canadian Alliance. Chrétien and his advisors believed that this strategy of contrasting Liberal (read Canadian) values with the alleged extremism of the Alliance would play especially well in Quebec, the province that historically has been most committed to collectivism and most supportive of government's role in social and economic life.

Despite some misgivings within his own caucus about the wisdom of calling an early election (barely three and a half years into the government's mandate) for a second time in a row, Jean Chrétien's political instincts were vindicated on November 27, 2000, when the Liberals cruised to a convincing election victory. The Liberals enjoyed their best showing in Quebec since 1980. Let us next examine various explanations of the Liberals' success in 2000.

EXPLAINING THE 2000 ELECTION
OUTCOME IN QUEBEC

As the data in table 5.1 indicate, the Bloc Québécois managed to increase its share of the popular vote slightly in 2000, winning 40 percent as opposed to 38 percent in the 1997 federal election, but its share of the seats in Quebec dropped from forty-four to thirty-eight. The Liberals exceeded many observers' expectations, winning 44 percent of the vote (37 percent in 1997) and thirty-six seats (twenty-six in 1997), while support for the Progressive Conservatives plummeted from 22 percent and five seats in 1997 to a mere 6 percent and one seat in 2000.[28] Of the ten seats that the Liberals picked up in the 2000 election, seven came from the BQ and three from the Conservatives. The Bloc also took one seat from the PCs.

A number of factors can be cited to explain these election results. First, during the federal campaign the Bloc Québécois became a lightning rod for voter unhappiness with the PQ government of Lucien Bouchard and its policy of forced municipal amalgamations in Quebec City and the island of Montreal. The Bloc lost three seats to the Liberals in the Quebec region—Québec-East, Louis-Hébert, and Portneuf—where voters were angry with the forced mergers. In all three the Liberals' margin of victory was less than 3,000 votes (and a mere 647 votes in Québec-East); the BQ might well have been able to retain these seats had disgruntled voters not used the Bloc as a proxy for the Parti Québécois.[29]

Secondly, the Liberals benefited disproportionately from the collapse of the Conservative vote. In 1997, the PCs won five seats and placed second in ten others in Quebec, taking 22 percent of the popular vote (811,410 votes). In 2000, the Conservatives retained only one seat, placed second in three others, and won just under 6 percent of the popular vote (192,153 votes). In fact, the Canadian Alliance outpolled the Conservatives in Quebec by almost 21,000 votes, even though they did not come close to winning a seat. The Liberals picked up three seats from the Tories in 2000—Chicoutimi, Compton-Stanstead, and Shefford. The latter two ridings are in the Eastern Townships near the U.S. border, close to former federal Conservative leader Jean Charest's old riding of Sherbrooke, which was won by the Bloc Québécois in a 1998 by-election after Charest left federal politics to become leader of the Quebec Liberal Party (QLP). All three Liberal gains came in ridings where sitting Conservative MPs defected to the governing party just prior to the election and were re-elected under their new party label.[30] André Bachand was the lone Conservative incumbent to win re-election, by a mere 363 votes, in Richmond-Arthabaska (also in the Eastern Townships and bordering the riding of Sherbrooke). These results appear to confirm that much of the Conservatives' electoral success in Quebec in 1997 was attributable to Jean Charest's personal appeal. With Joe Clark as federal Tory leader, the overwhelming majority of the party's supporters drifted to the Liberals rather than to the BQ.

Thirdly, the sharp drop in voter turnout affected the outcome of the 2000 election in Quebec, though perhaps not quite in the way that some observers initially believed. Nationwide, voter turnout in 2000 declined to a historic low of 61.2 percent (67 percent of registered voters turned out in the 1997 election, one of the lowest levels of the twentieth century). The biggest decline in turnout, 9.1 percentage points, from 73.1 percent in 1997 to 64 percent in 2000, occurred in Quebec.[31] Immediately after the election, some researchers and media commentators contended that the decline in turnout was possibly greater among Bloc Québécois supporters than it was among other partisans, reflecting the demobilization and demoralization of the sovereignty forces noted earlier. André Bernard, for instance, observed that "on November 27, 2000, the turnout was much lower than in 1997; the Bloc Québécois received approximately 18,000 fewer votes than in 1997."[32]

An analysis of voter turnout data from the 1997 and 2000 federal elections, however, quickly disproves this hypothesis: the greatest declines in turnout occurred in the predominantly Anglophone ridings of West Island Montreal. Mount Royal, for instance, experienced the sharpest decline in turnout in the province—18.8 percentage points between 1997 and 2000. This was also the riding with the least competitive race in the province: the Liberal candidate, well-known constitutional lawyer and human rights activist Irwin Cotler, won over 80 percent of the vote in 2000, while the second-place candidate, a Conservative, managed to obtain just 6 percent of the popular vote. Similar trends were evident in Westmount (drop of 16 percentage points in turnout; Liberal Lucienne Robillard won 60 percent of the vote), Notre-Dame-de-Grâce (drop of 15 percentage points in turnout; Liberal Marlene Jennings won over 60 percent of the vote) and St. Laurent (decline in turnout of 14 percentage points, Liberal Stéphane Dion won 74 percent of the vote).

In their careful analysis of the impact of voter turnout on the federal election in Quebec, Édith Brochu and Louis Massicotte find that on the whole the decline in turnout in ridings held by the Bloc Québécois was "unremarkable," except in sovereigntist strongholds such as Hochelaga and Laurier-St.-Marie, where the races were not competitive. They conclude that the most important feature of the 2000 election results in Quebec was the pronounced demobilization of Anglophone voters in safe Liberal seats. Indirectly, this demobilization reflected the sagging fortunes of the independence movement in the province: Anglophone voters, feeling that the threat of separatism was less acute in 2000 than it had been in 1997, could safely decide to stay home rather than go to the polls.[33]

In summary, the implications of the 2000 federal election were quite grim for the sovereignty movement in Quebec. Despite running a competent campaign—in stark contrast to their near disastrous effort in 1997—Gilles Duceppe and the Bloc Québécois were unable to make any gains among the "soft nationalists" who had voted for the Progressive Conservatives when Jean Charest was party leader. The Bloc had essentially stagnated, as had the Parti Québécois in the 1998 provincial election. Don Macpherson, the insightful columnist for the *Montreal Gazette*, concluded after the election that the "Bloc looks increasingly like the Creditiste Party in the 1960s—an anti-Liberal protest rump that rushed in to fill a vacuum left by a Conservative collapse, then gradually lost its purpose and its relevance and, after several elections, eventually faded away into history."[34] How valid is Macpherson's conclusion? Is the Bloc Québécois, and the independence movement as a whole, on the ropes?

REPERCUSSIONS OF THE 2000 FEDERAL
ELECTION ON THE SOVEREIGNTY MOVEMENT

Less than two months after the federal election, on January 11, 2001, Premier Lucien Bouchard unexpectedly announced his resignation as leader of the Parti Québécois and premier of Quebec. The proximate cause of Bouchard's departure was the Michaud Affair, a bitter internal party dispute over how to respond to some highly publicized anti-Semitic remarks made by Yves Michaud, former Delegate-General of Quebec in France (1979-84) and well-known PQ gadfly.[35] In his resignation speech, Bouchard claimed that the Michaud Affair was not a cause of his resignation, but that he did not have the stomach for any more discussions about either the Holocaust or ethnic voting patterns in the province. The fundamental reason for his departure, Bouchard stated, was that

> je reconnais que mes efforts pour relancer rapidement le débat sur la question nationale sont restés vain. Il n'a donc pas été possible d'engager une démarche référendaire à l'intérieur de l'échéancier rapproché que nous aurions souhaité. De même les Québécois sont-ils restés étonnamment impassibles devant les offensives fédérales comme l'union sociale, le programme de bourses millénaire, la création de chaires universitaires de recherche, l'adoption de la loi C-20, laquelle vise à rien moins que de restreindre notre capacité de choisir notre avenir politique.[36]

Bouchard's successor as PQ leader and premier was Bernard Landry, who had been minister of finance in Bouchard's cabinet. Landry, like Jacques Parizeau, is associated with the business-friendly wing of the PQ; both are hardliners on the issue of sovereignty. After assuming the leadership of the PQ, Landry played to *les purs et durs* in the party with a series of inflammatory comments about Canada and the federal system, the most notorious being his remark that Quebec would not "sell itself on the street for some bits of red rag."[37] Landry's aggressive posturing appears not to have had much of an impact on public opinion on the sovereignty issue. Survey data published by Léger Marketing indicate that support for sovereignty-association in Quebec has averaged about 44 percent over the last three years (1999–2001). Average annual support for the YES option reached its peak in 1996 (51 percent), and has declined slowly since then, stabilizing in the low- to mid-40s, notwithstanding Landry's incendiary rhetoric.[38] At the same time, support for the PQ government is in free fall, with over 70 percent of voters indicating that it is time for a change in government.[39] Interestingly, voter support in May and June 2002 seems to be coalescing behind a third party, the *Action démocratique du Québec* (ADQ)—which currently has but two members in the National Assembly—rather than the Quebec Liberal Party (QLP).[40] This perhaps reflects an attitude of "a plague on both their houses" among Quebec's voters, who are tired of the neverending constitutional wrangle and the apparent paucity of new and creative ideas on offer from the rival PQ and QLP.

Can it be concluded, then, that the sovereignty movement in Quebec is moribund, or at least on the ropes? Recent history teaches us to beware of such simplistic inferences. At best, we can say that most voters in Quebec (and, arguably, in Canada as a whole) are increasingly unhappy with the partisan choices confronting them, are fed up with constitutional politics, and are casting about for a viable political alternative. Things can change quickly in politics, and the Quebec electorate's infatuation with the ADQ may well be short-lived, especially as voters learn more about its unorthodox program, which grafts a desire for renewed federalism onto a package of right-wing economic proposals reminiscent of the Canadian Alliance's platform. Thus, the natural cycle of party fortunes in a first-past-the-post electoral system might well work in favor of the PQ and the Bloc in the not-too-distant future (and given the current difficulties of the federal Liberals—discussed further below—the Bloc's prospects have improved markedly in recent weeks).

There are, however, some substantial obstacles to the viability of the sovereignty project in the long term. In recent years, proponents of sovereignty have been casting about for a winning strategy that would avoid the trap laid for them by the federal Clarity Act—namely, a referendum on a clear question on Quebec independence *tout court*, which they would almost certainly lose. One alternative, proposed by Jean-François Lisée, a former advisor to both Jacques Parizeau and Lucien Bouchard, is to hold a referendum on extracting additional powers or resources from Ottawa.[41] The logic behind this proposal appears to be that a groundswell of public support for sovereignty would emerge in the wake of Ottawa's inevitable rejection of Quebec's demand for more. It must be said, however, that this strategy represents a dramatic scaling back of the sovereigntist dream, and it is difficult to believe that nationalist voters would be energized by what would likely be a very dry, technical debate. Instead of Daniel Johnson's ringing cry of "Equality or Independence" during the 1960s, voters would confront the much more mundane slogan, "Give us tax points, or give us sovereignty." All flippancy aside, it is unclear that this strategy for a referendum on decentralization would accomplish anything more than the traditional channels of federal-provincial diplomacy, where Quebec could potentially ally itself with other powerful, disgruntled advocates of decentralization like Alberta and Ontario. And the risks involved—losing yet another referendum—are much greater than those inherent in executive federalism.

Another strategy for re-energizing the sovereignty movement has been proposed by a number of Quebec intellectuals, and constitutes one of the main recommendations of the report of the Estates-General on the French language: the idea of a separate

Quebec citizenship. According to the Estates-General, the notion of Quebec citizenship is born out of the need for social cohesion; it is necessary "because we live in a period of great change and an era of confusion about language and belonging."[42] Some sovereigntists hope that a distinct Quebec citizenship, perhaps embodied in a "civic contract," will eventually forge a single identity (*Québécois*) out of the multiple identities (*Canadian, Québécois, immigrant*) that currently exist. Not surprisingly, representatives of a number of immigrant groups in Quebec have rejected this proposal as a nonstarter, one that is completely out of touch with the realities of an increasingly interdependent world.

CONCLUSION

The sovereignty movement in Quebec thus finds itself in perhaps the most difficult situation it has ever confronted. The generation that gave birth to the Parti Québécois is aging and, if Lisée's book, *Sortie de secours*, is any indication, it is demoralized as well. Young Francophones in Quebec, who are more likely to support the idea of sovereignty than their older counterparts, and who are most likely to have the single, unconflicted identity cherished by nationalists, are also less involved in traditional partisan politics than any other generation. At the same time, Quebec has one of the lowest fertility rates in the world, and thus will need to rely increasingly on immigration simply to replace the current population. As a society, then, Quebec will necessarily become more diverse, and the notion of a single, unambiguous *Québécois* identity will have less purchase over the entire population. In this rapidly changing social and political matrix, the dream of sovereignty appears to be less attainable than ever before.

Coming as it did just four months after the Chrétien government adopted the Clarity Act, the 2000 federal election indicated that the new rules of the constitutional game had had a profound effect on the balance of power between federalists and sovereigntists in Quebec. The sovereigntists' inability to cultivate a voter backlash against Ottawa's alleged infringement of the province's democratic rights provided Jean Chrétien and the federal Liberal Party with an important strategic advantage during the election campaign. The results of the election—significant Liberal gains at the expense of both the Bloc Québécois and the Progressive Conservatives—were deeply disappointing to the sovereigntist camp. Lucien Bouchard's resignation as leader of the PQ and premier of Quebec was at least partly attributable to this election outcome.

After exploring the political context of the 2000 federal election, a number of possible explanations can be assessed. Although such short-term factors as the backlash in the Quebec City region against the PQ's policy of forced municipal mergers had an impact on the results, the outcome also reflected a deeper demobilization and demoralization of the sovereigntist forces in Quebec. This demobilization, then, is likely to be exacerbated by a number of long-term demographic and political trends—the aging of the *péquiste* generation, for example, and the unavoidable reliance on increased immigration in the future simply to replace the population—making the dream of sovereignty more remote than ever before.

For those who believe in a united Canada, does this represent the best of all possible outcomes for the country? Sadly, recent events have indicated that while the 2000 federal election result might have represented an optimal outcome for the Liberal Party of Canada, it did not provide the ideal solution to the "Quebec problem." The pathetic spectacle of the Chrétien government's pork-barreling in Quebec, the funneling of millions of dollars in advertising contracts to friends of the Liberal Party under the guise of preserving national unity, suggests that the absence of a credible opposition to the "government party" has fueled a pathological hubris in the current administration. In the prime minister's own words: "Perhaps there were a few million dollars that might have been stolen in the process, but how many millions of millions of dollars have we saved because we have re-established the stability of Canada by keeping it a united country?"[43] This is about as effective an indictment of the current Liberal government's approach to the Quebec problem as is imaginable. The sovereignty movement may well be on the ropes, but as members of the PQ and the Bloc tirelessly point out, federalism as embodied in the policies of the current Liberal administration is equally bankrupt.

PART III

Cultural and Economic Forces

CHAPTER 6

My Heart Will Go on Living *la Vida Loca*: The Cultural Impact on the United States of Canada and Mexico

Mary K. Kirtz and Carol L. Beran

THE MOVIE *TITANIC* ENJOYED WORLDWIDE POPULARITY, but it also seemed to provide an excellent example of cultural interaction and cooperation accomplished without concern about cultural boundaries in North America. This movie, a Hollywood production about the sinking of a British ship, was directed by Canadian-American James Cameron, featured Québécois diva Celine Dion singing the theme song in her distinct Francophone accent, and was filmed mostly in Mexico, where the model ship was built. Perhaps such borderless cultural production might become a model for North Americans in the future, showing the harmonious blending of three different, yet related, cultural arenas. Upon closer examination, this model proves entirely too simplistic to demonstrate how the United States interacts with its two nearest neighbors and what their cultural impact is on the U.S.

Through the examination of patterns in immigration and language usage and exploration of the transformation of ethnic identities through American popular culture, we intend to determine those cultural impacts so far. By discussing the ways in which Canadian Americans and Mexican Americans are represented and viewed in the United States through these cultural markers, we will note the extent to which such socially constructed identities contribute to a new North American identity.

Immigration patterns, which give us a sense of who in the United States might be bringing cultural changes from their countries of origin, indicate that more Mexicans than Canadians come to the United States and that they tend to be less educated. Acceptance of language from Canada and Mexico reflects recent, if slow, trends toward greater acceptance of multiculturalism and awareness that language models the world for its speakers. The marker most readily apparent to a society at large, popular culture, shows a flourishing, if invisible, presence of Canadian involvement and an increasing visibility of Mexican American contributions to American culture.

We will also consider two particular initiatives since the 2000 election that will likely have a major impact on how immigrants, especially those from Mexico, interact with the larger culture: George W. Bush's No Child Left Behind Act and recent changes announced by the U.S. Immigration and Naturalization Service regarding rescue of illegal immigrants along the U.S.-Mexican border.

IMMIGRATION FROM CANADA AND MEXICO

A look at the immigration numbers in the United States makes it clear that many more people in the U.S. claim Mexican origin than Canadian. In the 1990 U.S. census (comparable data from the 2000 census was not available at the time of writing) 560,000 respondents described themselves as having undifferentiated Canadian ancestry, and 2,835,398 claimed French Canadian ancestry.

One of the hotly debated issues in Canada is the so-called "brain drain" of well-educated professionals to the United States. According to Statistics Canada for 1996, 49 percent of Canadian immigrants to the U.S. had university degrees. Furthermore, one in every thousand Canadian managerial workers and computer scientists, three in every thousand engineers, and five in every thousand doctors had recently immigrated permanently to the United States.

These statistics may seem alarming from a Canadian perspective, although Matthew Stevenson has pointed out that the approximately 180,000 Canadians who immigrated to the United States during the 1990s actually represent a downward trend. An almost equal number have come here under the transnational (TN) visas allowed under NAFTA. However, almost half of the immigrants return to Canada after five years.[1] While the brain drain may be a problem for Canada, it is a situation that clearly benefits the United States, providing a well-educated cadre that does not necessarily wish to stay in the States permanently.

FRENCH CANADIAN PRESENCE IN THE UNITED STATES

Just as Francophone Canadians constitute a "distinct society" within Canada, they are also present as a distinct group among Canadian immigrants in the United States. The highest concentration of people claiming French Canadian ancestry lives in New England. Almost 25 percent of Maine's population has French Canadian ancestry. This is not surprising, since drawing the 45th parallel across the state shows that two thirds of the state falls within the radius of Quebec and New Brunswick, both once part of New France. French Canadians have also scattered throughout the other New England states and New York. Although their presence is acknowledged, it is not easily recognized because many have anglicized their French surnames and they tend not to speak French on an everyday basis.

A more distinct version of the French presence exists in Louisiana. The Cajun patois is descended from the language brought from New France by the Acadians. Cajun cooking, popularized by New Orleans chef Paul Prudhomme, and zydeco music have become familiar to millions in mainstream American culture. An award-winning mystery series written by author James Lee Burke featuring a Cajun investigator, Dave Robicheaux, intrigues fans across the nation. Cajun culture, although no longer closely connected to its origins, retains a distinctiveness that has certain similarities to the distinctiveness of Mexican American culture in the Southwest.

HISPANICS OF MEXICAN DESCENT IN THE UNITED STATES

In the larger U.S. popular culture, the three major distinct Hispanic groups—Mexicans, Cubans, and Puerto Ricans—are seldom differentiated. "Hispanic" itself is a word created by bureaucracy during the Nixon administration, a bureaucracy which also divided Americans into five colors: white, black, yellow (Asian/Pacific Islander), red (Native American/Eskimo), and brown (Hispanic).[2] The term Hispanic is often eschewed in favor of the word "Latino," yet "Hispanic" can be seen as a term that constructs a link between cultures: "To call oneself Hispanic is to admit a relationship to Latin America in English."[3] One reason for the proliferation of Hispanic (or Latino) writers is the steady development of Hispanic Studies programs around the United States. As the Latino population continues to increase, so will such studies and the attendant increase in awareness of the impact of Hispanic/Latino culture in the United States. Yet as with all labels, we must be careful not to stereotype: Richard Rodriguez writes that he "sees only diversity among the millions of people who call themselves Hispanic."

According to the 2000 census, 12.5 percent of the U.S. national population is Hispanic. The census data also tells us that Mexico is, without question, the country of origin for the largest number of immigrants among the Hispanic groups: two-thirds of Hispanics in the United States are of Mexican origin (66.1 percent: 21.6 million). Mexican Americans tend to fall into a lower socioeconomic group than Canadian Americans, as census data shows: while 49.7 percent have high school diplomas, 33 percent of Mexican Americans have less than a ninth-grade education. Only 7.1 percent of this group boast bachelor's degrees, but 35.4 percent of its children live in poverty.

The first generation of immigrants, undoubtedly like their Canadian counterparts, comes because they hope for better lives. However, they come from a poorer, less-educated segment of the Mexican population, and this extends into the second generation, reflected in the fact that 25.8 percent of the Mexican-born population in the United States remains at the poverty level. This segment of the population has the second highest poverty rate among immigrants. Unlike Canadian immigrants, those from Mexico often need more help from social services, increasing their visibility in the public sector.

Mexican immigrants have brought Mexican culture to the southwestern part of the United States and beyond. Tex-Mex cuisine has long been popular in the border states. Mexican restaurants have proliferated, and Mexican foods such as chili peppers and tortillas are now readily available in many chain supermarkets. More recently, Chef Mark Miller's Southwestern Cuisine, nouvelle cooking with Mexican roots, has spread from his Coyote Café in Santa Fe, New Mexico, opened in 1987, to a larger audience through his cookbooks and widely available Coyote Cocina brand products. Fiestas such as San Francisco's Carnaval, which drew 125,000 people in May 2002, celebrate and increase awareness of Latino culture.[4]

Language Issues: French

Language constructs reality for those who speak it. Whereas recent immigrants generally continue to use their native languages, succeeding generations often assimilate linguistically, becoming bilingual or losing the language of their immigrant ancestors entirely. This is equally true of successive generations of both French- and Spanish-speaking immigrants.

According to the 1990 census, 17,143,907 Americans are of French Canadian descent. This number is considerably larger than the number who actually declare their ancestry as French Canadian. Historically, to be of French Canadian origin was not a point of pride in New England, and many people anglicized their family names and left their origins behind. Margaret Chase Smith, for example, never identified herself as being of French Canadian descent, but her mother's surname, Morin, had been anglicized to Murray.[5] Some 1,930,404 Americans speak some French at home. Massachusetts has the largest number of people calling French their mother tongue, but even if one includes occasional French speakers, the number in the United States comprises only 0.78 percent of the population. It is not surprising, then, that French Canadian culture has had a limited cultural impact even in the Northeast.

Efforts to revive French are limited. As part of the public school system curriculum, there are four French immersion elementary schools in Maine, located in Van Buren, Madawaska, St. Agatha, and Frenchville. In these schools, some classes are taught in French and specific cultural connections are explored. While other immersion schools exist in places such as Berkeley, California, and in the Washington, D.C., area, where interest in bilingualism is strong, they do not emphasize any connections to French Canada. In fact, "Joual," the Québécois vernacular French, has not generally been included in university French departments because it has been considered substandard. Its expression as a specific "North American French" has largely been discounted. There is, nevertheless, new hope for Franco-American recognition under the "Ethnic Studies" umbrella. For example, at the University of Maine there is now a Franco-American Studies Program.[6] The State University of New York (SUNY) at Albany has undertaken a Franco-American Database Project. The National Science Foundation is supporting a three-year study by Jane Smith of the University of Maine and Cynthia Fox of SUNY/Albany on the use of "North American French" in eight New England communities.[7] Other schools such as our own institutions, Saint Mary's College of California and the University of Akron, have introduced individual courses with titles such as "French in the New World" and "French-Canadian Literature," which reflect increased interest in literature written in French in the Americas. How much this will increase the awareness of French Canadian culture within the larger American culture remains to be seen.

Language Issues: Spanish

Spanish is clearly more commonly used in the United States than is French. Spanish-language television and radio stations, bilingual ballots, bilingual education, and ATM machines and voice mail that offer users the choice of English or Spanish reflect increasing acceptance of Spanish as a language commonly spoken in the United States. In March 2000, the Texas gubernatorial debate was held in English and Spanish.

However, there are signs that this may change, depending on immigration rates and assimilation by Mexican Americans into the larger linguistic culture. Third-generation Mexican Americans, two thirds of whom speak no Spanish, form the fastest growing segment of the Hispanic population in the United States. Their numbers are expected to triple by 2040. Not too surprisingly, then, a 1998 Spanish-language version of *The Emperor's New Groove* was pulled from theaters for lack of interest, and in 2002 an English-language radio station in southern California, KROQ, claimed a 40 percent Latino audience.

It is not likely, however, given continued immigration and continued areas with high concentrations of Spanish-speaking people (Hispanics comprise 32.4 percent of the population of California, and 44.6 percent of the population of Los Angeles County, according to the 2000 census), that this trend will eliminate Spanish as an important language, especially in the Southwest. Spanglish, the mainly spoken but, increasingly, written language that adds English words to Spanish (not unlike the transformation of French into Cajun in Louisiana or the increasing use of "Franglais" in Quebec, particularly in Montreal), may become more prevalent as the diaspora of Spanish speakers continues in the United States. "As an underground vehicle of communication, [Spanglish] has been around for over 150 years at least" and serves as "a bridge of sorts that unites the Latino community in the United States."[8]

CANADA AND MEXICO IN
U.S. POPULAR CULTURE

In another era, images of Dudley Do-Right and Speedy Gonzales might have served as a suitable introduction to a discussion of Canada and Mexico in U.S. popular culture. We have come a certain distance since then, although perhaps not as far as we would like to think. Over the last decade Americans have become increasingly aware of people of Canadian and Mexican origins among the population, for reasons that have as much to do with societal shifts in cultural awareness as they do with NAFTA and the recent elections. For example, there has been a surge in published work by Mexican American authors since the publication, more than two decades ago, of *Bless Me, Ultima* by Rudolfo Anaya. The growing list of Mexican American writers includes Sandra Cisneros and Denise Chavez, both of whose fiction is primarily about Chicanas in the United States. The experience of being Mexican in the United States is a shared concern amongst most Mexican American writers: Mexican American literature, ranging from the poetry of Francisco Alarcon to the plays of Cherríe Moraga, renders visible the lives of this ethnic group within the larger American culture.

Although many Canadian writers, including, for instance, Margaret Atwood, Robertson Davies, Alice Munro, and Michael Ondaatje, are recognized in the United States, the presence of Canadian American writers is more muted. Writers such as Jack Kerouac, Grace Metalious, and Annie Proulx are seldom identified as having Canadian roots. Of the three, only Proulx writes of Canada (in *The Shipping News*), but not of the experience of being Canadian in the United States.

In films and television, we have a dichotomy between Anglophone and Francophone cultural icons. English-Canadian film celebrities melt into the larger American culture: Dan Ackroyd, Leslie Nielsen, John Candy, Pamela Anderson, Jim Carrey, Michael J. Fox, Donald Sutherland, Keanu Reeves, William Shatner—none is thought of primarily as a "Canadian American." Carrey ranks among the top ten actors in Hollywood in terms of ability to assure financing, distribution, and huge box office receipts for any film they make.[9] The language barrier appears to have precluded the development of a similar roster of film celebrities from Quebec, with Genevieve Bujold serving as the exception that proves the rule.

The same holds true for entertainers. Nellie Furtado is the latest in a long line of Canadian singers assimilated into U.S. entertainment culture whether or not they live in the United States; among them are Shania Twain, Alanis Morrisette, Joni Mitchell, Sarah McLachlan, Neil Young, Diana Krall, Leonard Cohen, and k.d. lang. A review of a recent concert by Alanis Morrisette in the San Francisco area speaks of "her eccentric muse," without noting that she's Canadian.[10] The same San Francisco reviewer praises Nelly Furtado for "deftly packaging diverse influences into a pop formula" that merges "indie rock, R&B, hip-hop and Portuguese and other world musics," but doesn't mention Canada.[11] k.d. lang continues a trend toward feminism in American country music that goes back at least as far as Loretta Lynn; however, as the first country music star to question heterosexuality through both her appearance and music, she has also brought something new to Nashville.[12] lang notes that being "alternative" is not a drawback: "If I'd been an ordinary singer, I'd still be trying to get noticed in Canada."[13] Instead, lang has become an international "symbol for acceptance and freedom," a celebrity whose sexual orientation overshadows her Canadian ethnicity.[14] All of these singers easily blend into the larger American entertainment scene.

On the other hand, Celine Dion and Le Cirque du Soleil, differentiated by language, retain distinctiveness. Yet when Celine Dion's rendition of "God Bless America" became a big hit after September 11, 2001, few questioned the right of a Québécois diva who has sold more than 140 million albums worldwide to sing an American anthem.[15] Given that she also sang the universally adored and ubiquitously played *Titanic* theme song, "My Heart Will Go On," and has now signed a multi-year contract to perform in Las Vegas, it may be that Dion has transcended her Quebec roots and been subsumed into the American fold, a familiar phenomenon in this country.

Many of the Canadians well known in the popular culture of the United States have life stories that seem to fit into the template of the American Dream. Jim Carrey, for example, who dropped out of school to help support his parents and siblings, fits the rags-to-riches pattern. Similarly, Shania Twain sang to support her siblings after her mother and stepfather were killed in an accident; her current stardom is another example of that story. Celine Dion, the youngest of fourteen children, needed a beauty makeover before her singing talents could shine forth for a wider audience; although arthritis of the spine requires a massage therapist to travel with her, she continues to perform, illustrating both the Cinderella story and the American work ethic. Sarah McLachlan also exemplifies the American Dream: an adopted child, she began classical music training as a young child and studied piano, guitar, and voice for years before beginning her career. Even k.d. lang's alternative vision can be constructed as an example of the American virtue of individualism. Because Americans construct these stars in their own cultural likenesses, their ethnicity reinforces Americans' vision of themselves rather than challenging it.

Mexican American entertainers, on the other hand, are differentiated from the mass of popular cultural icons by language and by their expression of Latino, rather than mainstream American, culture: Ricky Martin and Jennifer Lopez, a Latina Pamela Anderson, both exude the kind of sexuality characterized as "Latin charm." Yet saying that indicates that those two represent one particular Hispanic stereotype, probably one that, like most stereotypes, obscures individuality as it attempts to classify many members of an ethnic group by salient traits of one or two highly visible people from that group.

Over the last decade, Mexican American actors, like their counterparts in other areas of popular culture, are invariably cast in roles reflecting their heritage. Consider the new PBS series *An*

American Family, which features an extended Mexican American family played by several well-established Mexican American actors, including Raquel Welch. Reflecting the kind of interchangeability of the various Hispanic groups in the American imaginary, however, we also see actors like Esai Morales, born in Brooklyn of Puerto Rican parents, playing the role of the elder son in this family. The series focuses on what it's like to be Mexican American in southern California, although the plight of other Hispanic groups, most notably illegal immigrants from Central America, are highlighted episodically. In fall 2002, "WB's *Greetings from Tucson* will join ABC's *George Lopez* as the second Latino family comedy."[16] Television shows tend to have homogeneous casts: all white, all African American, all Latino, perpetuating an image of racial segregation. Latino representation in American TV shows increased from 2 to 4 percent in the 2001–2, "season, yet most of these actors had secondary roles in which they were "overrepresented as service workers, unskilled laborers, and criminals."[17] Latino actors may now be targeted for the roles that once stereotyped African Americans because of a lack of organized pressure groups and because "maids, gardeners, parking valets and restaurant workers may be the only Latinos those in charge of the shows know." "It's their continued perspective of who we are," observes Latin actress Lupe Ontiveros, who says she has to assume an accent she doesn't have in order to get parts.[18] The repeated representation perpetuates a stereotype that reflects only one small aspect of Latino culture in the United States.

The same differentiation exists between Canadian Americans and Mexican Americans in television journalism. When we think of Canadian-born journalists such as Peter Jennings, Morley Safer, and Robert McNeil, their country of origin is incidental. (In an example that is the exact opposite of Celine Dion's reception for singing "God Bless America," however, Jennings was excoriated by viewers in mid-May 2002 when he refused to allow a country music singer to perform a blatantly hawkish song during a Flag Day program on ABC; callers to the morning C-SPAN show denounced Jennings as a mere "Canadian" and reiterated the typical exhortation for him "to go back where he came from.") In contrast, journalists of Mexican origin such as Richard Rodriguez and Linda Chavez tend to be viewed as spokespersons for their ethnic group. Perhaps only Ray Suarez of PBS has transcended this tendency.

In general, one can conclude that Canadian Americans, unless their language reveals their origins, form an invisible minority and can choose to keep their identity "closeted" within the larger American culture. As a visible segment of the population, Mexican Americans frequently have their origins spotlighted, whether they want this distinction or not. Speaking perfect English often proves insufficient to allow them to assimilate fully. Their visible presence within American culture, unlike the nearly invisible Canadian presence, challenges the culture to rethink old stereotypes and construct a new cultural identity to acknowledge a changing situation.

IMPACT ON TRANSNATIONAL RELATIONS

The presence of the Spanish language and Hispanic culture in the United States can, in certain ways, be contrasted to Quebec's language and cultural presence in Canada. Although there is no official sanction or deliberate effort on its behalf, Hispanic language and culture have pervaded American popular culture in a way that the French language and Québécois culture have not extended across Canada. This may be because the Hispanic presence is not bound to one specific region and also because there are three distinct, yet fluid, groups of Hispanics in the United States. Hispanics within the United States also construct a new, more transnational identity for themselves: "What Hispanic immigrants learn within the United States is to view themselves in a new way, as belonging to Latin America entire—precisely at the moment that they no longer do," writes Richard Rodriguez, the son of Mexican immigrants to California. In addition, Rodriguez notes that Americans' self-construction has altered in response to an enlarging Hispanic presence: "Because of Hispanics, Americans are coming to see the United States in terms of a latitudinal vector, in terms of south-north, hot-cold, a new way of placing ourselves in the twenty-first century."[19] We might add that Canadians are also contributing to overlaying the traditional east-west image with a north-south one.

THE "NO CHILD LEFT BEHIND" ACT

Although this discussion so far has covered a longer period, one initiative resulting from the 2000 election may have a significant impact on Mexican Americans as well as other groups. The bipartisan No Child Left Behind Act requires annual testing of all public school students in grades three through eight. Some analysts anticipate potential negative effects for Latinos and other minorities, including lower graduation and promotion rates, rising dropout rates, excessive emphasis on test practice, and not enough emphasis on thinking and analytic skills.[20] These factors could have a negative impact on the efforts of immigrant groups to increase their opportunities in the United States through education. Some experts favor a "multiple assessments" system in which additional information about a student's performance is collected to contextualize low test scores. Others contend that this act will force school districts to work harder to educate minority students, since scores of minority students must both be included in the school's average and reported separately.[21] Although the impact of the No Child Left Behind Act is not clear at this point, it definitely bears watching.

INS RESPONSE TO PROBLEMS ON
THE MEXICAN BORDER

Both heightened security concerns since September 11 and humanitarian concerns have prompted recent changes along the U.S.-Mexican border. Not all immigration from Mexico is legal. Over 1.6 million people were apprehended crossing the border illegally in 2000. In 2001, the number dropped to 1.2 million, a level not seen since the early 1990s. In 2000, 377 people died crossing the border; the number declined to 336 in 2001, and statistics for the first five months of 2002 suggest a further decline in deaths. On May 24, 2002, INS Commissioner James Ziglar announced that "the INS was installing six 30-foot tall rescue beacons" visible for thirty miles near areas where many deaths from desert heat have occurred. "If a migrant in distress can make it to the beacon and push a button, a rescue helicopter will be dispatched."[22] In addition, Hovercraft, horseback units, and "nonlethal pepper ball launchers" will be deployed along with increased helicopter surveillance in efforts to "heighten security and safety."[23]

Although questions should be raised about how illegal immigrants, presumably already frightened and wary, might reasonably be expected to react to the idea of pepper balls, lights, and helicopters, stopping deaths along the border seems a precondition to assuring that all who enter the United States from Mexico have a chance at the new life they seek. We can hope that the INS will work to enable those who want to come to the United States to do so legally and safely. At present, however, at the U.S.-Mexican border, a culture of affluence and power confronts a culture of poverty and need—and great courage.

One might also say that the impact of the events of September 11, rather than the 2000 elections, has brought greater visibility to Canadian border crossings. Since that time, many American politicians have been complaining about Canadian laxity and the need for greater vigilance, especially after it was erroneously reported in the news media that some of the terrorists had entered Maine through Canada. Although no one has yet called for the kinds of stringent policies practiced on the southern border, this new attitude appears to represent a view of Canada as "foreign," as "other," that has not been seen in recent times.

CONCLUSIONS

We can draw some tentative conclusions from the data presented above. First, the "invisibility" of Canadian contributions continues and no doubt will continue as they are subsumed into the larger English-speaking culture. The exception is the small renaissance of French Canadian identity in New England, which may grow as the nation continues its attempt to embrace multiculturalism. The relatively few people in the United States studying French Canadian culture may ultimately make a difference.

Secondly, Mexican Americans continue to assert their presence as a distinct American group even as they assimilate. The considerable expansion of Hispanic studies in the United States (coupled with a much smaller and slower growing expansion of Canadian studies) also suggests that the Mexican American presence will continue to develop greater visibility here. We can hope that Jeff Zucker, president for NBC entertainment, is correct in saying that Hispanic portrayals in the media will evolve to give a fuller picture of Mexican Americans: "As diversity increases, the span of roles increases."[24]

Impact on the Future

Data from the 2000 census indicates that the number of people in the United States who identify themselves simply as "American" has increased from 13 million to 20 million, with a particularly evident decline in people claiming European roots. At the same time, the surge in Hispanic immigration in the 1990s may contribute to a reshaping of the American identity.[25] In *Brown: The Last Discovery of America*, Richard Rodriguez suggests that the United States may yet become "brown," not merely in terms of skin color, but "in terms of culture [and] thought."[26] Rodriguez writes: "North of the U.S.-Mexico border, brown appears as the color of the future. The adjective accelerates, becomes a verb: 'America is browning.'" Yet Rodriguez cautions, "I do not propose an easy optimism," partly because he senses that "African Americans remain at the center of the moral imagination of America."[27] Some might argue that a *mestizo* culture can be seen as part of a larger hybrid culture, a new melting pot. However, if one takes the many ethnic groups that comprise America into account, including ones from Canada, it is possible to envision the emergence of a North American culture that is neither a *mestizaje* (the term Mexico uses for the marriage of races that comprise its population's mixture) nor a melting pot nor a mosaic (in which distinct pieces are held in fixed relationships to each other), but a salad bowl: in a salad, the dressing blends individual items and adds special flavor, yet individual entities can interact and alter their relationships easily.[28]

CHAPTER 7

A Tale of Two Elections:
What the Leaders' Rhetoric from the 2000
Elections Reveals about Canadian-American
Cultural Differences

Stephen Brooks

IN *HERE: A BIOGRAPHY OF THE NEW AMERICAN CONTINENT*, Anthony DePalma argues that the concepts of "here" and "there," used to underscore the separateness and distinctiveness of Canada, the United States, and Mexico, have diminishing relevance and resonance in the new North America being forged by free trade. "From 1993 to 2000," he writes, "North America evolved from being defined solely as three separate nations divided by two borders on one continent to being recognized as a community of shared interest, common dreams, and coordinated responses to problems that have no regard for borders."[1] Economic integration, he argues, has provided the main catalyst for more sweeping integration that ultimately, DePalma foresees, will produce a shared North American identity. This identity will not sweep aside national or regional identities, but will exist alongside them and, inevitably, dull the edge of national difference.

DePalma does not argue that full political integration is in the cards—at least not anytime soon. But he does argue that the cultural consequences flowing from the accelerated movement of goods and services, investment, and people across the borders that separate the United States from its northern and southern neighbors are already evident. He seems to be right, although the stubborn weight of history, psychological needs, insecurities and emotions, and self-interest on the part of those whose status, livelihoods, and/or power depends on separateness and difference, often obscures and operates to deny the process that DePalma maintains is already well advanced.

Is it true that the political culture of English Canada is significantly different from that of the United States? Did the rhetoric of party leaders in the 2000 Canadian and American election campaigns corroborate the conventional wisdom concerning Can-Am cultural differences? Although the rhetoric and messages of the Mexican parties and their leaders in that country's 2000 election campaign will not be examined here, if DePalma is correct, one would expect to find increasing convergence—particularly as the Mexican middle class grows in size and the roots of North American integration sink more deeply into Mexican society—between the messages used to connect with voters in Mexico and those characteristic of election campaigns in the United States and Canada.

POLITICAL CULTURE AND ELECTION RHETORIC

Seymour Martin Lipset has more than once remarked that, for students of comparative politics, Canada and the United States represent the closest thing to a laboratory for the testing of theories as one is likely to find in the messy, uncontrolled world of social behavior.[2] Two societies linked by shared histories, cultures, languages, and economic markets, whose border has been among the world's most open and whose similarities generally are more apparent to non-North Americans than their differences. And yet, of course, there are differences, the sort and magnitude of which have inspired disagreement for over two hundred years.

For half a century, Lipset's work has been at the center of the perennial debate over the ways and degree to which the political cultures of English Canada and the United States differ.[3] He is associated with the view that there are historically rooted differences between the two societies that are both persistent and significant. Lipset's earlier emphasis on Can-Am differences has, however, been qualified in more recent years by his belief—a belief shared by virtually everyone—that the Charter era in Canadian politics has been characterized by a significant shift toward a more American style of politics, evident in the far greater role that rights discourse and policy strategies that rely on the courts and other judicial tribunals have assumed since 1982. He has also argued that the electoral successes over the last several decades of Canada's chief left-wing party, the New Democratic Party (NDP), may have been wrongly interpreted as proof of considerably greater popular support for socialist values in Canada than in the United States. Institutional differences affecting the respective party systems of the two countries may well be more important than culture, he argues. The values represented by the NDP in Canada, Lipset says, both exist and have been influential on the left of the Democratic Party in the United States.

Leaving aside the important question that Lipset and others have raised about the degree to which such differences as the greater reliance on state enterprise in Canada or the higher levels of taxation and public spending in Canada can be explained by institutional and other factors that are not purely or primarily attitudinal, the differences between the political culture maps of Canada and the United States are neither as clear as some suggest nor consistent with the conventional wisdom, at least as this exists on the Canadian side of the border. That "wisdom" includes the three following assumptions: that Canada is a more compassionate society than the United States; that collectivist values occupy a more secure place in the Canadian political culture; and that there is a greater range of politically significant ideological expression in Canada than in the United States.[4]

In order to test various claims about the cultural differences between Canada and the United States, researchers have relied on a wide range of evidence, from polling data to such indirect measures of attitudes as policies, literature, crime statistics, and various forms of social behavior. There is as little agreement over the validity of the measures used to test arguments about Can-Am political cultural differences as there is over the nature of these putative differences. These disagreements will not be put to rest here. Instead, it is suggested that the examination of the political discourse of election campaigns, when parties and candidates are required by circumstances to market themselves to voters and, in doing so, both to associate themselves in citizens' minds with values and positions that significant groups of electors wish to see reflected in public life and to differentiate themselves from the competition, provides a good but neglected testing ground for arguments about Canadian-American differences.

Actions and the institutional embodiments of choices are certainly important. But it is a great mistake to ignore the words and symbols that are used to advocate and justify these choices. The carefully selected and laundered phrases that emerge from the arts of the pollster, focus group analyst, and professional speechwriter, no less than words created directly from the pen of a Lincoln or Laurier, constitute a sort of connective tissue of ideas and symbols between citizens and those who govern them (or aspire to). The craft of creating this connective tissue has changed dramatically, but the essential function of these ideas and symbols remains the same. And no less than in the days of Lincoln and Laurier, a Bush or Chrétien cannot afford to communicate in words and symbols that do not resonate sympathetically with a significant number of voters.

It is probably reasonable to predict that history will not remember either the 2000 presidential campaign in the United States or the 2000 general election in Canada as being of more than average importance. The prolonged aftermath of the 2000 American election has been excluded since only campaigns are being considered. Rather, I am speaking of the campaigns. In the case of Canada there was no big, dramatic issue that ripped apart the body politic, as the proposed Canada-U.S. Free Trade Agreement had in the 1988 Canadian election campaigns. Indeed, it was widely believed that the 2000 election was called by the Liberal government for no better reason than to take advantage of the Liberal Party's favorable standing in the polls and the fact that the main opposition party, the Canadian Alliance, had a new and rather untested leader, Stockwell Day, who appeared vulnerable on a number of fronts. Thus, the elections of 2000 provide a good occasion for comparing the rhetoric of leaders across the border.

In order to compare the political cultures of English Canada and the United States, the major speeches, campaign websites, party platforms, and leaders' debates from the 2000 Canadian and American election campaigns have been examined. For Canada the public pronouncements of Jean Chrétien (Liberal), Stockwell Day (Alliance), Alexa McDonough (NDP), and Joe Clark (Conservative) were reviewed. Gilles Duceppe, leader of the Bloc Québécois, on the grounds that his Quebec-based, sovereigntist party—the BQ only runs candidates in Quebec and is committed to the principle of independence for Quebec—was excluded. For the United States, the campaigns of George W. Bush (Republican), Al Gore (Democrat), and Ralph Nader (Green) were reviewed. Even though Nader won only a small fraction of the popular vote and no seats in America's Electoral College, his candidacy was far more significant than his numbers on election day might suggest. Major speeches and public pronouncements of the party leaders were trolled to determine whether the conventional wisdom concerning Can-Am political cultural differences was corroborated in the 2000 Canadian and American election campaigns. (See appendix for list of documents and public statements used.)

To distill the thousands upon thousands of words uttered by and on behalf of the three main presidential candidates and the four leaders of the main parties that contested seats in English Canada, their messages and meanings were organized along two axes. The first involves market values orientation, or what might be described as the degree of confidence in markets and outcomes that relies on unregulated personal choices. The second involves social values orientation, or what might be characterized as the degree of commitment to traditional values and institutions, particularly those based on religion and the traditional family. Figure 7.1 illustrates these dimensions. The estimation of where each leader's political rhetoric is situated on this map is not obvious and incontestable. Instead, this mapping exercise is to be a modest attempt at thinking systematically about Canadian-American cultural differences as these are reflected in election campaigns in the two countries.

MAPPING THE LEADERS' RHETORIC: THE 2000 CANADIAN ELECTION

The 2000 election was Jean Chrétien's to lose. As the leader of Canada's governing party, with a small majority in the Canadian House of Commons, Chrétien could have continued in office for another year and a half before facing the electorate. His decision

Figure 7.1. Mapping the Party Leaders' Rhetoric

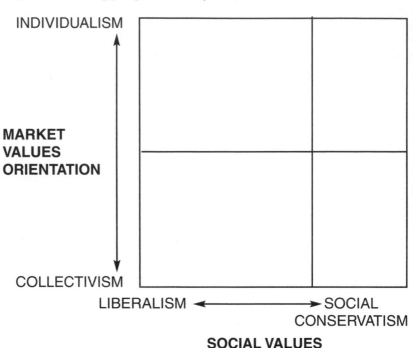

to call an election was generally and probably correctly viewed as a rather cynical attempt to secure a stronger majority at a time when the major opposition party, the Reform Party, had recently transformed itself into the Canadian Alliance, under a new and untested leader who appeared vulnerable on certain issues, and when support for separatism in Quebec—and therefore, presumably, for the Bloc Québécois—appeared to be soft. The possibility that the prime minister wished to stifle rumblings in his party about his leadership by calling and winning a third election cannot be ruled out. Reasons of electoral expediency and personal ambition aside, there was no crisis, issue, or set of circumstances that compelled the election call.

When there is no obvious issue in Canadian electoral politics, the pseudo-issue of leadership often substitutes for more substantive matters. But even with a well-liked leader—and Chrétien's "just folks" style, "*le petit gars de Shawinigan*," as he has always liked to describe himself, made him generally popular with Canadians— no party can entirely avoid addressing campaign issues that the media and the other parties place on the table. Instead of waiting for their opponents and critics to define the issues, the Liberals did what one would expect Canada's most successful political party to do. They went on the offensive, attempting to shape the campaign discourse around issues on which they believed themselves to be strong and the Alliance vulnerable. They did this by showcasing the third rail of Canadian politics, public health care.

From the opening salvos of press releases and public statements by Chrétien on the day the election was called, through the televised leaders' debates and the hours of paid political advertising, health care was the Liberals' preferred issue. The Chrétien/Liberal message was that the Liberal Party was committed to the protection of medicare and Ottawa's role in enforcing national standards in health care. "A new Liberal government will defend and vigorously uphold the values of medicare to ensure that all Canadians continue to have full and equal access to high quality health care."[5] This promise was accompanied by some of the most negative advertising ever seen in Canadian electoral politics, accusing the Alliance and its leader Stockwell Day of hiding their true agenda for health care, which the Liberals claimed was medicare's transformation into a two-tiered, American-style system with quality care for the affluent and inferior care for the rest of the population.

The core values and unifying themes of the Chrétien/Liberal message in the 2000 election campaign were the following: Canada's system of publicly-paid universal health care, and Ottawa's role in providing financing and maintaining national standards, must be protected; the nation should reinvest part of the budget surpluses that began to accumulate in the mid-1990s in the maintenance and expansion of social programs; the federal government should cooperate with provincial governments, including maintaining Ottawa's commitment to the interregional redistribution of wealth; and all Canadians deserve good government.

In fairness to the Liberals, it must be said that the party produced a wide-ranging platform, most notably in its campaign document, *Opportunity for All: The Liberal Plan for the Future of Canada*. The Liberal Plan was solidly in the Canadian tradition of brokerage politics, promising something for almost everyone in a sweeping catalogue of promises that ranged from investment in innovation to the enhancement of women's safety. But on the campaign trail, in the English-language televised debates and in their advertising, the Liberals emphasized the medicare issue above all others, linking it to the Chrétien/Liberal attacks on the credibility and alleged hidden agenda of the Alliance Party and its leader Stockwell Day.

When former president George H. W. Bush squared off against Michael Dukakis in the 1988 presidential election, Seymour Martin Lipset remarked that Canada had three center-left parties, all of them to the left of the Dukakis Democrats. His point was that, despite their differences on the issue of free trade, Canada's three main political parties shared a commitment to the principles of the welfare state, official bilingualism and multiculturalism, and were broadly similar in their views on constitutional reform (the Liberals, Conservatives, and NDP had unanimously supported the failed Meech Lake Accord in the House of Commons). The spectrum of policy and ideological divergence among Canada's chief national parties was, Lipset argued, comparatively narrow and in many ways offered Canadian voters a narrower spectrum of choices than their American counterparts experienced.

In the 2000 Canadian election this was true with a vengeance. Whereas the free trade issue had provided voters with at least the appearance of a real choice in 1988, issue-oriented product differentiation among the main parties and their leaders was almost absent from the 2000 campaign. Moreover, in terms of what the 2000 campaign revealed about the ideas, images, and symbols that Canada's national political parties use to evoke sympathetic responses among voters, the conclusion to be drawn is substantially identical to that which Lipset drew in 1988. Canada's chief political parties occupy a relatively narrow space on the idea/value spectrum, preferring to compete with one another in terms of leadership and the credibility of their promises, rather than offering voters significantly different sets of values and beliefs. Their refusal to engage in a battle over fundamental principles invites, of course, the sort of negative advertising that was so prominent a feature of the 2000 Canadian election that Jean Chrétien felt compelled to offer post-victory regrets for the tone of the campaign.

Health care has emerged in recent years as the valence issue par excellence of Canadian politics. Every party and its leader strive to be associated in the minds of voters with protection of medicare and the preservation of Canada from the putative evils of American-style health care. Just as the free trade issue in 1988 was about Canada's relationship to the United States, the health care issue evokes longstanding fears and emotions about Can-Am relations. When Alan Rock was Liberal minister of health he seemed incapable of criticizing health care reforms undertaken by the Conservative governments of Alberta and Ontario and the policy proposals of the Reform Party without using the derisive labels "American-style" and "two-tiered" health care. In the vocabulary of Canadian politics, "two-tiered health care" is understood to mean a system characterized by gross inequality between the rich and the rest of the population, as is believed to be characteristic of American health care, but also, and more controversially, levels of health care for those who are not rich that are far inferior to what all Canadians experience under their publicly-financed system of medicare. No Canadian political party wishes to be associated with such negative baggage, and all strove mightily in the 2000 campaign to convince voters that they represented the most credible defender of the values that Canadians tend to associate with the health care system.

When Canadians are asked to identify those features of their society that distinguish Canada from the United States, health care is invariably one of the first differences they mention. Encouraged by their politicians and opinion-leaders to believe that the different health care systems of Canada and the United States reflect significant cultural differences—Canadians portrayed as being more compassionate, egalitarian, and communitarian than their meaner-spirited, competitive, and individualist neighbors to the south—Canadians tend to react with Pavlovian alacrity to any suggestion that one of the chief embodiments of these putative differences and, as such, a bulwark for the defense of Canada's independent identity, may be under threat.

I would argue that the special place that the health care issue occupies in Canadian politics has had major consequences for the Canadian party system and Canadian political discourse. Chief among these is the deformation of the Canadian right and the narrowing of the range of rhetoric that party leaders use in competing for votes. By this I mean that it is extremely difficult in Canadian politics to talk about health care reform in any language that carries the suggestion of competition, privatization, and different standards for different income cohorts or that in any way suggests that Canadian health care should adopt elements of the American model. Talk of greater provincial autonomy in health care quickly becomes interpreted by critics as camouflage for the importation of two-tiered health care. Even the Canadian Alliance, Canada's only national right-of-center party, adopts the protective covering of the status quo rhetoric on medicare. Perhaps the most memorable moment during the terribly dismal English-language televised leaders' debates in 2000 came when Alliance leader Stockwell Day displayed a handwritten sign reading "No 2-tier health care" and then, in a gesture quite probably borrowed from Al Gore's combative challenge to Bush in the second presidential debate, left his lectern and approached Jean Chrétien, insisting that the Liberal leader either accuse Day of lying on health care or apologize for Liberal ads claiming that Day supported an American-style, two-tiered health system.

For his part, Day accused the Liberal leader of "ripping into health care" and, in language that was redolent of the Canadian left's desire to entrench a guarantee of universal, publicly-funded health care in the Charter of Rights and Freedoms, called for "legislated funding levels for health care." More spending on health was part of the Day/Alliance campaign rhetoric, as it was for all of the parties and their leaders. The third rail of Canadian politics was too hot for the Alliance to touch, as ideologically conservative parties in power in Alberta and Ontario have also discovered. Because the health care issue and the leaders' credibility on this issue were central to the 2000 Canadian campaign, this ensured that voters were offered relatively little choice in the values expressed by the parties and their leaders, all of whom clustered around the politically safe commitment to a non-American, universal, publicly financed system of medicare with increased spending levels.

An observer of the 2000 Canadian election campaign, and particularly of the leaders' debates and the war of televised advertising that took place, could have been excused for wondering

whether Canada truly had a right-of-center party. The prominence
of the health care issue and the party leaders' unanimous efforts to
associate themselves in the minds of voters with what might be
described as a "Canada Health Act plus more dollars" policy,
prevented the emergence of a competitive and diverse market of
policy ideas and associated values on this issue. This stood in sharp
contrast to the American presidential campaign, where the rhetoric of Bush and Gore on Social Security reform and, to a more
muted degree, education presented voters with fairly clear, ideologically distinctive choices.

Critics of the Canadian Alliance, including the leaders of the
other national parties, were quick to dismiss the Day/Alliance
commitment to the Canada Health Act—at one point in the
leaders' debate Day actually said that he stood by all five principles of the CHA and would add a sixth, legislated funding levels—and increased public spending on medicare as phony
camouflage for Alliance's "hidden agenda." They, not Day and
the Alliance, argued that voters in fact did have an ideological
choice when it came to health care and, more generally, the nature of Canadian society. But my point is not to determine
whether the Day/Alliance rhetoric was dishonest, but to examine the symbols, beliefs, and values that Day and the Alliance,
and the other parties and their leaders, used in order to evoke a
sympathetic response among Canadian voters. Judged against
the language the Day/Alliance campaign used to present itself to
voters and attack its opponents, the rhetoric of Canada's only
right-of-center party was barely distinguishable from that of the
centrist Chrétien/Liberal and Clark/Conservative campaigns.
The right could not find a clear and confident voice in the 2000
election campaign largely because of its vulnerability to the third
rail of Canadian politics.

Of course the 2000 Canadian election was not entirely about
health care and the party leaders' respective credibility on this

most crucial of valence issues in Canadian politics. The NDP attempted to focus voters' attention on the issue of the growing federal budget surplus and whether it would be reinvested in social programs or used to finance a tax cut for corporations and the affluent. The McDonough/NDP rhetoric was quite similar to that of Nader and the Green Party on many fronts, based on the idea of a conflict pitting powerful corporations against working people and families. The Day/Alliance rhetoric attempted to steer the campaign discourse toward the ideologically conservative issues of tax cuts and limited government, and the populist theme of greater citizen participation in governance. The social conservatism generally thought to be characteristic of Day and his party was muted, taking the form of carefully coded messages about tougher law enforcement, reform of the juvenile justice system, and support for the family. The Clark/Conservative rhetoric was as middle-of-the-road as that of the Liberal Party, as was to be expected of a leader and a party that seemed convinced they could recapture their past status as the other big brokerage party, competing with the Liberals in the broad center lane of the Canadian political highway. The Clark/Conservative preoccupation with discrediting Day and the Alliance on the right, and criticizing Chrétien's leadership and integrity and the performance of the liberal government on issues that had little or no ideological resonance, ensured that the Clark/Conservative message offered Canadian voters almost nothing that, in ideological terms, was distinguishable from the Chrétien/Liberal message.

The core values and unifying themes expressed in the rhetoric of the Day/Alliance, Clark/Conservative, and McDonough/NDP messages in the 2000 campaign are identified in table 7.1. The candidates' positions are then mapped according to the combination of market and social value orientations in figure 7.2.

TABLE 7.1.

Core Values and Unifying Themes in the Chrétien/Liberal, Day/Alliance,
Clark/Conservative, and McDonough/NDP Campaigns, 2000

Chrétien	Day	Clark	McDonough
• publicly-paid universal health care must be protected from American-style reforms	• limited government	• leadership	• people and working families vs. the powerful (banks, oil, etc.)
• part of budget surpluses must be reinvested in social programs	• protect and reinvest in health care	• restore integrity in government	• fair trade, not free trade
• cooperate with provincial governments, including Ottawa's role in the interregional redistribution of wealth	• restore eroded Canadian democracy	• protect and reinvest in health care	• health care system is catastrophically underfunded
• good government	• increase opportunities for citizen participation in governance		• social justice
	• respect provincial rights and equality of provinces		• increased government role in economic regulation
			• the environment must be a priority when making policy choice

Figure 7.2. American Presidential Candidates' Political Rhetoric

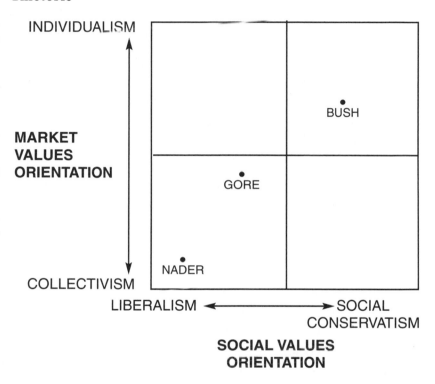

MAPPING THE LEADERS' RHETORIC:
THE 2000 UNITED STATES ELECTION

As the presidential candidate of the incumbent party, under whose watch the American economy had experienced an un-precedented period of impressive growth, Al Gore's position might have appeared an enviable one. Under Bill Clinton the Democratic Party had presided over large budget surpluses and had moved to the center of the political spectrum, supporting welfare reform. Issues that had previously tended to work to the advantage of Republicans—law and order, public finances, the state of the economy—became areas where the Democrats could claim success. Not everyone within the Democratic fold was happy with this shift to the center, but it certainly seemed to undercut what the Republicans were used to thinking of as their issue agenda.

In these circumstances the Gore campaign packaged its candidate and his message in a language that sought to retain and expand the centrist space the party occupied under Clinton, while at the same time invoking symbols and associations preferred by elements of the party and the electorate more sympathetic to communitarian and liberal values. This is a line that any serious Democratic presidential candidate must walk, but it was made more than usually difficult by the Nader candidacy on the left.

The core values and unifying themes of the Gore 2000 campaign included the following: powerful interests threaten the people's interests; the policies put in place since FDR's New Deal must be protected; government needs to be reformed, but it is not the enemy of the people; the litmus test of what government does should be its impact on families, particularly working families; and equality of opportunity is possible in America, but requires positive action on the part of government (through affirmative action, social programs that target the least advantaged, public education, and so on).

This was a very centrist message, but one that remained firmly committed to the values and policies of the New Deal Democratic Party. Of course the term "welfare state" has never been fashionable in American politics and was entirely absent from Gore's campaign rhetoric, as it was from that of Bush and Nader too. Gore's use of the terms "families" and "working families" was a politically safe, if somewhat elliptical way, of packaging the positive or welfare state in a way that was expected to generate a sympathetic response with the electorate.

The rhetorical hinge of Gore's campaign was the term "family." Family, working families, middle-class families—these words punctuated virtually all of Gore's speeches, providing an anchor for his message and policy proposals. The word "family" or "families" is used forty-six times in his acceptance speech at the Democratic Party's nominating convention. It is used ten times in Gore's relatively short introduction of Joseph Lieberman as his running mate (and then another twelve times by Lieberman in his acceptance speech). Family, especially working families, became a sort of Gore mantra on the 2000 campaign trail. This was not merely an attempt to consolidate the suburban support of the party of the so-called "soccer moms." Family, working families, and middle-class families were terms used by the Gore campaign in association with traditional Democratic policies and positions. Protection of the environment, reform of health care and Social Security, investment in education, tax cuts, and regulating the television, film, music, and tobacco industries were all packaged as family issues. The Gore/Democrat rhetoric attempted to establish an associational bridge between families, the positive state, and the time-honored tradition of the powerful versus the people.

Although many criticized the Gore candidacy as being too similar in its message and policies to the Republican candidacy of George W. Bush, this was simply not the case at the level of political rhetoric. The Gore rhetoric remained faithful to the values of the New Democratic Party, including the implicit idea that government action is necessary to ensure equality, freedom, and economic prosperity. But in a political culture in which mistrust of government is strong, the defense of the positive state cannot be as simple as this. It must be communicated in terms of symbols and beliefs that have a deep positive resonance. The "people versus the powerful" is a safe rhetorical formula with a long history in American politics. Gore played on this theme at almost every public speaking opportunity.

On the social-conservatism/liberalism scale, Gore's message was firmly on the liberal side, despite abundant references to God and family in virtually all of his major public addresses. His defense of affirmative action and *Roe v. Wade* on abortion—key litmus tests when it comes to matters of morality and justice in America—was unequivocal. In these respects the Gore/Democratic message was certainly as center-left as that of Canada's Liberal Party and Progressive Conservative Party.

At first blush, the Bush 2000 campaign was somewhat disorienting. The official campaign platform, *A Vision for America*, included a long shopping list of priorities and promises. But three of the first given on the list were issues normally thought of as Democratic ones. Education, Social Security, and Medicare—key components of the positive state—were included in the top five (first, third, and fifth, respectively). Taxes and national defense, issues generally thought of as Republican ones, rounded out the Bush/Republican top five.

On closer inspection, however, the way in which these issues were framed—if not the prominence given to them—was very much in the modern-day tradition of conservative Republicanism. The public rhetoric used by candidate Bush was deeply skeptical of government and strongly supportive of markets and individual choice in economic matters and of socially conservative values in matters of morality and the nature of the good society. If "families" was the Gore mantra in the 2000 campaign, "responsibility" was the Bush mantra. Whereas Gore's preferred rhetorical formula pitted the people against the powerful, Bush's implied that the real enemy of the people's interests was the government, Washington, and all those who did not trust the people to make their own choices about their children's education, their Social Security investments, their Medicare, and their tax surplus.

The core values and unifying themes of the Bush-Republican message in 2000 were the following: individuals and families should be provided with as much opportunity as possible to make their own choices about the disposal of their incomes and the education of their children; government is too large and too intrusive; the state's role in the provision of social services is not an adequate substitute for the involvement of churches and other faith-based groups for persons in need; policies should aim to encourage individual responsibility and reinforce the development of personal character; markets and competition do a better job than regulators and legislative controls in ensuring economic growth and widespread prosperity; freedom does not require that government do more than ensure educational opportunities and provide some other minimal support for a level playing field—it is compromised by the "soft bigotry" of affirmative action, quotas, and policies that categorize citizens on the basis of ascriptive characteristics.

This may sound like a very familiar message, and in some ways the Bush rhetoric was vintage Republicanism. However, they were packaged in a rhetoric that was reassuringly familiar but also intended to appeal to the huge centrist-independent segment of the electorate. "Compassionate conservatism," "armies of compassion," and "no child left behind" were among the terms Bush favored in describing his vision of an alternative to what these terms implicitly criticized, i.e., the big government, bureaucratic nanny-state preferred by liberals. The rhetoric of compassionate conservatism drew upon communitarian principles. Far from being a radically individualistic message, it emphasized the importance of communities, associations, and churches at the same time as it involved a reduced role for state agencies. Some will call this a phony or at least unrealistic communitarianism in contemporary America, but if the rhetoric is taken at face value—as I argue it should be, given that the point here is to understand what messages, symbols, and images evoke positive responses among Americans—it is clearly communitarianism in a way that seeks to locate the inspiration of and responsibility for compassion and caring outside the state.

The Bush/Republican message in the 2000 campaign was clearly on the individual side of the individualism/collectivism scale. But to be successful across the diverse constituencies that make up the American electorate, the conservative message must blend rhetorical elements that include personal choice, accountability (as in educational standards and testing), skepticism about government, and faith in the wisdom and goodness of the people. The Bush campaign did this with some success. This was best illustrated in the case of Social Security reform, the supposed "third rail" of American politics. By promising to protect Americans' old age income security by giving them more personal choice in the investment of "their money," the Bush rhetoric cleverly linked the values of compassion—caring for the retirement incomes of Americans—with those of personal choice and faith in the superior wisdom of the people over government when it comes to how to spend the people's money. The rhetoric was solidly conservative, but resonated more broadly with the electorate because it also evoked what I would characterize as a widespread communitarian spirit among Americans, but one whose link to the state is weaker than in Canada.

For much of the 2000 campaign, Ralph Nader and the Green Party stood at between 6 and 8 percent in public opinion polls. This dissipated by election day to a mere 2.74 percent—still enough for many Democrats to blame the Greens' candidate, Ralph Nader, for costing them the White House in a tight race. I would argue that the respectable poll numbers that Nader's Green Party maintained through much of the campaign accurately reflected the not insignificant support that existed, and continues to exist, in American society for the values championed by Nader.

The Green Party's 2000 campaign platform was significantly different from that of the two major parties. Democracy, social justice and equal opportunity, and environmental sustainability were the first three themes of the platform. When the Green platform finally turned to the economy, a priority in the other parties' platforms, the issue is framed in the context of economic sustainability. The values expressed in this document are ones that any Green or socialist party in Western Europe would find congenial. At the same time, however, these values are set in a context of historical allusions and evocative symbols that are firmly rooted in American culture.

The core values and unifying themes of the Nader/Green message in 2000 were the following: people must be provided with the means to wrest control of their lives, communities, and culture from the corporate elite; capitalism, and in particular the globalizing version of capitalism that has gained such momentum in recent decades, is fundamentally opposed to the values of a humane, compassionate, and democratic society in which social justice and protection of the environment are genuine priorities; trade liberalization, and the limits on national sovereignty that accompany the growing importance of the World Trade Organization and the rest of the international apparatus for the implementation and enforcement of global trade rules, represent the same threat to democracy and rights that other forms of tyranny and concentrated power represented in the past; the major parties and their candidates are stooges of the big corporate interests, a subservience that is guaranteed by a structurally corrupt system of campaign financing; Western Europe represents a model that the United States should emulate in matters of social policy; and the entire culture has become corporatized to such an invasive degree that only radical political and economic change can reverse this tide.

On the face of it, this may sound like a rather un-American message. It certainly is an undeniably radical message—who else talked about "corporate crime" and "corporate welfare" in 2000? At the same time, however, it is a message that Nader and the Green Party communicated in a language that was safely within the familiar comfort zone of the American political tradition—an absolute requirement if Nader expected to get onto CNN's *Larry*

King Live and the evening news broadcasts of the major television networks. Nader's acceptance speech at the Green Party's presidential nominating convention was masterful in weaving trenchant criticism into the familiar language of American populism, democratic ideals, and renewal.

More generally, the Nader/Green rhetoric relied heavily on references to "the people," "citizens," and community-level organization and popular movements. Unlike the major-party candidates, Nader's rhetoric did not rely on the terms "family/families," "working-class families," or "middle-class families." Nor did it rely on either a statist-collectivist or class-conflict language more familiar in European democracies. True to the longstanding tradition of American progressivism, the Nader/Green message was communicated in the language of conflict, but this was conflict between the "corporations" and the "people," between "citizens" and the "corporatists" (i.e., defenders of corporate power), and "concentrations of power" that threatened citizens' rights and well-being. The problem was framed in a recognizably American way and the proposed solutions relied on citizen action, community organization, and popular involvement rather than statist solutions of public ownership and dirigiste economics.

The Nader/Green message was situated toward the communitarian end of the communitarian-individualism scale, and toward the liberal end of the social conservatism-liberalism scale. Although packaged in language that was firmly within the American political tradition, the content of this message was certainly as collectivist as that of Canada's NDP and every bit as sympathetic to the social democratic vision of that party.

The core values and unifying themes expressed in the three American presidential campaigns are summarized in table 7.2. And as before, the candidates' positions are mapped according to the combination of market and social value orientations in figure 7.3.

Table 7.2.

Core Values and Unifying Themes in the Bush/Republican,
    Gore/Democrat, and Nader/Green Campaigns, 2000

Bush	Gore	Nader
• individuals and families should be provided with as much opportunity as possible to make their own choices about the disposal of their incomes and the education of their children	• powerful interests threaten the people's interests	• people must be provided with the means to wrest control of their lives, communities, and culture from the corporate elite
• government is too large and too intrusive	• the policies put in place since FDR's New Deal must be protected	• capitalist globalization is fundamentally at odds with democracy, social justice, and protection of the environment
• the state's role in the provision of social services is not an adequate substitute for the involvement of churches and other faith-based groups for persons in need	• government needs to be reformed, but it is not the enemy of the people	• trade liberalization and such organizations as the WTO represent a new form of corporate tyranny
• policies should aim to encourage individual responsibility and reinforce the development of personal character	• the litmus test of what government does should be its impact on families, particularly working families	• the major parties are stooges of big business; their subservience is guaranteed by a structurally corrupt system of campaign finance
• markets and competition do a better job than regulators and legislative controls in ensuring economic growth and widespread prosperity	• equality of opportunity requires positive action by government	• Western Europe represents a model that the United States should emulate in matters of social policy
• freedom and equality are compromised by the "soft bigotry" of affirmative action, quotas, and all policies that categorize citizens on the basis of ascriptive characteristics		

Figure 7.3. Canadian Party Leaders' Political Rhetoric

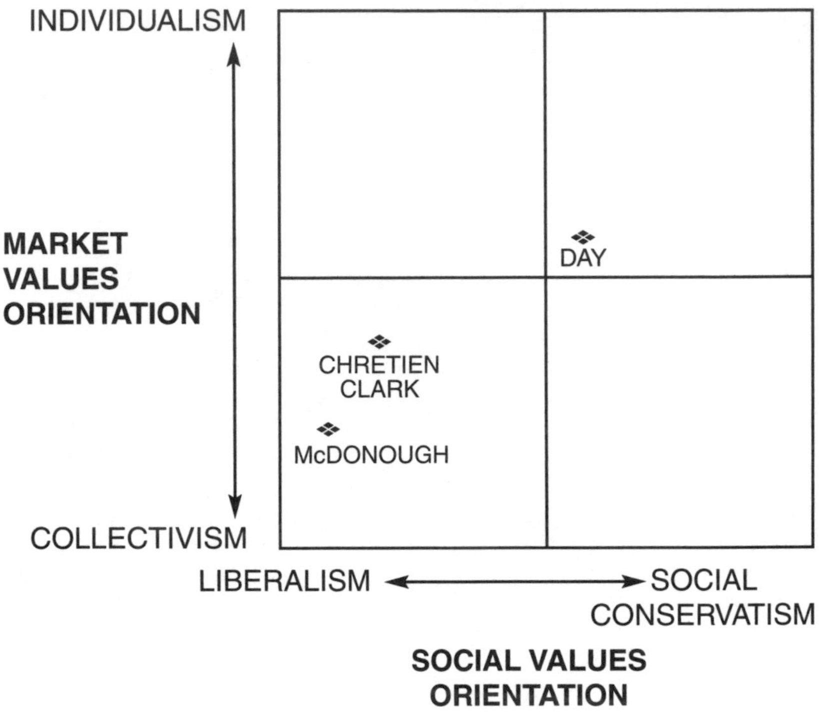

CONCLUSIONS AND DISCUSSION

Based on this analysis, it can be concluded that the Bush/Re-publican message was clearly more individualistic on the market values orientation axis than those of either Gore or Nader, and more individualistic than those of any of the Canadian party lead-ers. On the social values orientation axis, the Bush/Republican message was clearly more conservative than those of his American rivals, and even more socially conservative than the Day/Alliance message in Canada. The Gore/Democrat message was about as center-left on both the market values and social values axes as the campaign messages of the Chrétien/Liberals and Clark/Conserva-

Figure 7.4. American and Canadian Political Rhetoric

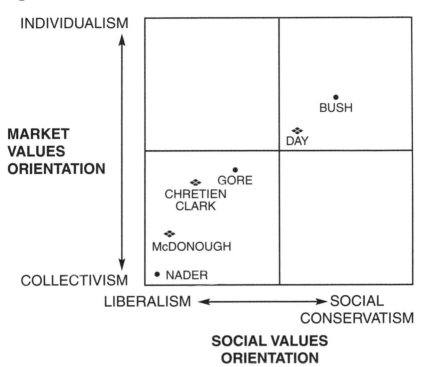

tives in Canada. On the left of the spectrum, the Nader/Green message was certainly as collectivist as that of Canada's NDP and its leader, Alexa McDonough, and every bit as sympathetic to the social democratic, statist program advocated by Canada's left-wing party. Figures 7.2 and 7.3 are merged in figure 7.4 so that the relative positions of the candidates in terms of market and social value orientations can be easily compared.

Mapping the rhetoric of the Canadian leaders and their parties on the same ideological grid used to plot the respective positions of the American presidential candidates, the range of ideological discourse is somewhat narrower, and there is a clear clustering of rhetoric toward the center-left of the ideological spectrum. The health care issue, in particular, operates to dissuade Canadian parties and leaders from using the language and symbols of individualism in selling themselves to voters. There is no evidence, based on the words and symbols that the parties and leaders used to sell themselves to the electorate, that the range of politically significant ideological expression in Canada was greater than in the United States. On the contrary, Lipset's observation about the tendency of Canada's main national parties to occupy the same center-left space appeared to be confirmed by the 2000 campaign.

This examination of the rhetoric relied on by the parties and leaders in the 2000 Canadian and American election campaigns began by identifying three widespread assumptions about the differences between Canadian and American political culture. None of the three is strongly supported by the evidence examined in the preceding pages. It may be that Canada is a more compassionate society than the United States—whatever one means by compassionate, and I fear that some merely assume that a greater state role is necessarily and by itself evidence of greater compassion—but the rhetoric of Canadian party leaders in 2000 was not more compassionate than that of the three contenders for the U.S. presidency. Nor is there strong evidence that collectivist values occupy a more secure place in the Canadian political culture, at least if the rhetoric of parties and leaders is a valid measure. The Gore/Democratic message was certainly as collectivist as that of the Chrétien Liberals and the Clark Conservatives. The McDonough/NDP message was no more collectivist than that of Nader and the Green Party in the U.S. Finally, there is no evidence to support the claim that there is a greater range of politically significant ideological expression in Canada than in the United States. On the contrary, based on the rhetoric of the parties and their leaders, it appears that the range of ideological expression is broader in American electoral politics than in Canada. In other words, American voters are offered a broader range of choice and more clearly distinguishable choices than voters in English Canada.

In this era of ever-increasing economic integration between the world's two largest trading partners—integration that is reinforced and deepened by the Canada-U.S. Free Trade Agreement and NAFTA and which has acquired greater comprehensiveness along defense and security fronts in this post–September 11 world— many question the ability of English Canada to maintain policies and political values that distinguish it from the United States. As the 2000 Canadian election campaign showed, any suggestions that Canada is becoming or could become "Americanized" is certain to sound alarm bells. Moreover, no Canadian party wishes to be associated with policies that may be portrayed as moving Canada closer to the status of the fifty-first state. Canadian elections continue to be opportunities for political leaders and their parties to proclaim loudly Canada's distinctiveness and resolve to chart its own political course, independent of its great neighbor to the south. The reality of increasing interdependence between Canada and the United States belies these proclamations and, in the end, may undermine the cultural and political foundations upon which they rest.

Documents and Public Statements Used in the Analysis

Canada

Chrétien and the Liberal Party

- *Opportunity for All: The Liberal Plan for the Future of Canada* (Official campaign platform of the Liberal Party)
- Daily campaign bulletins from the Liberal Party between October 22 and November 25, 2000
- Leaders' debate (November 9, 2000)

Day and the Canadian Alliance

- "Ready to Go! Ready to Govern!" (Speech delivered by Stockwell Day in Saskatoon, September 6, 2000)
- "The Next Step Towards a Stronger Economy" (Speech delivered by Day to Nepean Chamber of Commerce, Nepean, Ontario, June 7, 2000)
- "Renewing Canadian Democracy" (Speech delivered by Day in Toronto, June 19, 2000)
- "Canadian Values" (Speech delivered by Day at Owen Sound Legion Hall, Owen Sound, Ontario, June 5, 2000)

- *Your Principles* (Policy platform of the Canadian Alliance, January 2000)
- Leaders' debate (Toronto, Ontario, November 9, 2000)

McDonough and the NDP

- "The NDP Commitment to Canadians" (Official party platform, released October 30, 2000)
- Daily campaign bulletins between October 31 and November 26, 2000
- Leaders' debate (Toronto, Ontario, November 9, 2000)

Clark and the Progressive Conservative Party

- "Campaign platform" (downloaded from official PC Party website, November 2000)
- "Strengthening Canada's Communities" (official PC Party website, November 2000)
- Leaders' debate (Toronto, Ontario, November 9, 2000).

United States
Bush and the Republican Party

- "A Vision for America" (This was located at the George W. Bush for President Official Website, under "Issues")
- "A Period of Consequences" (Speech delivered by G. W. Bush at The Citadel, Charleston, South Carolina, September 23, 1999)
- "Agenda for the Greatest Generation" (Speech delivered by Bush at Langhorne, Pennsylvania, October 12, 2000)
- "No Child Left Behind" (Speech delivered by Bush to the Latin Business Association, Los Angeles, September 2, 1999)
- "Acceptance Speech" (Delivered at the Republican Convention, Philadelphia, August 3, 2000)
- Presidential Debates (held on October 3, 11, and 17, 2000), Boston, Mass., Winston-Salem, N.C., and St. Louis, Mo., respectively.

Gore and the Democratic Party
- "Issues (at the official campaign website for Al Gore)
- "Address to the American Legion National Convention" (Speech delivered by Al Gore at Anaheim, California, September 8, 1999)
- "A Vision for Leadership in the Twenty-first Century" (Speech delivered by Gore at Davenport, Iowa, January 3, 2000)
- "Gore Introduces Lieberman as Running Mate" (Speech given by Gore in Carthage, Tennessee, August 8, 2000)
- "Acceptance Speech" (Delivered by Gore in Los Angeles, at the Democratic Convention, August 17, 2000)
- Presidential Debates (held on October 3, 11, and 17, 2000), Boston, Mass., Winston-Salem, N.C., and St. Louis, Mo., respectively.

Nader and the Green Party
- Green Party Platform (ratified at the party's national convention, Denver, Colorado in June 2000)
- "Issue Summaries" (found at the official Nader campaign website, www.greenparties.org)
- "Acceptance Speech" (delivered by Nader in Denver, Colorado, June 25, 2000)

CHAPTER 8

The Economic Environment of the 2000 National Elections in Canada, Mexico, and the United States

Mark J. Kasoff

A NATION'S ECONOMIC PERFORMANCE about a year before a national election significantly frames the issues debated and can affect outcomes.[1] During prosperous and stable times, incumbent parties and candidates are frequently returned to office. The "ins" are usually thrown out when serious economic problems persist.

In the United States, political econometricians measure the impact of economic growth, inflation, unemployment, and changes in income, interest rates, and other variables on election outcomes. Equations predict shares for the two-party popular vote, which corresponds 97 percent of the time to Electoral College results.[2] Alan Abramowitz and Ray Fair have also found a strong anti-incumbent bias for parties seeking a third term in the White House and a significant advantage for incumbent presidents seeking a second term, especially Republicans.[3] Strong third-party candidates weaken the predictive value of these models, as was the case with Ross Perot in the Bill Clinton-George Bush campaign of 1992 and Ralph Nader in the 2000 George W. Bush-Al Gore race.

In 1993, Canadians were pessimistic about future economic prospects; economic growth was anemic, the unemployment rate was 11 percent, the federal budget deficit was $35 billion, and the Brian Mulroney-Kim Campbell Tory government had introduced the unpopular Goods and Services Tax (GST). The Liberal party platform called for abolishing the GST and reducing the budget deficit to the European Union standard of 3 percent of GDP.

The 1993 election produced decisive and astonishing results. A majority Liberal government was elected, while opposition forces fragmented along regional lines that persist to this day.[4] The once great Progressive Conservative Party of Sir John MacDonald was reduced to the Ottawa joke of "party of two sir?" when leader Jean Charest entered a restaurant. Liberal Finance Minister Martin moved swiftly to control federal spending while steady economic growth produced increased government revenues and budget surpluses.

The three North American Free Trade Agreement (NAFTA) countries of Canada, the United States, and Mexico held national elections in 2000. In Canada, the incumbent Liberal Party was returned for another five-year mandate. In the United States, the Supreme Court finally intervened in a fiercely contested election, declaring George W. Bush president, even though Al Gore received more popular votes. Mexico elected National Action Party (PAN) candidate Vicente Fox president, with no political party having a majority in the Chamber of Deputies. Seven decades of continuous rule by the Institutional Revolutionary Party (PRI) came to an end.

What were the domestic and international economic issues during these three national campaigns? Although Canada and the United States will be the primary focus here, all three national economies were doing well at the time in terms of economic

Figure 8.1. Change by Percentage in Gross Domestic Product

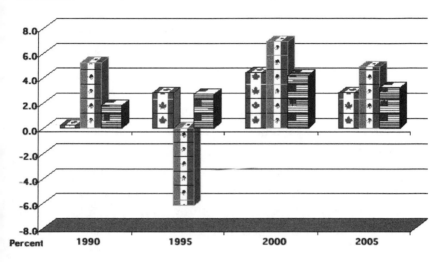

growth (see figure 8.1). The longest expansion ever recorded in the United States was still underway, with Canada enjoying similar prosperity. Despite several years of recovery, Mexican voters still remembered the peso crisis of 1994–95 that resulted in a shrinking economy and a rapidly depreciating currency. Canadian voters were reminded of lower taxes, government debt reduction, and spending increases in the context of economic growth, low unemployment and price stability. The U.S. economy was also doing well, and presidential candidates debated how to dispose of expected budget surpluses in an era of continued prosperity. In Mexico, budget matters were framed by difficulties associated with raising revenues.

DOMESTIC ECONOMIC CONDITIONS
SHAPE POLITICAL CAMPAIGNS

Economic indicators shape political campaigns, as exemplified by Clinton advisor James Carville's famous remark, "It's the economy, stupid!"[5] In Canada, surplus budgets provided the incumbent Liberal government with the means to restore funds to popular programs like medicare, reduce personal and business taxes, and to retire partially the accumulated national debt. Canada had the unfortunate distinction of having one of the largest debt overhangs (debt/GDP) of the advanced economies when the Liberals came to power in 1993. The federal debt peaked at 70.7 percent of GDP in 1996, but dropped to 51.8 percent by 2001.[6] The government moved quickly to bring expenditures under control, while tax revenues grew, along with 4.5 percent economic growth. Parties to the right of the Liberals, such as the Canadian Alliance and Progressive Conservatives, advocated bigger tax cuts and reductions in government spending, a strategy soundly rejected by the voters. Similar developments occurred in the United States after President Clinton assumed office in 1993.

Real GDP growth of 4 percent in 2000 saw the U.S. presidential candidates debate disposition of the huge budget surplus projected over the next decade. Governor Bush came down strongly for large across-the-board tax cuts, arguing continued economic growth would permit this while maintaining reasonable growth in federal spending. Vice President Gore argued for more modest tax cuts targeted at those in the middle and lower income brackets, and for using part of the surplus to assure the soundness of Medicare. With investors suffering from a serious case of what Federal Reserve Chair Alan Greenspan called "irrational exuberance," Bush proposed a partial privatization of Social Security. Rising stock prices would be the magic bullet to ease the financial strains of a system destined for insolvency in the years ahead. Gore opposed such speculation and uncertainty.

Other economic indicators were mostly favorable. In the United States, unemployment rates fell below what had been previously thought to be natural levels of 5 to 6 percent without increasing inflationary pressures. In Canada and the United States, prime lending rates stabilized around 10 percent, somewhat lower in Canada, while Mexican lending rates dropped steadily from their 1995 highs.

The North American economy deteriorated sharply one year after the election. Shortly after assuming office, President Bush saw the economy lapse into recession and the stock market go into a tailspin. The Canadian economy grew by barely 1 percent in 2001 while Mexico's GDP decreased by 1 percent. Loud calls in the United States for such policies as privatizing Social Security and providing for a prescription drug plan under Medicare were reduced to whispers. Surpluses as far as the eye can see have been replaced with annual deficits exceeding $100 billion. Surprisingly, during the 2000 campaign neither side proposed significant reductions in the federal debt, as was the case in Canada. Apparently debt reduction was not good politics in the United States.

INTERNATIONAL ECONOMIC ISSUES

All victorious parties supported free trade and NAFTA. Parties and candidates campaigning against globalization for environmental, labor standards, or economic nationalism reasons, such as the National Democratic Party (NDP) in Canada or the Green Party in the United States, did poorly at the polls. However, support for NAFTA is significantly nuanced in the three countries. About two-thirds of Canadians support NAFTA and increased economic relations with the United States and Mexico.[7] But Canadians fear becoming the fifty-first state, want stronger protection for cultural industries, and more effective ways to settle trade disputes with the United States. Mexico would like the

United States to liberalize regulations for guest workers and implement NAFTA rules allowing Mexican trucks to operate on U.S. highways. Regarding prospects for a common NAFTA currency (probably the U.S. dollar), Canada is opposed, Mexico feels this is likely decades ahead, while the United States is silent. A recent Leger poll in Canada found only 39.9 percent of Canadians in favor of a common currency, but 53.5 percent favored the concept in Quebec.[8] A later poll found only 23 percent of the citizenry support a common currency.[9]

President Bush took office vigorously advocating NAFTA's expansion to include all of the Americas. In May 2002, the Congress finally restored presidential fast-track negotiating authority, now called "trade promotion authority," which it had allowed to expire during the Clinton administration.

The Canada-U.S. Free Trade Agreement (FTA) of 1989 and NAFTA in 1994 led to greater economic integration in North America.[10] In all three countries, foreign trade as a share of GDP has risen (see figure 8.2). Shares rose from 51 percent to 86 percent in Canada, from 32 percent to 65 percent in Mexico, and from 20 to 26 percent in the United States. This translates to a

Figure 8.2. Foreign Trade as a Percentage of Gross Domestic Product

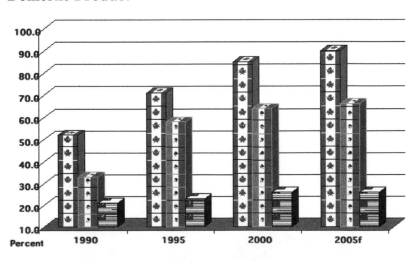

| Percent | 1990 | 1995 | 2000 | 2005f |

growth rate of 30 percent for the United States, 69 percent for Canada, and 103 percent for Mexico. Canada and Mexico are two to four times more dependent on foreign trade than the United States. Canada and Mexico have seen sales to the U.S. rise to 85 percent of worldwide exports. While trade shares have risen to nearly 30 percent in the United States, they are well below those in Canada and Mexico. Moreover, while Canada and Mexico are America's largest trading partners, U.S. exports are more regionally diversified. For Canada and Mexico, access to the U.S. market is a necessity.

Low levels of trade between Canada and Mexico persist despite the hopes for growth after NAFTA. These data may underestimate Canada-Mexico trade since increased amounts of value added probably pass through the United States. With interindustry and interfirm business growing as a percentage of total trade, Canadian exports to Mexico may show up as U.S. exports to Mexico (with additional value added in the United States). While the magnitude of the value-added export market has not yet been measured, it is probably significant for automobile-related trade.

U.S. ENERGY IMPORTS

About half of the oil consumed in the United States is imported. While countries like Saudi Arabia and Venezuela are important ongoing sources of supply, the importance of Canada and Mexico are underappreciated. Canada supplies about 10 percent of all oil and 15 percent of all natural gas used in the United States. In terms of crude oil and petroleum products, Canadian imports exceed those from any other country. Mexican sales to the United States have risen steadily while sales from Saudi Arabia and Venezuela peaked in the mid-1990s. Canada's proven reserves of crude oil exceed those for Saudi Arabia when the Alberta oil sands are included.[11] Extraction costs are approaching $10 per barrel U.S., well below world prices trading above $20 per barrel. OPEC actions restricting supply should keep oil prices at high levels and encourage North American energy integration. Canada and Mexico will account for larger shares of U.S. consumption in the future. The northeastern U.S. also purchases large amounts of electricity from Quebec.[12]

TRADE DISPUTES

A few high-profile trade disputes with the United States can strain long-term relationships. Canada and the United States continue to feud over sales of softwood lumber in the U.S. market, a dispute that dates back to the 1980s. When the latest Softwood Lumber Agreement (SLA) expired in March 2002, the United States slapped a 27 percent tariff on lumber imports. The United States argued that Canada's policy of charging stumpage fees for harvesting trees from public lands represents an unfair subsidy when compared to U.S. auction procedures. Previous rulings by the World Trade Organization (WTO) have not upheld the U.S. position, but Canada still entered into long-term SLAs to assure access to the U.S. market. This is big business, with Canadian sales averaging about $6 billion per year, about a third of the U.S. market. While the consumer side is better organized in the United States than ever before, taking out large ads in major national newspapers, it is not strong enough to influence public policy.[13]

The two countries fought a bruising battle over tomatoes as well. The United States charged Canada with dumping greenhouse tomatoes in the American market at unfair prices, strengthened by a preliminary finding by the U.S. International Trade Commission (ITC). Canada retaliated with its own tariff on U.S. tomatoes of all types. In April of 2002, the ITC reversed itself, finding that Canadian tomatoes were not being sold at subsidized prices. Canadian tariffs on U.S. tomatoes will no doubt be eliminated as well, but it is important to note that it took two years to resolve this dispute.[14]

President Bush announced tariffs on imported steel of up to 30 percent in early 2002. Exemptions were provided for less-developed countries and for Canada and Mexico owing to NAFTA. Should these tariffs continue, increased imports from Canada and Mexico can be expected. Many Canadians feel that recent U.S. actions reflect strong protectionist sentiments and a weaker commitment to free trade and open markets.[15] Canadians are also wary of the 2002 Farm Bill signed by President Bush, which vastly increases U.S. agricultural subsidies. Although this may be a reaction to higher subsidies in the European Union, this bill will adversely affect Canadian farmers, unless their government increases subsidies by a similar amount.

CURRENCY PERFORMANCE AND ISSUES

Shortly after NAFTA was signed in 1993, Mexico experienced severe balance of payments problems and a rapid fall in the value of the peso (see figure 8.3).

The Canadian dollar fell to an all-time low of $0.6175 U.S. on January 21, 2002.[16] Canada's interest rates, lower those in the United States since 1994 (see figure 8.4), coupled with higher productivity gains in the United States contributed heavily to the

Figure 8.3. Exchange Rates per U.S. Dollar

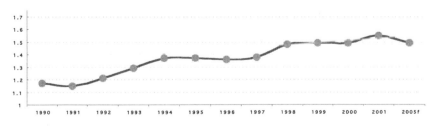

devaluation. By spring 2002, Canada became the first G-7 country to raise interest rates, with further increases to follow.[17] The Canadian dollar strengthened quickly, rising above $0.64 U.S. for the first time since December 2001.

During NAFTA's first year the Mexican peso averaged 3.38 to the U.S. dollar. In 1995, the peso fell by nearly 100 percent to 6.42 to the dollar. The Canadian dollar weakened steadily after the 1989 FTA, when one U.S. dollar rose from 1.18 to 1.37 Canadian dollars. During the 2000 election period, the peso stabilized and showed considerable strength, trading around 9.5 to the greenback.

Differential interest rates appear to be a factor determining foreign exchange rate valuations. In 2000, they averaged 9.23 percent in the United States, 7.27 percent in Canada, and 18.23 percent in Mexico.

Figure 8.4. Interest Rates

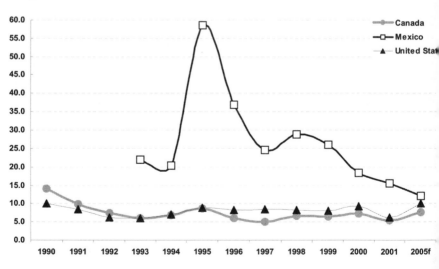

CONCLUSIONS

The 2000 elections took place in an environment of favorable economic conditions in Canada, Mexico, and the United States. As expected, the Liberals received another mandate in Canada, leaving the opposition remaining as badly fragmented as they were in 1993. In the United States, Vice President Gore received the most popular votes but a Supreme Court decision awarded George W. Bush the electoral vote. President Bush benefited from the anti-incumbency factor used in election forecasting models, while the Green Party probably swung some electoral votes away from the Democrats. Vicente Fox was elected president of Mexico after seven decades of rule by the PRI.

Increased economic integration in North America seems likely, along with a greater focus on border and security issues. With Canada and Mexico so dependent on the United States, some sort of customs union with a common external tariff seems likely, along with increased efforts to harmonize regulations, standards, and liberalize labor rules.[18] That said, a North American version of the EU, with a common market, a common currency, and a continental political body, seems unlikely to develop in the near future.

CHAPTER 9

Mexico's Linkage with North America after 2000: From NAFTA-Plus to NAFTA-Blues?

Isidro Morales

FROM THE BEGINNING OF 2000 to the fall of 2001, a kind of honeymoon existed between Mexico and the United States. Largely responsible was the increasing optimism of Washington elites about democratic change in Mexico, the North American Free Trade Agreement (NAFTA) partner still run by an authoritarian political clique whose members had inherited power through non-competitive elections since the late 1930s. Mexico's presidential elections in the year 2000 became a watershed. Vicente Fox suddenly emerged as the strongest and most credible rival to the Partido Revolucionario Institucional (PRI) candidate, Francisco Labastida, a man with a rather bureaucratic profile associated with political bosses of the now-named "old regime." In contrast, Vicente Fox, supported by the Partido de Acción Nacional (PAN), a conservative Catholic-based party, appeared to be a charismatic and credible leader whose major goal while campaigning was to eject the PRI's political clique from power and to inaugurate political openness and competition in the country. His campaign successfully attracted the support of some smaller center-left parties and groups, creating a major coalition reaching beyond the PAN's traditional constituencies that eventually delivered the presidency to Fox.

But another goal of Vicente Fox's campaign was to enlarge his political constituency beyond national borders. He campaigned intensively in New York and California, seeking the support of Mexican and Mexican American communities, whose electoral participation in the United States is becoming more and more decisive in key bilateral issues, such as illegal migration from Mexico and the social conditions of Mexicans in the United States. In many ways, Fox launched a double-edged diplomacy, the purpose of which was to send a message to both Washington and home. While campaigning in the United States, he announced that the major goals of his presidential term would include legalizing the status of some three million Mexicans already working in that country and the liberalization of labor markets between the two countries. Furthermore, he called for the creation of a stronger North American community, with the free movement of labor, institution building, and development-oriented policies at its core. The message was clear: Mexico was taking the lead in going beyond NAFTA while deepening continental integration, with labor mobility and a developmental approach as its main goals. By so doing, the new political elite hoped to enlarge its domestic constituency for supporting further integration within North America.

NAFTA-PLUS

Once in power, the government better framed what then became known as the "NAFTA-plus" project. In fact, Fox's alliances with center-left groups made it possible for Jorge G. Castañeda—a major critic of PRI's regime through his influential books and articles—to become the brain and the executor of Mexico's new foreign policy. This consisted of opening various international fronts to Mexico's participation. The very first one was to obtain a nonpermanent seat at the United Nations Security Council, through which Mexico could participate in global issues, such as peacekeeping operations, or more contentious ones like the right of intervention for humanitarian reasons. Another goal was Mexico's participation in strengthening its institutional commitments with principled international regimes. Castañeda has openly recognized, at the theoretical level, that his country is enmeshed in an international arena where Westphalian-based notions of sovereignty are being discarded. For him, the post–Cold War order cannot be ruled on the principles of non-intervention and self-determination, but on universal rules and principles held to be valid and enforced worldwide. This means intruding in the affairs of other countries when they breach those general principles. Those principles which advocate democracy and human rights became most important to Mexico, inasmuch as the Fox administration epitomizes, according to Castañeda's approach, the triumph of those principles.[1]

Hence, within this new foreign policy approach, principled institutions and international agreements are playing—and will continue to play—a major role in reinforcing Mexico's political openness and transparency. At the same time, principled regimes can both denounce those who breach international norms and pressure them to abide by the rules. This could explain Mexico's interest in participating in the creation of the International Penal Court or its historic vote at Geneva, after the UN-Human Rights Commission, challenging the respect and enforcement of human rights in Cuba.

The third front opened by the new foreign policy approach was the NAFTA-plus plan already sketched out by Fox during his presidential campaign. Fox's government devised a three-tier strategy centering on migration, development, and institution building. Migration became the core of the Mexican initiative, as earlier explained. Although its long-term goal was the full mobility of Mexican labor, legalizing the status of around 3 million illegal Mexican immigrants and protecting their basic social and human rights was its short-term target. In an accompanying move, Mexico started negotiating a guest-worker program, the scope and terms of which were never defined. The idea was to send the message that the borders were about to be opened for low-skilled labor. Second on the NAFTA-plus agenda was development. NAFTA, as it stands, is mainly a trade and investment plan favoring export-oriented industries and large corporations and investors. NAFTA has meant nothing for small inward-looking enterprises, peasants, or unions, let alone the deprived families amounting to half of the overall Mexican population. Though the development NAFTA-linked agenda has never been defined, Castañeda's own criticism of the agreement during the Salinas years was that it lacked a program of cohesion funds, similar to that existing in the European Union.[2]

Last but not least, the third tier of the NAFTA-plus plan was the ambitious idea of pushing for the creation of new trilateral institutions capable of dealing with issues currently handled at the unilateral or bilateral level. Common cross-border problems like environmental protection, drug trafficking, and migration could be better worked out with common goals and trilateral regional policies. Although the new institutional approach Mexico wanted was never defined at the official level, the intention to explore this possibility was consistent with Mexico's commitment in being further involved with principled international regimes. According to this rationale, it could be anticipated that deeper integration within North America, with stronger trilateral institutions, would give Mexico greater influence in dealing with common problems, as well as winning the support of a wider domestic constituency.[3]

Such an ambitious agenda, addressing both global and North American issues, was devised amidst great expectations in Mexico and abroad. North American economies were still growing, thanks to the impact of trade and investment liberalization conveyed by NAFTA and the booming years of the "new economy" in the United States. All three NAFTA partners experienced political change either at the executive or the legislative levels, with Mexico raising most of the optimistic expectations. The defeat of the PRI—the hegemonic party that had ruled the country for more than seventy years through noncompetitive, transparent, and pacific elections—became the sign that Mexico was becoming closer to its NAFTA and OECD partners than ever before.

At any rate, the Fox administration had the legitimacy and authority to launch a "new regime" policy approach, including this regional- and global-oriented diplomacy. However, the conditions on which this new diplomatic approach was based suddenly changed. The American economy went into recession around the beginning of the new century, due largely to its widespread global economic interests. The terrorist attacks of September 11, 2001, on the World Trade Center in New York abruptly changed all the parameters, notions, and strategies of American national and international security. And last but not least, the democratic awakening in Mexico and the lack of a partisan majority in Congress made it much more difficult for Fox to pursue his ambitious "new regime" political approach.

AFTER SEPTEMBER 11

The terrorist attacks of September 11 have already become a watershed in world politics. At the end of the Cold War, during 1989–1990, the so-called emergence of a "new world order" became commonplace. Nonetheless, it wasn't until the fall of 2001, after the dramatic collapse of the twin towers in New York, that a new world order started to emerge. Political and economic alliances are currently being remade all around the world, and traditional U.S. political and economic partners are obliged to react and adapt to the new security agenda drafted and implemented by Washington. Hence, Mexico's priorities have been subordinated to the primacy of American security.

Migratory policies were already a contentious issue between Mexico and the United States before the fall of 2001. Washington and local authorities of southern border states perceived Mexican migration as a judicial issue, i.e., Mexicans trespassing across the American border without documents or working permits and consequently breaking state and federal laws. On the other side, the Mexican perception was an economic one: there were pull factors on the U.S. side demanding Mexican labor and push factors in Mexico side provoking a surplus of a low-skilled labor force.[4]

Illegal Mexican immigration to the United States came under the spotlight when local authorities in American border states attempted to suppress any rights of those illegal aliens, and abuses inflicted by patrol and police members while attempting to deter that migration became evident—including physical and in many cases fatal attacks. The heavy-handed penalization of illegal cross-border movement and the plethora of related physical and social abuses prompted Mexico, under the Fox administration, to frame the issue as either an economic or a human rights question. Mexican consulates all over the United States began to advocate for the protection of Mexicans' rights in the United States, regardless of whether they were legal aliens or not.

Mexico also realized that, in the short- and medium-terms these migration questions could only be handled at the bilateral level, in the best of cases, and not with the trilateral approach the third tier of the NAFTA-plus design anticipated. Although Canada has a stake in working on immigration issues with the United States, human migration between these two countries is different than that between Mexico and the United States. Canada, rather, suffers from a "brain drain" (Canadian-trained professionals such as doctors emigrating to the United States for higher salaries and benefits) while simultaneously promoting immigration into Canada. As a result, bilateralism remains the best approach for these two countries in dealing with emigration to the United States. Furthermore, any negotiation for reaching a type of "guest workers" program would require legalization of the status of millions of illegal migrants in the United States—either they are Mexicans or not. The last amnesty to those illegal aliens was granted in 1986, in the midst of major negotiations involving Washington political groups and the federal government.

However, after September 11, 2001, human, trade, and information flows across borders became a security issue for the United States. Although Washington's definition of its new transnational enemies and challenges came promptly, it took longer to define the new security architecture for dealing with the changing nature of the threat. North America became the first territorial zone in which security borders were redrafted. In December 2001, Washington announced the shift of its security perimeter in order to include its Canadian partner, with whom it would share the establishment and functioning of "smart borders." In March 2002, the security perimeter as defined by Washington was extended to Mexico, including the "smart borders" mechanisms already in place with the Canadians. By one year after the terrorist attacks, it had become clear that enlarging the U.S. security perimeter to include its North American partners was part of a major plan aiming to reduce the risks of physical, biochemical, and cybernetic attacks on American territory. This tactic, called "The National Strategy for Homeland Security," is based on four pillars—intelligence and warning, security in borders and transport, domestic counter-terrorism, and infrastructure protection—all of them to be supervised and administered by the newly conceived Department of Homeland Security. Due to the subordination of border issues to this security architecture, the U.S. Immigration and Naturalization Services and the Customs Service, among other agencies, have been integrated into the new department.[5]

According to Washington's new security scheme, "smart borders" and transport are intertwined, in the sense that every community in the United States—whether small or large—is connected within a worldwide transport infrastructure. Harbors, railroads, airports, highways, energy grids, virtual networks, and any flow conveying people or commodities are currently considered part of that worldwide transport infrastructure. The goal of smart borders is to promote the efficient and safe transit of people, goods, and services across borders using modern technology.[6] Canada and Mexico are now committed, even in their own territories, to cooperate with U.S. authorities to ensure the security of the North American transport network.

It is clear that September 11 changed the parameters in which Mexico formulated its NAFTA-plus strategy. The migration agenda that reflected economic and human rights was reformulated according to the U.S. guidelines: human flows were not only to be divided between legal and illegal but also between safe and unsafe. The smart borders mechanism aims to detect, measure, and evaluate those distinctions. Furthermore, the new security agenda and architecture devised by Washington since fall 2001 suggests that the United States is ready to move from unilateral or bilateral formulas, as long as this protects its own interests. Migratory policies will be decided at the national level, but policies aiming to protect U.S. national territory call for the creation of security strategies that must be shared by its two border partners.

But September 11 also made clear that the domestic setting in which Fox's new foreign policy was anchored had also changed. Castañeda's first reaction after the New York attack was to invoke Mexico's "unconditional" support for the American government.

This statement, and the way the Ministry of Foreign Affairs attempted to legitimize Mexico's support of U.S. military action against Afghanistan, was highly criticized by opposition parties in the Mexican Congress. The criticism became more acute after Cuban president Fidel Castro's sudden and controversial visit to Mexico, and once Mexico made explicit its condemnation to human rights violations in Cuba. Exploiting the lack of a majority party in Congress, opposition parties identified Castañeda's new foreign policy as a departure from the nationalistic and non-interventionist foreign policy principles, traditionally invoked by old-regime politicians when they wanted to distance themselves from or even criticize U.S. foreign policy. The opposition saw Castañeda's position as too close to American interests. Tensions between opposition leaders and the executive branch reached a peak when President Fox had to cancel a short visit to the United States and Canada because a majority vote in the Senate refused to accept his petition to leave the country. The message was clear: the new foreign policy had no constituency in Congress.

In spite of these setbacks on the foreign and domestic fronts, Castañeda successfully negotiated a so-called "Alliance for Prosperity," facilitating the transfer of technology and resources between the United States and Mexico. The alliance was announced in the midst of a summit of the three North American heads of state, held in Monterrey in March 2002. It was based on four premises: a) access to private investment for small- and medium-sized enterprises; b) transfer of technology through targeted projects involving small entrepreneurs and American universities; c) upgrading of infrastructure; and d) promotion of institutional interconnectedness.

A major goal of this alliance is reducing the costs of remittances made by Mexicans living in the United States, regardless of their legal status. According to this plan, money originating from the United States can be used to help finance private construction projects (mainly private dwellings) for migrants' families still living in Mexico. Also announced were plans to disperse credits obtained in the United States in Mexico. In addition, the alliance considered the promotion of American franchises and tourist-oriented development projects. These market-based mechanisms had as a goal halting illegal immigration to the United States by rooting Mexican families to their own localities. This new economic alliance also claimed it would market Mexican handicrafts in the States through institutional mechanisms and teach medium-sized enterprises to get funding for their projects. Plans for new investment in infrastructure—such as transport, power transmission, telecommunications, among other sectors—was also announced, as well as coordination among major multilateral institutions, such as the World Bank, and regional ones, like the Inter-American Development Bank, in order to fulfill this task.[7]

Though this new "alliance for prosperity" was proclaimed as a major success for Mexico within its NAFTA-plus agenda, it was in fact far from the three-tier approach envisaged at the beginning of the Fox administration. Although it was publicized when Fox, Bush, and Chrétien met in Monterrey, this alliance involved only the United States, and not Canada. Washington made no commitment to a unilateral transfer of funds for deprived regions of Mexico. Any reference to income disparities among the country's different regions was omitted, let alone the increasing number of poor households. In fact, this alliance was instead announcing the privatization of development policies, originally accomplished by public development banks and public programs targeting deprived populations through the transfer of resources from the better off. Ironically, this new alliance anticipated that Mexicans living in the United States would become major actors in propelling development in their native country. Their remittances suddenly became a strategic means for funding development programs in

Mexico, while at the same time the entrance of Mexican labor in the United States had become more and more securitized.

In fact, this new prosperity alliance was announced and highlighted in such a way that the extension of the U.S. security perimeter into Mexico and the establishment of smart borders on the Mexican side—two approaches also discussed during the Monterrey summit—were minimized by the media. Although (as of this writing) no official statement has been released by the Mexican government regarding this continental strategy conceived by Washington, it is clear that Mexican cooperation will be required somehow. Will this be the trade-off for the "prosperity" deal?

A few days later, a decision by the U.S. Supreme Court made more evident the contradictory terms under which the new prosperity alliance was negotiated. In a split vote, the Court ruled against the National Labor Relations Board, which was asking for wage relief for an illegal Mexican worker fired by an American business once it was discovered that he wanted to create a union. The Court grounded its decision in the illegal status of the Mexican worker, although it said nothing about the illegality of the U.S. firm's hiring of an illegal alien. The Mexican Ministry of Foreign Affairs offered only a timid response.[8] It became evident that relying on the remittances of Mexican workers living in the United States for funding development projects in Mexico was not a sound business. Furthermore, the Supreme Court decision, which set a precedent for similar cases to come, showed clearly that negotiating any immigration deal between Mexico and the United States was still far from easy. Immigration policies and decisions are still so fragmented in the States that to reach a single and unified position vis-à-vis Mexican migration is almost impossible. It became evident that in migration issues, as in development and institution-building, a holistic approach was not the best way to deal with the Washington agenda. A piecemeal approach was the only way to follow through.

This once again became apparent during the hot summer of 2002, when American farmers contended that Mexico was not honoring a treaty signed in 1944, through which the United States and Mexico shared water coming from the Colorado and Bravo rivers. According to this treaty, the United States delivers an amount of water, estimated on a five-year basis, from the Colorado River to Mexican farmers; in exchange, American farmers benefit from water coming from the Bravo River. For the period 1997–2002, Mexico was delivering much less than agreed in the treaty, alleging drought and a change in agricultural production in northern states, which had become more water-intensive. Though the water war did not escalate and spill over to other border issues, it was clear that many problems between Mexico and the United States should be handled on an ad hoc basis. But summer 2002 was hot not only due to water shortages. It also marked the end of the NAFTA-plus approach initiated by Fox while campaigning for the presidency. In June and July, he twice cancelled visits to Texas, during which a short encounter had been scheduled with President Bush. The water war was the reason for the first cancellation, and the execution of a Mexican convicted of killing a U.S. anti-narcotics officer the reason for the second. This last decision boosted the Mexican president's political support in Congress, even among the PRI and Partido de la Revolución Democrática (PRD) opposition parties. In early September, just after President Bush threatened Iraq with a possible unilateral intervention if it did not comply with United Nations resolutions, and a little before the sad anniversary of the terrorist attack in New York, Mexico announced its decision to suspend its commitments with the Inter-American Treaty of Reciprocal Assistance (the Rio Treaty). These two decisions marked a major change in the North American approach pursued by Mexico.

NAFTA-BLUES

The sudden cancellation of President Fox's visit to the United States, alleging human rights violations in that country, along with the announcement that Mexico was defecting from the Rio Treaty, marks the end of the NAFTA-plus undertaking begun in 2000. Mexico seems to be returning to basic bilateral relations, having apparently given up on taking a continental approach to what it perceived as being North American issues. If there is any room for a continental approach in the short- to midterm, it will only be found in those areas where American interests lie. If this was true during the NAFTA negotiations, it became even more evident after the terrorist attacks on New York. Mexico and Canada suddenly became part of a domestic U.S. territory in relation to the "securitization" of American borders. And the new security agenda, both domestic and international, is being shaped and enforced by Washington's perceptions and definitions of its enemy and the threat it poses.

In this sense, Mexico's decision to renounce its Inter-American Treaty membership can be interpreted as a declaration of independence, both at the regional and global levels, from U.S. security policies. At the North American level, institution building and trilateral agreements are not possible. As a result, Mexico will probably shift its efforts to multilateral forums, in order to increase its leverage with its powerful neighbor when dealing with bilateral issues. As it did in the Cold War years, Mexico will probably focus on reinforcing and creating new international legislation and institutions as a means to deter and contain U.S. unilateralism in security and strategic issues. It seems likely that Mexico will be tempted to join in coalitions with those countries interested in drafting new legislation and changing perceptions regarding international terrorism, the right of intervention for humanitarian reasons, and the like, a fine example being its participation in the creation of the International Penal Court. The Fox administration's original vision of Mexico as a major global activist may have to be curtailed, as its dealings on bilateral hot-button issues with the United States and its need to enlarge its own political constituency domestically will divert significant resources. As in the Cold War years, however, Mexico will be a sought-after and perhaps necessary presence in global forums, if only to clarify its differences on some global issues vis-à-vis its neighbor.[9] This independent move in global affairs will target both domestic and international audiences, and by so doing, enlarge the political support Fox still needs domestically to govern his country.

At the continental level NAFTA will probably remain an investment and trade regime, and it will be in nobody's interest to attach any other agenda to it, in order to avoid any risk of contaminating any other bilateral issue. In other words, contentious issues among its countries, such as migration, drug trafficking, security, border issues, and the like, will remain framed by and treated within national and bilateral agendas. However, some linkages across agendas are also possible. If in fact Mexico has become part of America's security space, there are many sensitive issues that require intergovernmental accommodation. If people, goods, transport services, chemical stocks, and the like, have become potential security threats, cooperation between the armies, police, intelligence services, and customs officers of the two countries (three if we include Canada) will be necessary. And the good will and aid of the Mexican government is essential to such an endeavor. Mexico will need to restructure and modernize its security agencies, which have been permeated by corruption and drug dealers. At the same time, it will be in the Mexican government's interest to keep its territory safe from any major threat to national and continental security. The United States won't offer any major concessions if Americans perceive security threats as coming from Mexico. Linkages between security and immigration issues can be anticipated in the future U.S.-Mexican relations. One of Mexico's major challenges will be to change American perceptions of Mexican emigrants as "undesirable people" in the context of those "smart borders"—in other words, as people suspected of being dangerous to American security. At least a minimum of global activism on Mexico's part will be necessary and desirable. This would give Mexico the standing to denounce eventual abuses done in the name of "continental security" in international forums.

The Mexican government also needs to link global activism with its domestic politics. Denouncing the Inter-American Treaty might be the first case of this type of linkage. As previously stated, Fox's "new" foreign policy led to criticism and animosity from opposition parties. It raised the costs of establishing political coalitions to launch new policies, at a time when President Fox did not have a majority in Congress. After two years in power, Fox and his party urgently needed to demonstrate that they could steer the country without resorting to the PRI's old methods and solutions. A major fiscal reform proposal ended up making only slight changes to the fiscal regime the original proposal attempted to attack. A plan to move Mexico City's current airport was cancelled due to the activism of furious peasants who denounced the irregularities involved in the expropriation of their land, the proposed site of the new airport. President Fox was forced to cancel a short visit to the U.S. and Canada, as already noted, because the Senate, still dominated by the PRI, did not accept the grounds for his trip. And when, more recently, the government announced a restructuring of the electricity and energy sectors, for which a qualified majority vote is needed in Congress, electricity unions marched in the streets, denouncing the "selling of the country" to U.S. corporations. There is a growing perception among political circles and public opinion leaders that Fox and his cabinet have become hostages of a divided Congress.

How will Washington—and to some extent, Ottawa—perceive this shift in Mexico's foreign policy? The answer to this question is crucial. If Washington perceives Mexico's "independent" globalism as a non-cooperative strategy vis-à-vis key U.S. strategic interests, bilateral issues will become more difficult to handle, exacerbating the misperceptions and mistrust between the two countries, which could eventually affect the ongoing democratization of Mexico. In contrast, if Washington accepts Mexico's independent activism in global issues as a trade-off for enlarging the domestic support of its current administration, progress on both the security and migratory agendas of the two countries can be anticipated, with no risk of affecting Mexico's political transition. In both scenarios, NAFTA will remain as it is, because entrepreneurs, corporations, consumers, and political leaders of its three countries have already realized its benefits. In the first scenario, however, a climate of misperception and confrontation over bilateral issues could eventually politicize some NAFTA-based issues, increasing the costs of an eventual deepening of the agreement or its enlargement through the long and more difficult negotiations of a hemispheric deal. Misperception and confrontation would inevitably spill over into North American security concerns, making enhanced cooperation with American and Canadian officials increasingly difficult for the Mexican government. Under the second scenario, the possibilities of a political contamination of the agreement remain much lower. The gains, whether great or poor, obtained from bilateral negotiations could eventually contribute to revive some parts of the original NAFTA-plus formula Fox attempted to push vis-à-vis the United States and Canada at the beginning of his administration.

PART IV

Epilogue

CHAPTER 10

Beyond Trinity: Parties and Elections in Central America

Manuel Orozco

UNTIL THE LATE 1980S, the politics of elections in Central America were linked to the prevalence of dictatorships, military rulers, and warfare. For many years, political leaders struggled to gain the right to vote or to participate in free and fair elections. As a consequence, Central American countries have entered into a process of democratization in which elections continue to be an important part.

To understand the deepening integration of North America, and of the whole Western Hemisphere—potentially moving beyond the "reluctant trinity" of the United States, Mexico, and Canada, it is necessary to look at two elements. First, it is important to understand the key characteristics of Central American elections from a historic perspective, while considering the recent challenges faced by countries such as Nicaragua and Costa Rica. Second, we should address the constraints Central American party systems face internally and externally within the context of the democratization and modernization of their political systems.

PARTIES AND ELECTIONS IN
CENTRAL AMERICAN HISTORY

Four key factors have determined the fate and influence of power and politics in Central America: the level of social stratification; the concentration or fragmentation of power; the ways in which violence and repression are employed; and the form in which resistance to authority has occurred. These four factors have traditionally functioned through *caudillo* politics: a highly stratified society with significant levels of social inequality, concentrated power and authority in the hands of a *caudillo*, be this a dictator or military ruler, the extensive use of violence and repression as a method of managing everyday life, and limited social resistance to these practices due to repression and the presence of a culture of violence.

Within this context political parties were historically subsumed by the forces of powerful economic elites, dictators, and the military. Dictators and military rulers of various kinds, including Jorge Ubico in Guatemala, Anastasio Somoza Garcia in Nicaragua, Tiburcio Carias in Honduras, and Maximiliano Martinez in El Salvador (see figure 10.1), have plagued Central American political history. Each sought to control political power by strengthening the armies they commanded and buying off parties.

This does not mean that political parties were inactive; table 10.1 lists the parties active in Central America today, the years in which they were founded, their ideologies, and positions on the right-left spectrum. The earliest parties supported or rejected political schemes related to regional federation proposals; these have been replaced by a wide variety of parties. First, the rise of "liberalism," which in Latin America meant the separation of church and state, produced competing parties, some with pro-liberal positions or with the opposite pro-conservative stances. During the period of dictatorships and military rule, such parties sought to accommodate their ideologies to those in power by seeking limited demands. Second, in many Latin American countries, new political parties were created

Figure 10.1. Dictatorships and Military Rule, 1930–1990s

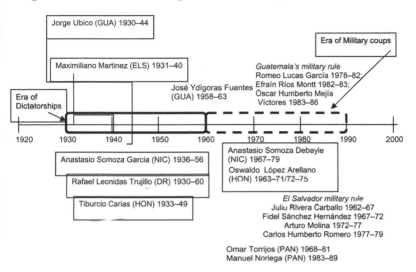

in the 1940s and 1950s, ascribing to Christian Democratic ideologies. There were also Communist parties whose existence was briefly permitted during the period preceding the Cold War, but were then banned, and regained legal recognition in the 1960s. Other socialist and social-democratic parties have appeared since then, some of which were involved in the civil wars of the 1970s and 1980s, such as the FSLN in Nicaragua and FMLN in El Salvador. In addition, new conservative parties, such as ARENA in El Salvador, have developed in recent times, some tied to the civil wars as well.

Within dictatorial regimes, parties coexisted with military forces in order to survive, acquiescing to the demands of clientage systems dominated by generals or economic elites. In some countries, Guatemala and El Salvador, for instance, the military rulers created their own political parties, headed by retired army officers. Even when elections were permitted, fraud was a prevalent practice or the military intervened in the political and electoral process. The tables below show the various forms of access to power, the main authorities in charge, and the significance of military participation, which limited opportunities for pluralism and competition.

TABLE 10.1.

Political Parties in Central America

Country and Party	Founded	Ideology	Positioning
Nicaragua			
Partido Conservador de Nicaragua (PCN)	1940	Conservative	Right
Partido Liberal Nacionalista (PLN)	1940	Liberal	Right
Partido Liberal Constitucionalista (PLC)	1967	Liberal	Right
Partido Socialista Nicaraguense (PSN)	1944	Socialist	Center Left
Partido Social Cristiano (PSC)	1957	Social Democrat	Center Left
Frente Sandinista de Liberacion (FSLN)	1960	Socialist	Left
Costa Rica			
Partido Republicano (PR)	1940	Conservative	Right
Partido Unidad Social Cristiano (PUSC)	1985	Christian Democrat	Center
Partido Accion Cuidadana (PAC)	2001	Social Democrat	Center Left
Pueblo Unido (PU)	1978	Socialist	Center Left
Partido Communista (PC)	1940	Communist	Left
Partido Liberacion Nacional (PLN)	1948	Communist	Left

TABLE 10.1. (*continued*)

Country and Party	Founded	Ideology	Positioning
Guatemala			
Frente Republicano			
Guatemalteca (FRG)	1988	Conservative	Right
Partido Accion Nacional (PAN)	1990	Conservative	Right
Union Centro Nacional (UCN)	1990	Conservative	Right
Partido Democrata			
Cristiano (PDC)	1955	Christian Democrat	Center
Unidad Revolucionaria			
Nacional (URNG)	1982	Socialist	Center Left
El Salvador			
Alianza Republicana			
Nacional (ARENA)	1981	Conservative	Right
Partido Conciliacion			
Nacional (PCN)	1961	Liberal	Right
Partido Democrata			
Cristiano (PDC)	1960	Christian Democrat	Center
Frente Farabunto			
Marti (FMLN)	1981	Socialist	Left
Honduras			
Partido Nacional (PN)	1902	Conservative	Right
Partido Liberal (PL)	1891	Liberal	Right
Partido Democrata			
Cristiano (PDC)	1980	Christian Democrat	Center
Partido Communista de			
Honduras (PCH)	1954	Communist	Left

TABLE 10.2.

Forms of Access to Power, 1950–1980

Forms of Access to Power	El Salvador	Guatemala	Honduras	Nicaragua	Central America
Election	26.70%	50.00%	33.30%	44.40%	37.50%
Fraud	20.00%			33.30%	12.50%
Congress	13.30%	8.30%	25.00%		12.50%
Coup	26.70%	33.30%	41.70%	11.10%	29.20%
Revolution				11.10%	2.10%
Other	13.30%	8.30%			6.30%

Source: Data compiled by the author

TABLE 10.3.

Main Authority in Charge, 1950–1980

Main authority in charge	El Salvador	Guatemala	Honduras	Nicaragua	Central America
Civilian	26.70%	16.70%	41.70%	11.10%	25.00%
Civic/Military	26.70%			11.10%	10.40%
Military	46.70%	83.30%	58.30%	77.80%	64.60%

Source: Data compiled by the author

Thus, except for Costa Rica, most political parties in Central America prior to the 1980s operated under significantly restricted schemes of political participation due to the presence of dictatorial regimes. Table 10.4 offers a typology of party systems in Central America.[1] Elections were racist, fraudulent, and both pluralism and competition were largely absent. Resistance to the state was also commonplace, often in the form of guerrilla warfare.

TABLE 10.4.

Types of Political Parties in Central America

Regime Type	Party System	Country and Period
Dictatorial	Hegemonic system	El Salvador, 1950–1979
		Nicaragua, 1936–1979
	Restricted pluralism	Guatemala, 1963–1982
	'Artificial' two-party scheme	Honduras, 1965–1971
Democracy	Dominant party	Costa Rica, 1953–1978
	Tolerated pluralism	Costa Rica, 1953–1978 (legislature)
		Honduras, 1982–2002
	Two-party system	Costa Rica, 1982–2002
		Nicaragua, 2000–2002

However, by the 1980s the demand and struggle for democracy led to a process of liberalization that attempted to reconstruct or redefine political traditions in many ways. The struggle between a conservative state, its elites and followers, and the larger community of people struggling to increase their participation of society in national life gradually transformed a process of military and violent confrontation to conditions of dialogue, negotiation, and political reform. This struggle has generally undergone four stages.

First, negotiations to end the civil wars occurred in all the countries which had such conflicts. Guerrilla forces such as the Contras, FMLN, Morazanist Front, Cinchonero, URNG and others, negotiated to end civil wars in order to democratize their countries. One fundamental aspect of this process is the inclusion of electoral politics and the protection of human rights as both an element of and a condition for negotiation. Second, all over Central America, social forces, increasingly including governments, engaged in efforts to improve human rights. This struggle took two forms: on the one hand there was (and is) an attempt to reverse the culture of violence that became endemic in the region; and, on the other hand, there was increased pressure to implement efficient administrative measures of justice and human rights. Within this context, Central Americans sought to face the past by investigating abuses.

Third, social forces organized in various ways to transform democracy from a process of exclusion to a process of engaging in active participation in everyday problems by promoting democracy from below. Fourth, electoral politics were legitimized. The nations of Central America recognized that as a fundamental aspect, democracy demands the election of governmental representatives with participatory and competitive political parties at work. Many of these competing parties were involved in demanding free and fair elections. From the end of the 1980s and through most of the 1990s, a number of Central American countries underwent these experiences. Although far from achieving true democracy, especially in the Guatemalan and Nicaraguan cases, these forces continue to treat it as a work in progress. Ending internal conflict, dealing with the past, participating in electoral processes, and strengthening civil society have been central to the region's democratic successes.

Political parties, however, continue to face serious challenges. Although electoral fraud is no longer an issue, the lack of representation of parties has affected the progress, of democratization in the region. Other problems involve the prevalence of *caudillo* politics within each political party, preventing younger cadres from achieving positions of authority.

The Politics of Reform: Nicaraguan Elections

An agreement between the two major political forces in Nicaragua, culminating with the November 2001 election changed the political dynamics and prospects for democracy in that country. The forced imposition of a two-party system led to the decomposition of democratic institutions and the gradual exclusion of citizen participation in politics.

A democratic transition was inaugurated in Nicaragua after national elections were held in 1990 and Violeta Chamorro declared the victor. Chamorro was concerned with achieving national reconciliation, pacification, and state reform. Although her government inherited deep political polarization, and small-scale violence continued after the war, she was able to demilitarize the state, increase political participation, and peacefully guarantee a second democratic election in 1996.[2] For the first time in Nicaragua one democratically elected government passed power to another popularly elected government. Arnoldo Alemán became the new president, and the FSLN remained the dominant opposition party.

Alemán's victory consolidated key political allegiances and deepened a division between traditional, pro-status-quo groups (Liberals) and populist, pro-labor-rights organizations (the Sandinistas). The preference for Liberals reflected Nicaraguan traditionalism and conservative values, the negative memories associated with life under the FSLN, and support for a free-market economy. The support for the Sandinistas reflected a rejection of Somocismo, as well as an orientation toward policies that sought to redistribute wealth and was grounded in populist rhetoric. Alemán has adopted an undemocratic style of rule. He surrounded himself with traditional politicians, some of whom had worked with the Somoza dictatorship, and technocrats, who maintained structural adjustment measures and emphasized strengthening the construction and agricultural sectors. His rule, conservative economically and politically, has angered many sectors of society, the Sandinistas included, but Alemán has made pacts with the Sandinistas to secure important power positions. As a consequence the country has no legitimate and viable political opposition.

Democracy was most strongly undermined when Alemán and the FSLN negotiated a political formula that protects his influence after his term ends. The pact is also designed to exclude other political forces from electoral competition or at least make participation extremely difficult. It was accompanied by consistent abuse of political authority and government corruption at all levels.

Negotiating Exclusion: Constitutional and Electoral Reforms

Elite pacts have been an important method of achieving democratic change. Graeme Gill has also explained, however, that real democratization is achieved by involving broader social sectors, not just the political elites.[3] In the history of Nicaraguan politics, however, elite pacts between any two dominant forces have traditionally been anti-democratic, as they have sought to eliminate potential and existing opposition forces. Table 10.5 lists the major political agreements in Nicaraguan history. In contrast, the 1995 agreement on constitutional reforms was reached as a result of different political forces working in concert to produce positive changes.

However, the Alemán government, in agreement with the FSLN, designed a political formula that returned to the old practices of 'pactism.' Furthermore, it has endangered the future of democracy by establishing an almost perfect legal framework for excluding political parties through a form of neocaudillism. Shortly after Alemán's electoral victory in 1996, he encouraged former president Daniel Ortega to recognize defeat and move to establish a political agreement that would work for both.[4] (In fact, once Alemán came to power, he engaged in private conversations with Ortega in order to resolve a property dispute.) By 1998, the talks had moved on to achieving a political agreement, through

TABLE 10.5.

Political Pacts in Nicaragua

Year	Pacts
1857	Pact between Liberals and Conservatives: "Thirty years of Conservative peace"
1893	Pact of Sabana Grande and Momotombo: Conservatives negotiate presidential succession
1910	Dawson Pact: shared government, elections, and continuity between Liberals and Conservatives
1927	Pact of Espino Negro (this pact continued A. Sandino's struggle against U.S. intervention)
1940	Washington Pact: Liberals, Conservatives, and U.S. government
1950	The General's Pact: agreement between Somoza García, and the Conservative Party
1972	Pact Kupia Kumi or Agüero-Somoza Pact: agreement between Somoza Debayle and Conservatives
1990	Transition Protocol: FSLN and UNO agreement about the transfer of power
1995	Framework Law: national political elites' agreement on constitutional reforms

Source: Information elaborated by the author.

constitutional reforms, to create a power-sharing scheme by dividing appointments to governmental institutions, such as the Supreme Court, the Comptroller's Office, and the Supreme Electoral Council (SEC). To the Sandinista faction supporting Daniel Ortega, this agreement represented an important stepping stone toward achieving political power in 2001. To Alemán supporters, it represented a consolidation of their current grip on power, as well as protection of the economic benefits they had achieved while in government. During formal negotiations in 1999, a number of issues were addressed, such as Alemán's demand for re-election, the division of Managua into three municipalities (which decreased its administrative and political influence), and the distribution between Liberals and Sandinistas of appointments to the Supreme Court, the Electoral Councils, and other key governmental institutions.

By August 1999, after eleven meetings, the two sides had drafted a final version of the political agreement to be legalized through constitutional reforms. Despite national opposition and rejection of the pact by public opinion and civil society, the reforms were published as law in the official government newspaper, *La Gaceta*, in January 2000. The reforms included more than nine changes to the Constitution, including reform of the electoral law. The electoral law also established constraints on the formation of political parties. Two of the most damaging reforms were, first, lowering from 45 percent to 40 percent the votes needed to win an election in a first round, or to 35 percent if the leading party has a 5 percent lead over the other parties, and second, the requirement to garner loyal endorsements from 3 percent of registered voters in order to participate in an election. The following tables illustrate the reforms to the Constitution and electoral law.

Exercising Exclusion: Constraining Citizens

Key to democratic practice is the ability of citizens to express themselves in different political contexts: as individuals with political opinions, as citizens organized in civil society groups or in social movements, as citizens who belong to political parties, or as citizens who choose to run for government offices. Political parties, candidates, and citizens represent the means for political competition and participation. The Alemán government and the FSLN with Daniel Ortega as its leader designed an almost perfect political formula that excludes all three from choosing how they

Figure 10.2. The Constitutional Reforms

- DUAL NATIONALITY: The Constitution allowed the existence of dual nationality. This reform is a very important one as it provides incentives to Nicaraguans living abroad to retain or reaply for their Nicaraguan nationality while being citizens of another country. The intent or at least effect, was politically oriented, namely to legalize the status of a number of Alemán supporters who were U.S. citizens.

- LEGISLATIVE SEAT TO A PRESIDENT: This reform stipulates that after serving a term, the president automatically joins the Legislative Assembly. This change means that Alemán will continue to influence politics, now from Congress after 2001.

- SUPREME COURT OF JUSTICE MAGISTRATES: The number of its members increased from 12 to 16 members and was between the FSLN and Liberals.

- A BOARD IN THE COMPTROLLERS OFFICE: The authority of the office changed from one person to a five member board, also composed ideologically.

- SUPREME ELECTORAL COUNCIL: The membership increased from five to seven members and three deputies. The formation followed an ideological divide.

- PRESIDENTIAL IMMUNITY: The number of votes required to remove the immunity of a president changed from a simple majority into a two thirds majority.

- ELECTORAL VICTORY: A candidate running for office can win an election with 40% of the vote (this was changed from 45%). However if a leading candidate has 35% of the votes and is 5% ahead of the candidate in the second place, then such candidate wins the election.

The Electoral Reforms

- PARTY FORMATION: In order for a political party to run, it must have 3% of support from those registered to vote. This equals about 73,000 registered voters.

- PARTY LOYALTY: Citizens can only express support for one political party with their signature. Supporting more than one party invalidates their endorsement.

- PARTY ORGANIZATIONAL STRUCTURE: A political party must have a complex structure comprised of a nine member national directorate, seven member departmental directorates, and five representatives in each of the municipalities.

Figure 10.2. The Constitutional Reforms (continued)

- LEGAL RECOGNITION: Political parties must achieve legal recognition at least one year before a national election, and six months before a municipal election. This year, opposition parties had only four months to achieve recognition to participate in municipal elections.
- NATIONAL PARTICIPATION: Parties must participate in all contests of a national election.
- PARTISANSHIP OF ELECTORAL AUTHORITIES: Electoral Authorities must be formed by the two major political parties. In case of an alliance they would be formed by the leading party of that alliance. In the current scenario, this meant the FSLN and the PLC.
- MUNICIPAL ELECTIONS: Parties could be allowed to obtain 80% of signatures and representatives in 80% of municipalities and still be recognized as new parties.
- LOSS OF RECOGNITION: If the party earns less than 4% of votes in an election it has to apply again for recognition for the next election.
- POPULAR SUBSCRIPTION: Candidates have to be party members. Independents are not allowed.
- MUNICIPAL DIVISION: Managua was to be divided into three municipalities, resulting in gerrymandering.
- ALLIANCES: To form an alliance two requirements exist. All alliance member parties must obtain the 3% support from registered citizens, and the alliance must be lead by a political party, not by a new coalition.

want to participate in politics. Political parties are legally constrained through the reforms by eliminating their chances to run for government, as the requirements are highly demanding. Fragmentation followed as groups attempted to form coalitions and disagreements ensued. It has also prevented the creation of regional parties or parties interested only in legislative seats, not in presidential runner-ups. Candidates wishing to participate in electoral contests have been prevented from doing so in various ways. They cannot run as independents, nor just for legislative seats. Citizens have been discouraged from voting if their preferences are for a third party, which is the case for approximately 30 percent of the population. Moreover, the electoral law stimulates abstention. (The law and constitutional reforms have also been constrained by political maneuvering and through abuses of governmental authority.)

After the reforms were implemented, a political machine emerged designed to enforce a new *caudillo* system, organized through hierarchical settings, from top to bottom. The Supreme Court judges, Supreme Electoral Council members, Bank Superintendency chief, and Comptroller's Office Board now divided its membership under two political flags, the FSLN and PLC. The previous heads of the Supreme Electoral Council, Rosa Marina Zelaya, and the Comptroller's Office, Agustin Jarquin, were eventually removed from their positions.[5] The new members had tainted the posts with their idelogical views. Zelaya stated, for example, that "the positions from the Electoral Affairs Division, and the General Directorate of Informatics represented the vertebral column of the elections, [and these are] positions held by Sandinista member Adonai Jiménez and Narciso Aguilera respectively."[6] Jarquin, on the other hand, had suffered jail time for alleged fraud, charges which in fact were Alemán's way of intimidating the comptroller's investigation of corrupt activities by the president.[7]

After the January implementation of the reforms, all political parties began to organize and form alliances to comply with the requirements. A significant number of small parties immediately decided not to participate, overwhelmed by the excessive demands placed on them by the CSE. At least seven political groups, however, sought to engage in the political game. Among them were the Movimiento Renovación Sandinista (MRS), Partido Liberal Independiente (PLI), Unión Social Cristiana (USC), Movimiento Democrático Nicaraguense (MDN), Pronal, Camino Cristiano (Christian Way), and Partido Conservador de Nicaragua (PCN). Attempts to form coalitions were part of the strategy, while the

FSLN and PLC were hoping some of these parties would be excluded. It was important to the Sandinista party to remove the MRS (and its alliance group, the Third Way) from the political landscape in order to run unchallenged as the party of the left. Alemán's party, the Liberal Constitutionalist Party (PLC), wanted PLI and other smaller liberal groupings out of the electoral game as well.

By February and March 2000, these political opposition parties sought to establish alliances as a third force to confront the two parties that had compacted with each other, abusing the constitution and the legal framework to protect their status quo. Eight political groups agreed to form an implicit alliance supporting one party, the MDN, without formally declaring their alliance, thus avoiding the unrealistic quest of gathering the seventy-thousand-plus signatures per party. Unfortunately the implicit alliance broke down before it was formed, with fifteen MDN leaders (some who were close friends of Alemán) fearing a Sandinista victory, endorsing the Conservative Party and splitting from the movement.[8] The alliance, reorganized with five parties supporting the MRS, still moved forward and submitted 86,000 signatures to request legal representation to participate in the November 2000 municipal election. The Supreme Electoral Council rejected their petition. The council argued that 25,981 signatures had been eliminated because they appeared in other parties' lists; 31,829 were annulled for having invalid identification numbers; and 9,115 were annulled because they were said to appear twice in the list.

The MRS demanded the right to compare the signatures with the registration polls, but the SEC denied them that right without justification.[9] This refusal to comply with the demands of a political party may be linked to the SEC's inability to prove its verification work. In fact, according to the former director of the registrar's office of the SEC, Maria Teresa Alemán, the institution does not have a system to guarantee the verification and validity of signatures provided by registered voters.[10] The MDN and MRS experience was only one case of the political maneuvering emerging from reforms.

The exclusion of the Conservative Party's Pedro Solórzano from the electoral game is another example of the use of formal institutions to inhibit political participation. Solórzano, a leader of the Conservative Party, was a favorite in Managua's municipality. Fearing a victory by Solórzano, the reforms redrew the municipal districts, leaving this leader outside Managua's boundaries. Solórzano contested the redistricting and continued his electoral campaign.

In August, however, after the Conservative Party had submitted its request for participation (fulfilling the requisites demanded by the SEC), Solórzano was prevented from participating due to the council's allegation that the candidate had submitted two addresses, and then that he had reported no address, thus violating article 173 of the electoral law, which demands that a candidate must have resided in the municipality for at least two years.[11] Solórzano allowed William Báez to run for mayor instead.

Yet another example of censorship and rights violations is the case of José Antonio Alvarado. Alvarado was a major supporter of Alemán and had been as minister of defense. However, he had grown critical of the way Alemán was conducting his presidency and was particularly critical of the proposed meeting of a constituent assembly in lieu of holding national elections.

Following that pattern, Alemán would have to remain in power longer, until the assembly drafted a new constitution. Alvarado wanted to form a new political party, the Liberal Democratic Party. As a result of Alvarado's criticisms of Alemán and his attempt to form a new party, the minister of government, René Herrera, nullified Alvarado's nationality, arguing that there were legal discrepancies that could not be reconciled. Although Alvarado had U.S. citizenship, in 1990 he had regained Nicaraguan citizenship after applying for it. The government, however, had nullified his nationality days after he had announced the formation of a new party and voiced his criticisms of Alemán.[12]

Only four political parties (FSLN, PLC, PCN, and the Christian Way) ran in the 2000 municipal elections. One month before the deadline for forming a political party for the 2001 national elections, a high degree of uncertainty prevailed in Nicaragua. Political divisions and intimidation had plagued the country. Alemán used his power to discourage, weaken, or intimidate its opponents, inside or outside its ranks. In the end, despite a partial victory by the PLC, which won 94 of 151 municipalities, the Sandinistas prevailed in some of the key municipalities in the country: Managua, León, and Chinandega (and the Conservatives won Granada).

The short-term outcome of the reforms and the municipal elections suggests that the FSLN and PLC have succeeded in becoming the two dominant parties: the Sandinista group and the PLC rightist group with strong ideological links to the Somoza legacy. The legal framework and the political authorities' monopoly on enforcing the laws of exclusion have secured electoral victories and the ability to distribute political power for the two parties. Pedro Solórzano, a potential presidential candidate for the Conservative Party, was investigated on charges of corruption while a council member of Managua's municipality. These allegations appeared just weeks before the deadline to register candidates and parties before the SEC.[13] Eventually, Solórzano gave in to political pressures and endorsed the Liberal party, thereby creating uproar among various opposition leaders.[14]

The Electoral Contest in 2001

The election of 2001 was one of the most contested campaigns in recent history. The two main candidates' margins of victory were very close. Until October 2001, opinion polls showed that the FSLN was leading, but only by one percentage point. Ortega had received the endorsement of Agustin Jarquin (the leader of the Social Christian Unity Party) in exchange for the vice presidency (or the presidency itself) and the possibility of legislative seats lost by the USC in 1996.[15] The FSLN counted some 30 percent of popular support. With a third party, weakened by internal fights and political intimidation by Alemán and the Sandinistas, the "third force" functioned as a spoiler, which could attract a significant percentage of votes, but not enough to compete in a second round.

Given the PLC's loss of popularity, due to Alemán's widespread corruption—reported almost daily in the national press—its chances of winning were slim but not impossible.[16] The political landscape of Nicaraguan politics showed three major parties in the contest: the FSLN with Daniel Ortega as candidate, the PLC with Enrique Bolaños, and a weak Conservative Party with Alberto Saborío as its newest candidate. Bolaños, a former member of COSEP, the private enterprise council, was Alemán's vice president and has been strongly criticized for supporting Alemán and not standing against his corrupt practices while in office.

The continued political pressure on the Conservative Party eventually weakened its leaders and provoked a split in the party, ultimately leaving the group debilitated politically. Because the Conservative Party was viewed by the opposition as the only alternative within the electoral process that could function as a "third force," leaders of various movements sought to form alliances with the party. However, traditionalists within the party (such as the former mayoral candidate, William Báez) opposed the idea of integrating non-Conservative groups.

Figure 10.3. Arnoldo Alemán's Decline in Popularity

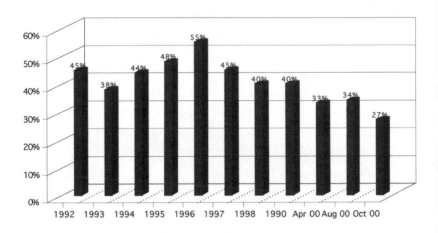

Two of the main political groups seeking to form coalitions with the party were the Liberal Democratic Party, led by José Antonio Alvarado, and the National Unity Movement (MUN), led by former general Joaquin Cuadra. Alvarado succeeded in gaining the support of the Conservative leadership to run as the vice-presidential candidate. However, the Supreme Electoral Council, siding along party lines, and with the Liberal Party's support, rejected Alvarado's candidacy for vice president, arguing that he was not a Nicaraguan citizen. As a result, the then presidential candidate, Noel Vidaure, supported the option of integrating Carlos Tunnermann as an outside force. (Tunnermann had worked with the Sandinista government in the 1980s.) Tunnermann accepted the offer. In July, however, another crisis emerged within the Conservative Party dealing with the selection of legislators for the election.[17]

The MUN, in particular, had agreed to support the party in exchange for giving Joaquin Cuadra Managua's deputation. The tension between traditionalists and reformists led to the party's split after Vidaure's resignation over the Conservative leadership's re-

TABLE 10.6.

Public Opinion Polls in Support of Presidential Candidates

Candidate	Daniel Ortega	Enrique Bolaños	Noel Vidaure	Undecided
February	33.4	24.8	14.1	27.7
May	34.1	28.8	13.6	23.5
July	37.3	35.5	8.0*	19.2
September	40.0	43.0	5.0	12.0

* The July poll captured the demise of Vidaure and the crisis of the Conservatives. *Confidencial*, edición no. 244: June 10–16, 2001, Empate técnico Bolaños-Ortega, *La Prensa*, August 9, 2001. Polls conducted by Borge & Asociados.

jection of Cuadra as a Conservative legislator. The result was a decline in support for the party, as voters moved to support the Liberal Party. Table 10.6 shows how support for the Liberal Party increased thanks to the crisis within the Conservatives. The table also shows that the number of undecided voters had declined significantly. These results can also be observed in figure 10.4, showing the surveys of different polling companies.

The scenario prior to the national election raised questions as to the implications of a Sandinista victory tainted by an illegitimate pact.[18] The legacy of the FSLN remained fresh in people's minds, and public dislike of Daniel Ortega was very significant. Although he received support from a large segment of society, polls showed that 48 percent of the population would never vote for him.[19]

The end result of the election was an overwhelming victory for Enrique Bolaños, who received 56 percent of the votes, versus 42 percent for the FSLN. His rupture with Alemán, the electoral sup-

Figure 10.4. Nicaragua's 2001 National Elections: Survey Results

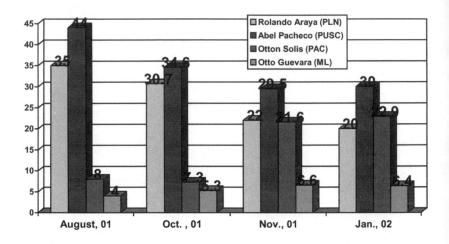

port gained over time, and fears about a Sandinista return tipped the balance to Bolaños' side. The Sandinista defeat demonstrated the party's inability to garner more than 40 percent vote for the third consecutive time (see table 10.7).

TABLE 10.7.

Nicaraguan Elections since 1990

Party	1990	1996	2001
FSLN	40.8	37.70	42.28
Other	5.3	11.15	1.41
Liberals*	53.9	51.06	56.30
FSLN defeat	13.1	13.36	14.02

*In 1990 the party running was the UNO.
Source: Supreme Electoral Council.

A TWO-PARTY SYSTEM IN FLUX: COSTA RICA

Neither of the traditional leading Costa Rican political parties, National Liberation (PLN) and Social Christian Unity (PUSC), won the presidency in that country's national elections, held in February 2002. Costa Rican voters stunned politicians by giving their support to at least four different parties, breaking down the two-party framework that had prevailed for over fifty years. This election marked a new political stage, in which traditional leaders will seek to accommodate changing demands from society, and new political players will take the opportunity to promote alternative social and political agendas.

Two key questions weigh on the future of Costa Rican politics. The first is whether the traditional two-party balance of power will change into a multi-party system. The second is how the new president will meet social demands and growing dissatisfaction with national political leaders.

Trends Prior to the Election

Costa Rican citizens have traditionally expressed their support for a two-party system. Since the mid-fifties, voters chose between the traditional PLN and a coalition group until 1983 and the Partido Unidad Social Cristiana (PUSC) thereafter. These tendencies led scholars to conclude that "what was previously a bipolar system, with one strong party (National Liberation Party, or PLN) and a shifting series of ad hoc opposition coalitions, has become a stable two-party system."[20]

Historically, an important aspect of political debate in Costa Rica has been the role of the state and its capacity to address social demands. In particular, after the economic crisis of the early eighties, when Costa Rica experienced high levels of external indebtedness, a rising fiscal deficit, and unemployment, the nature of the welfare state was subjected to scrutiny by the public and the elites. Scholars and policy experts then referred to a crisis of the welfare development model implemented in Costa Rica and sought ways out of that crisis and model.[21]

As part of the process of economic adjustment, most Costa Rican administrations during the eighties and nineties adopted outward-looking strategies emphasizing state reform, which included a combination of policies oriented toward diversification of markets, privatization, trade liberalization, reduction of government subsidies, and changes in fiscal and monetary policy.[22] To some extent, Costa Rica's economic restructuring closely followed the model advocated in the Washington Consensus. However, successive governments balanced different formulas to increase the growth rate through state reform without completely dismantling the welfare system that characterized the country.

In the 1990s, the political debate turned partly around the extent of privatization, the effects of economic liberalization on society, and the management of the fiscal deficit. In April 1995, President Jose Figueres (son of Jose Figueres Ferrer, former president and founder of the PLN) sought to continue a strategy of advancing economic reforms by securing an agreement with the opposition Social Christian Unity Party. The country's elites embarked on a process of "concertación" (understanding or agreement) with broad sectors of society in order to face emerging economic and social challenges.[23] Moreover, in 1998, President Miguel Angel Rodriguez inaugurated his term with a national dialogue that opened the door to a debate about political inclusion and modernization of political parties.

Although the efforts of Figueres and Rodriguez were positive, events relating to privatization schemes of the telecommunications and electricity industries led to a decline of "concertación" and growing social opposition to Rodriguez and the PLN. Since 2000, criticism has grown over social conditions in the country and the pace and effects of privatization. Economists argued that despite the economic liberalization process that led to increasing growth rates (particularly in 1999 with the arrival of Intel), poverty rates actually increased by one percent in 2000.[24] Public opinion polls showed dissatisfaction, and people demonstrated in the streets over the Congress's lack of consultation about privatizing the Costa Rican Institute of Electricity. While this debate was developing, tensions within the parties were increasing over their capacity to attract support for the upcoming 2002 election. Sensing criticism and popular dissatisfaction and speaking before Congress in May 2001, President Rodriguez proposed the formation of a semi-parliamentary system in Costa Rica as a formula to improve democratic governance.

From the Electoral Campaign to the First Round

The leading parties found themselves challenged in this changed political landscape. Criticism within the parties about the lack of access for women and young political cadres in decision-making structures, a very high rate of voter abstention, and growing discontent within the PLN about moving away from its social democratic tradition were key issues on the national agenda. In addition to these challenges to and changes in the two historically dominant parties, third forces emerged with greater strength to voice their views about increased participation. During the Rodriguez administration there were non-traditional political parties holding seven legislative seats and representing 24 percent of the electorate.

The internal selection process of presidential candidates in the two leading parties was marred by relative confrontation between traditionalist and reformist groups. In each party, important developments took place that signaled or reinforced dissatisfaction with the parties. The PLN's first problem was low voter turnout. The contest in the PLN involved selecting one of three candidates. The first was Rolando Araya, nephew of former president

Luis Alberto Monge and an ally of former president Oscar Arias. He was the party's favorite.[25] Second was Jose Miguel Corrales, a traditionalist leader who had run for the presidency in 1998, losing against Rodriguez. He had lost support due to his previous defeat. Finally, Antonio Alvares Desanti represented the younger generation of the Liberación Nacional but was perceived as inexperienced. Although the vote was disputed, Araya won 50 percent of the votes, compared with 30 percent for Corrales.[26]

The selection process in the PUSC presented a different scenario in that a relatively new actor in the party, Abel Pacheco de la Espirella, received significant support. His opponent, Rodolfo Méndez Mata, a traditionalist leader supported by former president Rafael Angel Calderon and his minister of the presidency, lost the vote in a landslide defeat. Seventy-seven percent of PUSC voters gave their support to Pacheco.[27]

A major surprise was the strong emergence of the Partido Acción Ciudadana (PAC) created by Otton Solis, a former minister of President Oscar Arias. This new party was supported by Walter Coto, former secretary general of the PLN, Margarita Penon, former first lady, and Rodrigo Carazo, son of former president Carazo Odio. The party represented a significant group dissenting from the PLN. According to some analysts, the 1995 political agreement between Figueres Olsen and Calderón Fournier and the support in April 2000 to approve the privatization of the telecommunications company were the triggering factors that provoked the split within the PLN.[28] The formation of the PAC, as well as the mobilization of other smaller parties, initiated a new process in the debate: as the parties gained support during the contest, they began to receive the label of 'emerging parties' and signal the question about the fate of a two-party system in Costa Rica.

The polls showed growing support for the emerging parties, particularly for the PAC, and declining support for the PLN. Between

August 2001 and January 2002, the number of voters supporting the PAC tripled. Most importantly, the polls showed growing dissatisfaction among voters over the major candidates. In April 2001, a poll conducted by a research center showed that 60 percent of Costa Ricans were unsatisfied with the way the country's democracy was functioning.[29]

A key issue in this campaign was Pacheco's popularity. His appeal to voters and the citizenry at large was due to his approach to mainstream Costa Ricans as a man who speaks the language of the people. Moreover, to the PUSC, he represented a fresh way to look at the traditional political cleavages and signaled new hopes for the party. Although support for him vis-à-vis the other parties declined, his popularity continued to affect the political process.

The political discourse during the campaign focused on the rule of law, improving the judicial system, corruption, employment, participation of women in politics, privatization, and free trade. Crime and public safety in particular were key issues for voters. Crime in Costa Rica had gradually increased over the previous decade, producing a greater sense of insecurity in the population,

Figure 10.5. Costa Rican Elections: Opinion Polls

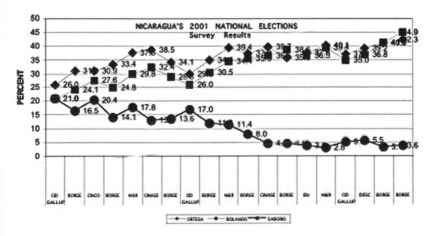

highlighted in its identification as the number one problem in the country.[30]

Although Costa Ricans have generally acknowledged that state interventionism was somewhat detrimental to the country's economy and welfare, there has been reluctance to move toward a complete reduction of state involvement in some economic activities. This debate and ambivalence is illustrated in the opposition to the privatization of the telecommunications company. There has also been opposition to or criticism of other privatization initiatives such as those of the airport, the oil refinery, and the water companies. In a similar vein, free trade was criticized by others, such as some agricultural groups, arguing that it could negatively affect small farmers.

Some voter abstention, undecided voters, and an often disillusioned electorate characterized the elections. A survey conducted by Procesos, an NGO, and the political science department at the University of Costa Rica a few days prior to the election, confirmed both disappointment with politicians and parties and the intention of some not to vote. A little over half of the respondents expressed the view that Costa Rica was heading in the wrong direction ("*Costa Rica va por el camino equivocado*"), with women responding more pessimistically (53 percent) than men (47 percent).[31]

The April 2002 Outcome and Future Perspectives

The February election surprised many groups. First, for the first time in the country's history, a president was not elected in the first round. Second, the election results showed significant support for non-traditional third parties. Third, voters' disappointment in political leaders was reflected in the increasing rates of abstention. Finally, women gained significant prominence in the election.

The inability of any party to win in the first round represented a major blow to their capacities to defeat the opposition. The PLN probably suffered the greatest loss, as its political clout had been declining over time and they had expected to regain strength in 2002. The table below shows that Acción Ciudadana reached a very close third place behind the PLN, reflecting remarkable success for a new and third party.

TABLE 10.8.

Election Results from February 3, 2002, Votes

	PUSC	PLN	PAC	ML*	Abstaining
Parties	38.57	30.99	26.16	1.68	32.00

*ML: Movimiento Libertario
Source: Tribunal Supremo de Elecciones.

However, support for third forces gained even more momentum in the election for the legislative assembly. The balance of power shifted from the two dominant parties into three blocs with close voting power. Table 10.9 shows the division in the number of seats held before and after the election. At least two major changes occurred. First, Acción Ciudadana enjoyed a strong showing, winning fourteen seats. Second, the number of women in the legislature increased from eleven to nineteen *diputadas*, exactly one-third of total legislators.

The news of a second round moved each party to reconfigure its strategy. The two traditional parties, the PLN and the PUSC, reorganized their campaigns and opened new wounds within each group. In particular, the PUSC appointed Lineth Saborio, causing friction by rejecting Luis Fishman, an ally of former president Calderón Fournier. Laura Chinchilla was named to direct the PLN's campaign in the second round. Opinion polls indicated that

TABLE 10.9.

Legislative Seats in Parliament

Party	Total Legislators	
	1998–2002	2002–2006
PUSC	27	19
PLN	23	17
PAC	0	14
PML	1	6
PRC	1	1
PIN	1	0
PALA	1	0
Total	54	57

Source: Asamblea Legislativa and Tribunal Supremo Electoral

Pacheco would win the second round. In fact, the election results showed that Pacheco won on April 7 by a large margin, with 58 percent of the votes, against Araya's 42 percent, but with 39 percent of voters abstaining.

The challenge for all political parties remains to increase citizen interest in and support for the political process. In one of the most important studies on contemporary democratic politics in Costa Rica, analyst Jorge Rovira showed that, starting in the mid-eighties, the two-party system began to weaken in the legislature. In 1986, 90 percent of voters chose legislators from one or the other party, but that number dropped to 76 percent in 1998. When asked whether the 1998 election results were altering the two-party framework, Rovira replied that the parties were showing signs of weakening and that the two-party system was not in danger as long as the small parties showed sufficient strength to challenge the status quo.[32] However, the question of a two- versus multi-party system remains relevant because in the 2001 election power shifted even more significantly to the extent that the two parties received less than 70 percent of votes.

Analysts agree that that there is no question that the balance of power has shifted. To some this shifting balance may have a longer duration but is contingent on emerging political groups strengthening their own power. Carlos Sojo stresses that, with four political groups in the legislature, circumstances may favor the formation of alliances; otherwise political stagnation could occur.[33] Cecilia Cortes asserts that there is also another emerging power, that of the women in the legislature who represent one-third of the assembly.[34] What seems to be the key to the future of the party system is whether the PAC will become stronger and increase its capacity to create larger coalitions and attract new political elites. Rodriguez believes that part of that skill will involve the PAC's not falling prey to the internal fragmentation produced by personal infighting, which has occurred within the Fuerza Democratica, the third party in the 2001 legislature.[35]

The implications of these political changes will be fourfold. First, there is a significant chance that Costa Rica will move from a two-party to a multi-party system. The immediate effect will be a reconfiguration of the ideological and political landscape that prevailed before 2001. Second, there will be a shift from the traditional political party leadership to new political leaders who will advocate different agendas or question prevailing ones. Third, the decision-making process will be constrained by debate over social policy, privatization, and free trade. As the political map has shifted from center to left of center, questions about privatization and free trade will dominate the debate. As a result the ratification of the free trade agreement with Canada may be the first test of the extent to which Costa Rica is prepared to continue economic liberalization. Finally, the political maneuvering will oscillate between consensus building and coalition building in an effort to prevent stagnation or paralysis between the executive and legislative branches.

These issues will define the future political scenario of Costa Rica and the direction in which the country will head with regard to political party and state reform, free trade, and citizenship participation.

POLITICS AS USUAL: GUATEMALA, EL SALVADOR, AND HONDURAS

The characteristic political dynamics of the Central American countries of Guatemala, El Salvador, and Honduras are often troubling. The Central American peace agreements (Nicaragua in 1990, El Salvador in 1991, and Guatemala in 1996) ended decades of war and ushered in a new era of democratization and stability in the region. Since then, free and relatively clean elections have been held on a regular basis, civil liberties and freedom of expression have been protected, and civilians are in control of the region's military forces. Despite recent progress, however, major obstacles, including political fragmentation, weak political parties, and corruption, continue to impede further democratic development.

Guatemala

Guatemala most recently held presidential elections in 1999. During the first round, Alfonso Antonio Portillo Cabrera, representing the Frente Republicano Guatemalteco (FRG), secured 1,037,775 votes, for a total of 48 percent. Oscar Berger Perdomo of the Partido de Avanzada Nacional (PAN), received 660,404 votes, 31 percent of the total. The Unidad Revolucionaria Nacional Guatemalteca (URNG, founded in 1982 when major guerrilla groups united to form this party) finished in third place with only 12 percent of the vote. Finally, the Partido Libertador Progresista (PLP) came in last with a mere 3 percent of the total vote. In the second round, Perdomo received only 32 percent of the votes, while Portillo secured a decisive victory, receiving more than 68 percent of the total votes cast.

Since taking office, the government of President Alfonso Portillo has sought to integrate liberal forces and indigenous leaders into his cabinet. He has faced significant opposition from a still influential and often retrograde army as well as from Congress and the private sector. Portillo has not been an effective leader, and his government is widely considered to be corrupt. Crime rates in Guatemala continue to rise and affect the average citizen. Judicial systems are also ineffective, to the extent that in some rural areas, peasants have executed criminals vigilante-style. Racial and ethnic differences are major sources of conflict in the country, which must be confronted as Guatemala continues its process of democratization.

El Salvador

The presidential elections in 1999 declared Francisco Flores of the Alianza Republicana Nacionalista (ARENA) the winning candidate, having received 51 percent of the vote in the first round. The Frente Farabundo Martí Para la Liberación Nacional (FMLN) and the Unión Social Cristiana (USC) finished in second place, with 29 percent of the vote. The Centro Democrática Unido (CDU, formerly Covergencia Democrática, CD) placed third, with 7 percent of the total votes cast, while the Partido Demócrata Cristiano (PDC), came in last, with only 6 percent of the vote. Like Guatemala, El Salvador also experienced a high rate of voter abstention in 1999. In fact, it reached a notable 61.4 percent, an increase of more than 6 percent since previous elections (1994) and, moreover, the highest rate of abstention recorded in El Salvador since 1989.

El Salvador has experienced a stronger process of democratization relative to its neighbors, but discontent is growing over the government's inability to control crime and promote economic growth. The large increase in the number of private security guards protecting the wealthy exemplifies both problems. The two earthquakes that hit El Salvador in 2001 only increased poverty and insecurity. Currently, the governing ARENA party is losing the confidence of the country's voters, but the opposing FMLN remains too divided to capture a national election. The March 2003 legislative campaigns illustrate the political struggle over control amidst the challenges these two parties face.

The political outcome of the legislative and municipal elections held on Sunday, March 16, 2003, in El Salvador reaffirmed the country's political landscape of competitive party elections but also raised questions about the country's future agenda. While the drive toward free trade and privatization has characterized the agenda of the ruling party, ARENA, the decline in growth rates, crime, and the decline in popularity of current President Francisco Flores were demonstrated in the electoral results.

Contrary to the expectations of many, including pollsters, the opposition party, FMLN, emerged triumphant in this election. It retained control of key municipal governments and the same number of legislators in the assembly (thirty-one out of eighty-four seats). The ruling party, on the other hand, lost municipalities and two legislators (retaining twenty-seven of eighty-four). However, the conservative and traditional ally of ARENA, the National Conciliation Party (PCN), won sixteen seats, three more than in 2000, which guaranteed the continuity of a conservative majority in Congress.

The results caught some by surprise, because the FMLN had undergone serious divisions between orthodox factions within the party and reformist groups that highlighted a crisis of legitimacy. Prior to the election, a segment of the reformist groups had formed their own political coalition that ran independently. But they received less than 2 percent of the vote and elected one legislator as part of a coalition formed with two other parties. Moreover, public opinion polls showed less than 30 percent of the vote going to the FMLN.

One important result of the election was the FMLN victory in the city of San Salvador after a close battle between the two leading parties. For the FMLN, winning the capital municipality meant a continuation of its control of the most important city in El Salvador.

To many observers, these electoral results were clearly a defeat for ARENA, which had ruled the country through three consecutive governments. However, discontent with the government has been widespread. Despite ARENA's attempts to reorganize its leadership, it could not address key issues. The public perception remains that the economy has worsened since President Flores took office. El Salvador's economic growth has not increased above 2 percent between 2000 and 2004. Crime has not improved and continues to affect the poor predominantly. In addition to domestic violence, youth gangs are a troublesome reality. According to police reports, three gang members die daily in turf fights and it is estimated that there are at least thirty thousand young Salvadorans involved with these groups. There is also increasing discomfort over the effect of privatization on society. The attempt to privatize the health care sector produced opposition among low-income sectors.

Overall, the electoral results are not simply a defeat for ARENA but also a warning about the need to renew the social contract with the people. ARENA has lost the leadership in the assembly and as a result will face a major challenge in the upcoming 2004 election.

The next twelve months will be critical with regard to various issues. First, the debate over the possible ratification of a free-trade agreement with the United States will most likely meet with opposition from the FMLN. Second, the presidential elections in 2004 have opened a window of opportunity for an FMLN victory. On the other hand, Salvadorans still tend to lean toward the right

Figure 10.6. Municipalities Won/Lost by Party and Legislators per Party

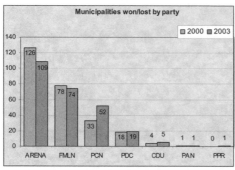
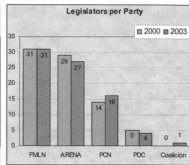

in presidential elections. On legislative issues, the FMLN will continue to face opposition from ARENA, the PCN and the Christian Democratic Party (PDC). More importantly, however, if the current head of the FMLN, Schafik Handal, were to be selected as a presidential candidate, voters would be less likely to vote for the FMLN and might abstain from voting altogether due to his lack of leadership. Electoral apathy and voter abstention in El Salvador continue to be pressing issues as the current level of voter turnout remains at 41 percent—low enough to pose a predicament in the presidential elections of 2004.

Honduras

Honduras' last national election, in November 2001, was characterized by political manipulation. Members of the opposing Liberal Party (namely, Rafael Pineda Ponce, who also served as the president of Congress and was a Liberal presidential candidate at the time) attempted to block Ricardo Maduro (of the National Party) from running for the presidency. The Liberals based their contention on a constitutional technicality that questioned Maduro's nationality and thereby challenged his legal right to run for president in the national elections. Eventually, an agreement was reached that allowed Maduro to run as a National Party candidate, but not until March 2001—a mere eight months before the election.[36]

Five candidates represented their respective parties in the 2001 presidential elections. Ricardo Maduro Joest of the National Party (Partido Nacional) received 1,137,734 votes, which accounted for 52.21 percent of the total, so a second round of voting to declare a victor was not necessary. Maduro's competition included Rafael Pineda Ponce of the Partido Liberal, which received 964,590 votes, or 44.26 percent of the total. The Partido Innovación y Unidad (PINU) placed third and obtained 31,666 votes, which represented a mere 1.45 percent of the total. Finally, the Partido Demócrata Cristiano de Honduras (PDC) received only 21,089 votes or .97 percent of the total. Interestingly, the abstention rate of 33.73 percent in the Honduran presidential election was rather low vis-à-vis its Central American neighbors, but represented more than a 5 percent increase since the prior 1997 elections (see table 10.10).

Upon assuming office, President Maduro launched a campaign against corruption and for crime prevention. In an unprecedented initiative, Congress is debating whether to strip fifteen legislators of their immunity from prosecution.

CONCLUSION: DEMOCRATIZING THE PARTY SYSTEMS IN CENTRAL AMERICA

Electoral processes in Central America have progressed dramatically towards participatory, competitive politics. The region is making significant progress toward liberal democracy, and the countries of Central America are gradually approaching a political synergy similar to that described by Anthony DePalma in the opening essay of this book. More importantly, the concurrence of

TABLE 10.10.

Past Elections in Contemporary Central America

Country	Winning Party	Second Place	Third Place	Fourth Place	Percent Abstention
Guatemala (4-year term)					
1985	DCG (34)	UNC (18)	PDCN-PR (12)	MLN-PID (11)	30.0%
1985 (second round)	DCG (63)	UNC (30)			34.6%
1991 (second round)	MAS (68)	UNC (32)			58.0%
1995 (first round)	PAN (36.6)	FRG (22.1)			53.2%
1995 (second round)	PAN (51.2)	FRG (48.78)			63.1%
1999 (first round)	FRG (48)	PAN(30)	URNG (12)	PLP (3)	61.0%
1999 (second round)	FRG (68)	PAN (32)			
El Salvador (5-year term)					
1989	ARENA (50)	PDC (34)	PCN (4)	CD (4)	44.0%
1994 (first round)	ARENA (49)	FMLN-CD (25)			47.0%
1994 (second round)	ARENA (68)	FMLN-CD (32)			54.5%
1999	ARENA (51)	FMLN-USC (29)	CDU (7)	PDC (6)	61.4%
Honduras (4-year term)					
1989	PNH (53)	PLH (45)	PDC (1.5)	PIU-SD (1.3)	23.0%
1993	PLH (53)	PNH (40)			35.0%

TABLE 10.10.
(cont.)

1997	PLH (53)	PNH (42)	PINU (2)	PUD (1)	28.0%
2001 (Nov. 25, 2001)	PNH (52.2)	PLH (44.3)	PINU (1.5)	PUD (1)	33.7%
Nicaragua (5-year term)					
1984	FSLN (70)				25.0%
1990	UNO (55)	FSLN (41)	MUR (1)		14.0%
1996	AL-PLC (51)	FSLN (37)	PCCN (4)	PCN (2)	24.0%
2001 (Nov. 4, 2001)	PLC (56.3)	FLSN (43)			
Costa Rica (4-year term)					
1990	PUSC (51.4)	PLN (47.2)	PU (1)		18.0%
1994	PLN (50)	PUSC (48)			19.0%
1998	PUSC (47)	PLN (44)	FD (3)	IN (2)	
2002 (Feb. 3, 2002) first round	PUSC (38)	PLN (31)	PAC (26)	PML (2)	
2002 (April 7, 2002) second round	PUSC (58)	PLN (42)			39.0%

Figure 10.7. Voter Abstention in Previous Elections (Percentage), 1996–2001

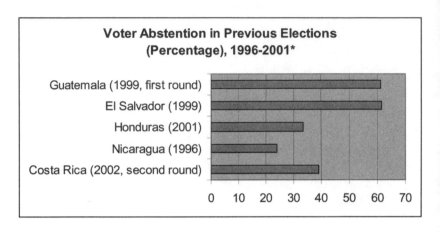

interests within these different and independent countries is drawing the region closer to rest of the North American community.

It is important to carefully follow the political processes in Central America during negotiations over free trade with the United States. Central America has supported a free trade agreement with Mexico, and some countries in the region have also negotiated individual agreements with Canada. The negotiations with the United States concern legislatures and governments, as well as ordinary citizens, as the impact on households and economies will be dramatic. The approval of the trade agreements is contingent on how civil society responds to the possible setbacks of free trade and to the ratification by the legislatures. In recent elections the process of economic integration with North America has been debated, and the governments and various sectors of society have envisioned a deeper relationship that encompasses goods and labor. In fact, the synergy in the region goes beyond governmental coordination to include transnational linkages among people and migrants. In consequence, governments are studying and reacting to increasing demands of Central Americans in the United States,

Canada, and Mexico concerning the right to hold dual citizenship and vote abroad.

Central American political systems are thus facing both a national process of democratic consolidation and emerging transnational demands that result from a gradual integration with North America. The continued democratization of the party systems in Central America will be critical to this process.

Notes

CHAPTER 1

1. Press conference at the National Press Club, Washington, D.C., August 24, 2000.
2. Ibid.
3. Fox speech at The Center for Democracy, Washington, D.C., August 24, 2000.
4. Transcript of the presidential debate on October 4, 2000.
5. Miami, Fla., August 25, 2000.
6. Ibid.
7. *Globe and Mail* (Toronto), November 10, 2000.
8. On January 11, 2001, a disgruntled and sorely disappointed Lucien Bouchard resigned as premier of Quebec, saying he had failed to keep his promise to make Quebec independent.
9. From an address to the National Policy Research Conference in Ottawa on November 30, 2000.

CHAPTER 2

1. Enrique Krauze, *La Presidencia Imperial: Ascenso y Caída del Sistema Político Mexicano, 1940–1996* (Mexico City: Tusquets Editores, 1997).
2. These figures were taken from "México Social," edited regularly by the Banco Nacional de México, and the electoral database at the Centro de Investigación para el Desarrollo, CIDAC.
3. A brief review of these three main parties' histories and programs can be found in Mónica Serrano, ed., *Governing Mexico: Political*

Parties and Elections (Macmillan-ILAS Series, Institute of Latin American Studies, University of London, 1998).

4. Beatriz Magaloni and Alejandro Moreno, "Catching All Souls: Mexico's Partido Acción Nacional," in Scott Mainwaring and Timothy Scully (eds.), *Christian Democracy in Latin America: Electoral Competition and Regime Conflicts* (Stanford: Stanford UP, 2003).

5. Volker G. Lehr, "Modernización y movilización electoral, 1964–1976: Un estudio ecológico," *Estudios Políticos* 4, no. 1 (1985): 54–61, and Juan Molinar Horcasitas, *El tiempo de la legitimidad. Elecciones, autoritarismo y democracia en México* (México City: Cal y Arena, 1991).

6. Juan Molinar Horcasitas, *El tiempo de la legitimidad. Elecciones, autoritarismo y democracia en México* (México City: Cal y Arena, 1991).

7. Jorge I. Domínguez and James A. McCann, "Shaping Mexico's Electoral Arena: Construction of Partisan Cleavages in the 1988 and 1991 National Elections," *American Political Science Review* 89 (1995): 34–48.

8. Alejandro Moreno, "Party Competition and the Issue of Democracy: Ideological Space in Mexican Elections," in Mónica Serrano (ed.), *Governing Mexico: Political Parties and Elections* (Macmillan-ILAS Series, Institute of Latin American Studies, University of London, 1998) and "Ideología y voto: Dimensiones de competencia política en México en los noventa," *Política y Gobierno* 6, no. 1 (1999): 45–81.

9. Alejandro Moreno, *Political Cleavages: Issues, Parties, and the Consolidation of Democracy* (Boulder, Co.: Westview Press. Series on Latin America in Global Perspective, 1999).

10. Beatriz Magaloni and Alejandro Moreno, "Catching All Souls: Mexico's Partido Acción Nacional," in Scott Mainwaring and Timothy Scully (eds.), *Christian Democracy in Latin America: Electoral Competition and Regime Conflicts* (Stanford: Stanford UP, 2003).

11. The empirical evidence for this chapter comes from a collection of surveys conducted in Mexico between 1990 and 2002. A list of the surveys includes: 1) The Mexican samples of the *World Values Survey*'s second, third, and fourth waves, administered in 1990, 1996/7, and in 2000, respectively, to slightly over 1,500 respondents in each wave. The Mexican samples of the *World Values Survey* were conducted in 1990, 1996/7, and 2000 among 1,531, 1,511, and 1535 Mexican adults, respectively. They are part of the ICPSR archives, at the University of Michigan. The fourth-wave survey was conducted in February 2000, sponsored by Grupo Reforma, and conducted by the Departments of Survey Research at newspapers *Reforma, El Norte, Mural,* and *Palabra.* 2) A national exit poll administered to over 3,000 voters as they left their corresponding polling places in the 2000 elections. I compare these results with those from a national exit poll conducted in the 1997 elections. The 1997 exit poll was sponsored by the Partido Acción Nacional and conducted by *Arcop,* on July 6, 1997, among 3,452 voters. The 2000 exit poll was sponsored by Grupo Reforma and conducted on July 2, 2000, among 3,377 voters by newspaper *Reforma* and its affiliates. 3) Four national pre-election polls conducted between April and June 2000 and pooled into one single database. The national pre-election polls were conducted in early April, early May, late May, and mid-June, 2000, by the newspaper *Reforma* and its affiliates. Each survey had slightly over 1,500 respondents (with the exception of the April one, which had slightly over 1,600) from all thirty-two federal entities. For the analysis in this chapter, the four polls were pooled into a single database of 6,289 cases. All the surveys listed here are national representative samples of Mexican adults or voters, and were conducted face-to-face in the respondents' homes or as they left their polling places, in the case of the exit polls.

12. Between one-fourth and one-third of Mexican respondents, depending on the survey, do not place themselves on the left-right

scale. In this analysis, I assigned an average placement to those who did not originally place themselves on the scale. The general averages fell between categories six and seven on a ten-point scale.

13. The original measure is a ten-point self-placement scale.

14. Alejandro Moreno, "Ideología y voto: Dimensiones de competencia política en México en los noventa." *Política y Gobierno* 6, no. 1 (1999): 45–81.

15. The shift to the right probably reflects the influence of the PRI's also historic primary to select its presidential candidate. The 2000 survey was conducted in February, four and a half months before the presidential election and with campaigns officially running, but, most importantly, three months after the PRI primary of November, 1999, and after Fox and others had started to advertise widely on television. Very intense negative campaigning and mudslinging characterized the primary contest, but it boosted voter interest in the PRI.

16. Alejandro Moreno, "Party Competition and the Issue of Democracy: Ideological Space in Mexican Elections," in Mónica Serrano (ed.), *Governing Mexico: Political Parties and Elections* (Macmillan-ILAS Series, Institute of Latin American Studies, University of London, England, 1998).

17. According to Moreno (1999b), the liberal-fundamentalist dimension is empirically observable in many Latin American countries, and it provides a useful tool to analyze party competition across the region.

18. Alejandro Moreno, "Party Competition and the Issue of Democracy: Ideological Space in Mexican Elections," in Mónica Serrano (ed.), *Governing Mexico: Political Parties and Elections* (Macmillan-ILAS Series, Institute of Latin American Studies, University of London, 1998).

19. Empirically, these dimensions result from a theoretically-guided principal components factor analysis based on the Mexican sam-

ples of the 1997 and 2000 *World Values Surveys* pooled into one single dataset.

20. Herbert Kitschelt, *The Radical Right in Western Europe* (Ann Arbor: University of Michigan Press, 1995), Herbert Kitschelt et al., *Post-Communist Party Systems: Competition, Representation, and Inter-Party Cooperation* (Cambridge: Cambridge University Press, 1999), and Alejandro Moreno, *Political Cleavages: Issues, Parties, and the Consolidation of Democracy* (Boulder, Co.: Westview Press. Series on Latin America in Global Perspective, 1999).

21. Ronald Inglehart, *Modernization and Postmodernization: Cultural, Economic, and Political Change in 43 Societies* (Princeton: Princeton University Press, 1997), and Ronald Inglehart and Wayne E. Baker, "Modernization, Cultural Change, and the Persistence of Traditional Values," *American Sociological Review* 65 (February 2000): 19–51.

22. Alejandro Moreno, "Party Competition and the Issue of Democracy: Ideological Space in Mexican Elections," in Mónica Serrano (ed.), *Governing Mexico: Political Parties and Elections* (Macmillan-ILAS Series, Institute of Latin American Studies, University of London, 1998) and "Ideología y voto: Dimensiones de competencia política en México en los noventa," *Política y Gobierno* 1 (1999a): 45–81.

23. Moreno, 1999a.

24. The model is based on a multinomial logit regression that uses vote choice as the dependent variable and a number of independent variables that have been of theoretical and empirical relevance in the literature of Mexican voting behavior. The model is then applied to the different types of survey data (exit polls and pre-election polls). The vote for PAN or Fox is taken as a basis for comparison in the results shown in the tables. See for example Domínguez and McCann 1995; Magaloni 1997; Buendía 1997; Magaloni and Moreno, 2003.

25. Beatriz Magaloni and Alejandro Poiré, "Sincere and Strategic Party Switching in the course of the Presidential Campaign," in Jorge I. Domínguez and Chappell Lawson (eds.), *Mexico's Pivotal Democratic Election: Campaigns, Voting Behavior, and the 2000 Presidential Race* (Stanford: Stanford University Press, 2004).

26. The official vote for Congress in 2000 is not broken down by party in the case of the Alliance for Mexico (PRD) and the Alliance for Change (PAN), but opinion polls showed that support for the Green party alone was about 2 to 4 percent.

27. Beatriz Magaloni and Alejandro Poiré, "Sincere and Strategic Party Switching in the course of the Presidential Campaign," in Jorge I. Domínguez and Chappell Lawson (eds.), *Mexico's Pivotal Democratic Election: Campaigns, Voting Behavior, and the 2000 Presidential Race* (Stanford: Stanford University Press, 2004).

28. Alejandro Moreno, "The Effects of Negative Campaigns on Mexican Voters," in *Mexico's Pivotal Democratic Election*, ed. Domínguez and Chappell Lawson.

29. Alejandro Moreno and Roy Pierce, "The Impact of the PRI Primary of November 1999 on the Mexican Presidential Election of July 2000," unpublished manuscript.

30. Alejandro Moreno, "Mesa 1: Encuestas preelectorales, serie incluyendo últimas encuestas (Estimación de los votantes probables)," in *El papel de las encuestas en las elecciones federales: Memoria del taller Sumiya 2000*. Federal Elections Institute (IFE), Mexican Association of Research Agencies (AMAI), and Colegio Nacional de Actuarios, 2000, and Alejandro Moreno and Patricia Méndez, "Cómo llegó: La debacle y el triunfo". *Reforma*, December 1, 2001.

CHAPTER 3

1. James W. Ceaser and Andrew E. Busch, *The Perfect Tie* (Lanham, Md.: Rowman & Littlefield, 2001). See also John C. Green and

Rick Farmer, *The State of the Parties*, 4th ed. (Lanham, Md.: Rowman & Littlefield, 2003).

2. Larry J. Sabato, *Overtime* (New York: Longman, 2002).
3. Ibid.
4. John C. Green et al., "Murphy Brown Revisited: The Social Issues in the 1992 Election," in *Disciples and Democracy: Religious Conservatives and the Future of American Politics*, ed. Michael Cromartie, (Grand Rapids, Mich.: Eerdmans, 1994), 43–66.
5. These data were made available by the Interuniversity Consortium for Social and Political Research. All analysis and interpretation are solely the responsibility of the authors.
6. These data come from a poll by the Gallup Organization, May 18–May 21, 2000 (N=1,011). Data provided by the Roper Center for Public Opinion Research, University of Connecticut.
7. David K. Ryden, "Out of the Shadows, but Still in the Dark? The Courts and Political Parties," in *The State of the Parties*, ed. John C. Green and Rick Farmer, 4th ed. (Lanham, Md.: Rowman & Littlefield, 2003), 79–94.
8. Gerald M. Pomper, "Parliamentary Government in the United States: A New Regime for a New Country," in *The State of the Parties*, ed. John C. Green and Rick Farmer, 4th ed. (Lanham, Md.: Rowman & Littlefield, 2003), 267–86.

CHAPTER 4

1. The Canadian Election Study is based on a rolling cross-section survey of 3,651 interviews conducted by the Institute for Social Research at York University and Jolicoeur & Associés. It follows in the tradition of previous Canadian election studies conducted in 1979, 1984, 1988, 1993, and 1997.
2. Blais et al., *Anatomy of a Liberal Victory: Making Sense of the Vote in the 2000 Canadian Election* (Peterborough: Broadview Press, 2002), 13.

3. Mordecai Richler, "More Proof That Pundits Can't Be Trusted," *National Post*, December 2, 2000, A18.

4. Conrad Black, "The Most Boring Election in History." *Wall Street Journal*, November 30, 2000, A22.

5. Peter Gzowski, "Where Do They Stand? How Would We Know?" *Globe and Mail*, November 11, 2000, A13.

6. Statistics Canada. http://www.statcan.ca/.

7. Ibid.

8. Blais et al., *Anatomy*.

9. Samuel Popkin, *The Reasoning Voter: Communication and Presidential Campaigns* (Chicago: University of Chicago Press, 1991).

10. Shanto Iyengar and Donald Kinder, *News That Matters: Television and American Opinion* (Chicago: University of Chicago Press, 1987).

11. Thomas Nelson and Donald Kinder, "Issue Frames and Group Centrism in American Public Opinion," *Journal of Politics* 58, no. 4 (November 1996): 1055–78.

12. Doris Graber, *Processing the News: How People Tame the Information Tide* (New York: Longman, 1984).

13. Milton Lodge, Marco Steenbergen, and Shawn Brau, "The Responsive Voter: Campaign Information and the Dynamics of Candidate Evaluation," *American Political Science Review* 89, no. 2 (June 1995): 309–26.

14. Diana C. Mutz, "Effects of Horse-Race Coverage on Campaign Coffers: Strategic Contributing in Presidential Primaries," *Journal of Politics* 57, no. 4 (November 1995): 1015–42.

15. Blais et al., *Anatomy*, 35.

16. Blais et al., *Anatomy*, 73.

17. Barry Cooper, *Sins of Omission: Shaping the News at CBC TV* (Toronto: University of Toronto Press, 1994), chapter 1.

18. Blais et al., *Anatomy*, 40.

19. Ibid.

20. Thomas Hartley and Josephine Mazzuca, "Fewer Canadians

Favour Legalized Abortion under Any Circumstance," *The Gallup Poll* (Toronto: Gallup Canada, December 12, 2001).
21. Blais et al., *Anatomy*, 145.
22. Blais et al., *Anatomy*, 175.
23. Lydia Miljan and Barry Cooper, *Hidden Agendas: How Journalists Influence the News* (Vancouver: University of British Columbia Press, 2003) 92.
24. Reginald Bibby, *Fragmented Gods: The Poverty and Potential of Religion in Canada* (Toronto: Stodart Publishing, 1993).
25. Blais et al., *Anatomy*, 71.
26. Blais et al., *Anatomy*, 80 n. 12.

CHAPTER 5

1. A feat not accomplished since Mackenzie King had won three in a row in 1935, 1940, and 1945.
2. Robert A. Young, *The Struggle for Quebec* (Montreal and Kingston: McGill-Queen's University Press, 1999), 87.
3. Reginald Whitaker, *The Government Party* (Toronto: University of Toronto Press, 1977).
4. The referendum question asked voters whether they agreed "Quebec should become sovereign after having made a formal offer to Canada for a new economic and political partnership."
5. Voter turnout was an astonishing—by Canadian standards, at any rate—93.5 percent. See Québec, Directeur-général des élections, http://www.dgeq.qc.ca/information/.
6. The amendment of section 93 was not implemented until after the 1997 federal election, which returned the Liberals to power.
7. Formerly a political scientist at the Université de Montréal, Dion was elevated to the cabinet, along with Pierre Pettigrew, in January 1996. Dion, Allan Rock, and Marcel Massé were members of a special cabinet committee charged with elaborating a strat-

egy for dealing with the Quebec question in early 1996. See Young, *Struggle for Quebec*, 102.

8. Ibid.

9. A third question asked the Court whether international or Canadian law would have precedence in the event of a conflict between them. For more on the Supreme Court reference see Young, *The Struggle for Quebec*, 108–9, and David Schneiderman, ed., *The Quebec Decision* (Toronto: Lorimer, 1999).

10. In March 1997 Duceppe replaced Michel Gauthier as leader of the Bloc Québécois. Gauthier had succeeded Lucien Bouchard when the latter resigned in January 1996 to become leader of the Parti Québécois and premier of Quebec.

11. Thus the third question put before the Court, namely whether international or Canadian law would take precedence in the event of a conflict between them, was moot.

12. Supreme Court of Canada, *Reference Re the Secession of Quebec*, para. 138. The entire judgment is reprinted in Schneiderman, ed., *The Quebec Decision*, 14–71. The cited passage is on page 64.

13. *Reference Re Secession*, para. 151, in Schneiderman, ed., *The Quebec Decision*, 69.

14. *Reference Re Secession*, para. 153, in Schneiderman, ed., *The Quebec Decision*, 69–70.

15. Canada, House of Commons, 2d session, 36th Parliament, 48 Elizabeth II, 1999.

16. *Clarity Act*, s. 1(4)(b).

17. Bill C-20 does not spell out what exactly constitutes a "clear majority," stating only that the size of the majority, along with the percentage of eligible voters and other relevant matters, will be taken into account by the House of Commons. *Clarity Act*, s. 2(2).

18. Canada, House of Commons, 2d Session, 36th Parliament, Legislative Committee on Bill C-20, *Evidence*, February 23, 2000. Online at http://www.parl.gc.ca/InfoComDoc/36/2/CLAR/Meetings/Evidence/clarev08-e.htm.

19. In a survey conducted between May 1 and May 8, 2000, Ekos Research Associates, Inc., found that Joe Clark had fairly high levels of trust among voters, was better known and had more widely acceptable platform ideas than his Canadian Alliance counterparts (either Preston Manning or Stockwell Day), but that his positioning on the Clarity Bill was unpopular. The sample size was 3,530 and the margin of error +/- 1.6 percent, 19 times out of 20. See "The Political Landscape: Continued Liberal Dominance, Resurgent CA, Conservatives Fading." This and other surveys can be accessed in the Ekos archives available on the Web. http://www.ekos.ca/media.

20. Québec, Assemblée nationale, First session, 36th legislature, December 15, 1999.

21. *An Act Respecting the Exercise of the Fundamental Rights and Prerogatives of the Québec People and the Québec State*, ch. 1, art. 2 and 3 (emphasis added).

22. Ekos Research Associates, Inc., "Fin de siècle: Fin de la souveraineté? Quebeckers think the unthinkable," December 14, 1999. The sample consisted of 803 respondents in Quebec and 2204 Canadians outside Quebec. Margins of error were +/- 3.5 percent in Quebec and +/- 2.1 percent in the rest of the country, 19 times out of 20. The study is available online at the Ekos webpage (see note 19 above).

23. Tammy McNamee, "The Clarity Bill: Examining Liberal Party Hegemony in the Transitional Party System" (M.A. major research paper, Wilfrid Laurier University, 2000), 55. McNamee cites an editorial, "The Centre Stops Being Soft" in *The Economist*, December 18, 1999, which argues along similar lines.

24. Young, *Struggle for Quebec*, 91. As a result of the vote, Bouchard walked out of the convention and rumors spread that he was considering resigning as party leader. Bouchard stayed put, of course, and he gradually asserted control over the party apparatus (if not over the most militant advocates of independence, *les purs et*

durs): over 90 percent of delegates supported his leadership at the PQ convention in May 2000.

25. Ekos Research Associates, Inc., "The Quebec Political Landscape," March 5, 1999. Sample size was 1,006 in Quebec and 1871 in ROC.

26. Angus Reid Group, "Issues and Attitudes in a 1998 Post-Election Quebec," December 1, 1998. Sample size was 1,000 and the margin of error was +/- 3.1 percent, 19 times out of 20. The survey was accessed online at http://www.angusreid.com.

27. Bloc Québécois, *Le Québec gagne à voter Bloc* (Montreal, 2000; English version). Accessed online at ¡www.blocquebecois.org¡. Sovereignty is mentioned only once, at the beginning of the pamphlet, in an excerpt from the BQ's declaration of principles. The thrust of the document concerns the Bloc's role in defending Quebec's interests within the federal system and in holding the federal Liberals accountable, just as an opposition party should do. For an insightful analysis of the 2000 federal election campaign, and the relatively minor role played by the issue of sovereignty, see Stephen Clarkson, "The Liberal Threepeat: The Multi-System Party in the Multi-Party System," in *The Canadian General Election of 2000*, ed. Jon H. Pammett and Christopher Dornan. (Toronto: The Dundurn Group, 2001), 13–57.

28. Claire Durand, a sociologist at the Université de Montréal, argues that pollsters systematically underestimate Liberal support in Quebec, perhaps (though this is only speculative) because respondents in surveys are reluctant to admit to supporting the federalist party. In 2000, the underestimation of Liberal support, when all polls were averaged together, was approximately 4 percent. See Durand's paper, "Electoral Surveys in the 2000 Canadian Campaign: How Did They Really Fare?" http://www.fas.umontreal.ca/socio/durandc/menurecherche.htm, n.d.

29. André Bernard, "The Bloc Québécois," in Pammett and Dornan, *Canadian General Election of 2000*, 139–40.

30. The three defectors were André Harvey in Chicoutimi, David Price in Compton-Stanstead, and Diane St.-Jacques in Shefford.

31. In spite of this pronounced decline, Quebec still had the third-highest turnout among the provinces and territories in the 2000 election. Only Prince Edward Island (72.7 percent) and New Brunswick (67.7) registered higher turnout rates. I have calculated Quebec turnout rates from raw data supplied by Elections Canada. There is a very slight difference (one-tenth of one percent) between the figures for Quebec voter turnout reported in the *Official Voting Results* for the 37th General Election and those calculated from the raw data.

32. Bernard, "The Bloc Québécois," 141.

33. Édith Brochu and Louis Massicotte, "Élections fédérales de novembre: Coup de loupe sur un scrutin," *Le Devoir*, February 26, 2002, A7.

34. Don Macpherson, "The Evil of Two Lessers: Neither Liberals nor the Bloc Can Hold Heads High as Apathy Ruled in Quebec," *Montreal Gazette*, November 29, 2000.

35. Michaud made his remarks—inter alia, he claimed that Jews feel that they are the only people to have suffered in the history of humanity—in a radio interview in early December and repeated them in testimony before the Estates-General on the Situation and Future of the French Language in Quebec. I have written in greater detail about the Michaud Affair in "Sclerosis or a Clean Bill of Health? Diagnosing Quebec's Party System in the 21st Century," in *Quebec: State and Society*, ed. Alain-G. Gagnon, 3rd ed. (Peterborough, Ont: Broadview Press, 2004).

36. Québec, Premier ministre, "Allocution à l'occasion de la démission du premier ministre du Québec," January 11, 2001. Available at the website of the Association internationale des études québécoises. http://www.aieq.qc.ca/bouchard.htm.

37. This remark was actually made before Landry officially became leader of the PQ, in January 2001, at a party caucus meeting.

Landry's outburst was occasioned by the federal government's offer of an $18 million subsidy to the province for the renovation of the Aquarium de Québec. One of the strings attached to this money, however, was that the Canadian flag (the "bits of red rag" in question) be allowed to fly and bilingual signs be posted at the renovated site. This offer prompted Landry's crude metaphor.

38. The data on "Referendum Voting Intentions" are available at Léger Marketing's website, http://www.legermarketing.com/english/set.html. Sample size was generally close to 1,000, and the surveys were conducted approximately 10 or so times each year. The margin of error for a sample this size is +/-3.5 percent, 19 times out of 20.

39. Léger Marketing, "Opinions of Quebeckers toward Provincial Politics and More Particularly the ADQ," May 2002. http://www.legermarketing.com/english/set.html. Sample size was 1,001, with a margin of error of +/- 3.5 percent, 19 times out of 20.

40. Léger Marketing finds that the ADQ and the Quebec Liberals are running neck and neck, with 35 percent of voters saying that they would vote Liberal if a provincial election were to be held and 32 percent supporting the ADQ (the PQ stands at 26 percent). See "Opinions of Quebeckers Toward Provincial Politics," May 2002.

41. See Lisée's book, *Sortie de secours* (Montreal: Boréal, 2000). For commentary on the Lisée proposal, see Gordon Gibson, "Will Separatists Settle for a Half a Loaf?" *National Post*, January 18, 2001. Online at http://www.vigile.net/01-1/gibson.html. See also Alexander Panetta, "PQ Strongly Considers Referendum to Ask Ottawa for More Cash: Landry," *Montreal Gazette*, June 4, 2002.

42. Québec, Commission des États généraux sur la situation et l'avenir de la langue française au Québec, *Le français, une langue pour tout le monde* (Québec, 2001), 12 (my translation).

43. Shawn McCarthy, "Shut Down Campaign, PM Orders Martin," *Globe and Mail*, May 31, 2002, A1.

CHAPTER 6

1. Matthew Stevenson, "Canada's Other Brain Drain: The Continuing Exodus from Quebec," *Political Options/Options Politiques* (October 2000): 63–66, page 64, www.irpg.org/po/archive/oct00/stevenso.pdf.

2. Richard Rodriguez, *Brown: The Last Discovery of America* (New York: Viking, 2002) 94, 103, 105, and 108.

3. Rodriguez, *Brown*, 110.

4. "Carnaval Celebrants Grin and Bare It Despite S.F. Fog," *San Francisco Chronicle*, May 27, 2002, B1.

5. Robert E. Chenard, "Historical Perspective on Waterville's 19C Franco-Americans," http://members.mint.net/frenchcx/frcanwtv/htm.

6. Roger Roy, "An Analysis of the Assimilation of French-Canadian Language and Culture into American Language and Culture: How French-Canadian Became Franco-American and then Became Invisible" (Graduate research essay for EDU 690 Social Context of Higher Education, University of Maine).

7. Juliana L'Hereux, "North American French as an Academic Subject." www.happyones.com/franco-american/Julian/North-American-French.htm.

8. Ilan Stavans, "Spanglish: Tickling the Tongue," *World Literature Today* 74.3 (Summer 2000): 555.

9. "Tom, Tom and Julia . . . The Names Say It All," *Globe and Mail*, February 6, 2000, R2.

10. Neva Chonin, "Morissette Does Her Own Thing," *San Francisco Chronicle*, May 7, 2002, D3.

11. Neva Chonin, "Furtado in Control at Warfield," *San Francisco Chronicle*, February 16, 2002, D1.

12. Paula Martinac, *k.d. lang* (Philadelphia: Chelsea House, 1997), 89.

13. Quoted in David Bennahum, ed., *In her own words: k.d. lang* (New York: Omnibus, 1995), 18.

14. Bennahum, *In her own words*, 7.
15. "Celine's New Album," *Globe and Mail*. February 7, 2002, R2.
16. Tim Goodman, "Families, Frisco Formulas for Fall," *San Francisco Chronicle*, May 27, 2002, D1.
17. Jonathan Curiel, "Lack of TV Diversity Hit," *San Francisco Chronicle*, May 15, 2002, A2.
18. Mireya Navarro, "Hollywood's Dirty Little Broom Closet," *San Francisco Chronicle*, May 17, 2002, D13.
19. Rodriguez, *Brown*, 117.
20. Andrew Mollison, "Researchers Attack Bush's Education Reforms," *San Francisco Chronicle*, March 16, 2002, A4.
21. Ibid.
22. Mary Jordan, "Fewer Migrants Caught on Border," *San Francisco Chronicle*, May 24, 2002, A14.
23. "INS Unveils New Plan, Devices for Border," *San Francisco Chronicle*, May 24, 2002, A9.
24. Quoted in Mireya Navarro, "Hollywood's Dirty Little Broom Closet," *San Francisco Chronicle*, May 17, 2002, D13.
25. "More People Say That They're Just 'Americans,'" *San Francisco Chronicle*, June 8, 2002, A8.
26. Anthony Walton, rev. of *Brown: The Last Discovery of America* by Richard Rodriguez, *New York Times Book Review*, April 7, 2002, 7.
27. Rodriguez, *Brown*, xii.
28. Rodriguez, *Brown*, 164.

CHAPTER 7

1. Anthony DePalma, *Here: A Biography of the New American Continent* (New York: Public Affairs, 2001), 354.
2. Seymour M. Lipset, *Continental Divide: The Values and Institutions of the United States and Canada* (Washington, D.C.: Canadian-American Committee, 1989).
3. Seymour M. Lipset, *Revolution and Counterrevolution: Change and*

Persistence in Social Structures (New Brunswick, N.J.: Transaction Books, 1988).

4. James Laxer, *Discovering America: Travels in the Land of Guns, God, and Corporate Gurus* (New York: New Press, 2001). See also, Neil Nevitte, *The Decline of Deference: Canadian Value Change in Cross-National Perspective* (Peterborough, Ont.: Broadview Press, 1996).

5. For a fuller description of this analysis, see Stephen Brooks, "A Tale of Two Elections: What the Leaders' Rhetoric from the 2000 Election Tells Us about Can-Am Political Culture Differences" (paper delivered at the Biennial Meeting of the Canadian Studies in the United States, San Antonio, Tex., November 2001). Readers may also contact the author at brooks3@uwindsor.ca.

CHAPTER 8

1. Ray C. Fair, http://fairmodel.econ.yale.edu/. Randall L. Jones Jr., *Who Will Be in the White House: Predicting Presidential Elections* (New York: Longman, 2002), and James F. Campbell and James C. Garand, eds., *Before the Vote. Forecasting American Election Politics* (Thousand Oaks, Calif.: Sage Publications, 2000).

2. Jones, *Who Will Be in the White House*, chapters 8 and 9.

3. Fair, http://fairmodel.econ.yale.edu/.

4. Mark J. Kasoff and Christine Drennen, eds., *Canada: A Fractured Political Landscape*, Canadian Studies Center, Bowling Green State University, Bowling Green, Ohio, 1994.

5. Jones, *Who Will Be in the White House*, 79.

6. *National Post*, April 29, 2002.

7. *Globe and Mail*, April 29, 2002.

8. United Press International, September 10, 2001.

9. *National Post*, April 29, 2002.

10. Earl H. Fry and Jared Bybee, *NAFTA 2002: A Cost/Benefit Analy-*

sis for the United States, Canada and Mexico (Canadian-American Center, University of Maine, Orono, 2002).

11. Nick Schultz, "Canadian Energy Policy and Trade with the United States," in Kasoff and Drennen, 2003.

12. Michel Tremblay, "Hydro-Québec and TransÉnergie: Continuity in a Changing Environment," in Kasoff and Drennen, 2003.

13. *Wall Street Journal*, April 24, 2002.

14. *AuCanada*, "Bruising Battle over Tomatoes," Canadian Studies Center, Bowling Green State University, Bowling Green, Ohio, 2002.

15. *National Post*, April 29, 2002.

16. *Globe and Mail*, May 22, 2002.

17. *Globe and Mail*, April 25, 2002; Federal Reserve Bank of Cleveland, *Economic Trends*, May 2002.

18. *Globe and Mail*, March 6, 2002.

CHAPTER 9

1. Jorge Castañeda, "El nuevo activismo internacional mexicano," *Reforma*, September 23, 2001a, Section Enfoque 15–17; "Los ejes de la política exterior," *Nexos* 23 no. 288 (December 2001b) 66–74; and "El factor externo y consolidación de la democracia en México," *Reforma*, February 24, 2002, 10A.

2. For Castañeda's critical view on U.S.-Mexican relations before becoming minister of foreign affairs, see Castañeda, 1996.

3. Robert Pastor has made an effort to articulate a greater post-NAFTA vision for North America. He advocates institutional deepening, among other things, in order to deal with continental problems that hitherto were handled under national or bilateral agendas. However, Pastor's position does not represent the official positions of any NAFTA members. See Robert Pastor, *Toward a North American Community* (Washington, D.C.: Institute for International Economics, 2001).

4. For a comprehensive view of migratory problems between Mexico and the U.S. see SRE, 1997.
5. George Bush, *The Department of Homeland Security*, www.whitehouse.gov/homeland/, 2002a.
6. *"Estrategia nacional para la seguridad del territorio nacional. Resumen ejecutivo,"* Office of the Press Secretary, www.whitehouse.gov/news/releases/2002/07/200207-16.es.html. 2002; and George Bush, *"Securing the Homeland and Strengthening the Nation,"* www.whitehouse. gov/homeland/, 2002b.
7. Eduardo Sojo, et al., "Sociedad para la Prosperidad: Reporte a los Presidentes Vicente Fox y George Bush," Monterrey, Mexico, March 22, 2002, electronic copy.
8. A declaration was released from a top official of that ministry, suggesting that Mexico was considering bringing the case before the Inter-American Human Rights Commission, but eventually did not.
9. Mr. Castañeda's most recent address before the General Assembly of the United Nations, condemning any unilateral action against Iraq in the global war against terrorism, suggests that Mexico is heading in that direction. See *Reforma*, September 14, 2002.

CHAPTER 10

1. Alvaro Artiga, *La Política y los Sistemas de Partidos en Centroamérica*, (San Salvador: 2000).
2. Manuel Orozco, *International Norms and Mobilization of Democracy*, (London: Ashgate, 2002).
3. Graeme Gill, *The Dynamics of Democratization: Elites, Civil Society and the Transition Process* (New York: St Martin's Press, 2000).
4. "Alemán llama a Ortega a concertar pacto de gobernabilidad en Nicaragua," *La Prensa* (Honduras), November 23, 1996, http://www.laprensahn.com/caarc/9611/c23002.htm.

5. Both had resigned from their positions; their continuation was not desired by the new members. Moreover, they were not interested in supporting the new establishment.

6. "Desconfianza impera en el ámbito pre-electoral" *Inforpress Centroamericana*, July 28, 2000.

7. The extent of corruption in Aleman's government is the subject of another paper. However, suffice it to say that in 1999 the comptroller had identified a number of anomalies and abuses of government resources on behalf of the president. The most public case was the use of resources to build infrastructure at the president's farm, La Chilamapa, the construction of a special road leading to the president's home, and a number of contracts. His wealth was estimated to have increased by millions of dollars. *Confidencial* (Managua) 5, no. 206, August 27–September 2, 2000.

8. "A Society Scandalized," *Envio* (June 2000).

9. "The Air is Thick with Electoral Fraud," *Envio* (July 2000).

10. "Indeciso proceso electoral en marcha," *Inforpress Centroamericana* (Guatemala), April 28, 2000.

11. "Entre Partidos te veas: candente ambiente pre electoral" *Inforpress Centroamericana* (Guatemala), August 18, 2000.

12. "Renuncia evidencia lucha por el poder" *Inforpress Centroamericana* (Guatemala), May 26, 2000.

13. "Contraloría va contra Solórzano," *La Prensa* (Managua), October 11, 2000.

14. Consuelo Sandoval and Nidia Ruiz López, "Solórzano sorprende a políticos," *La Prensa* (Managua), March 17, 2001.

15. "No tengo la alternativa ideal," *Confidencial* (Managua) 5, no. 206, August 27–September 2, 2000. In late March 2001 Daniel Ortega announced the endorsement of Jarquín and the alliance with the Christian Way.

16. "Presidente Alemán admite desgaste," *La Prensa* (Managua), October 19, 2000.

17. "Renuncian candidatos conservadores," *La Prensa*, July 17, 2001.

18. A poll showed that Ortega had the lead in the election with 31 percent. Shortly after this poll, he endorsed the alliance with the Christian Way. "Encuesta nacional de CINCO: Ningún ganador a la vista," *Confidencial*, 233, March 18–24, 2001.

19. "Milagro Electoral de Enrique Bolaños," interview with Victor Borge (Borge y Asociados) by Adolfo Pastran, August 9, 2001.

20. John Peeler, *Building Democracy in Latin America* (Boulder: Lynn Reiner, 1998), 174.

21. Edelberto Torres Rivas, *Costa Rica crisis y desafíos* (San José: Departamento Ecuménico de Investigaciones [DEI], 1987).

22. Eliana Franco and Carlos Sojo, *Gobierno, Empresarios y políticas de adjuste* (San José: FLACSO, 1992).

23. "Pactos, descrédito, inestabilidad" *La Nación* (San José) 1995.

24. "Modelo económico impulsa crecimiento con pobreza," *Inforpress Centroamericana*, December 1, 2000.

25. Araya joined the party very young, was president of the youth movement, legislator, minister, and president of the party.

26. "Complicado panorama para elecciones," *Inforpress Centroamericana* (Guatemala) June 22, 2001.

27. INCEP, *Reporte Político/Panorama Centroamericano No. 171: Llegaron las internas partidarias para designación de candidatos*, Guatemala, June 2001, 5.

28. *Inforpress*, June 2001.

29. IDESPO, *La población costarricense del gran area metropolitana frente a su participación ciudadana y sus valores políticos*, Heredia: IDESPO, May 23, 2001.

30. Juan Manuel Villasuso, Jenny Díaz, and Laura Chinchilla, *Gobernabilidad democrática y seguridad ciudadana: El Caso de Costa Rica* (Managua: CRIES, 2000).

31. Florisabel Rodríguez (Director of Procesos), interview by author, March 22, 2002.

32. Jorge Rovira Mas, *La democracia de Costa Rica ante el siglo XXI*, San José: FLACSO, 2000.

33. Carlos Sojo (director of FLASCO), interview by author, San José, Costa Rica, March 21, 2000.

34. Cecilia Cortes (Director of Funpadem), interview by author, San José, Costa Rica, March 23, 2002.

35. Rodríguez interview.

36. "Liberales aceptan inscribir a Maduro," *Inforpress Centroamericana* (Honduras), March 2, 2001.

Bibliography

"Alemán llama a Ortega a concertar pacto do governabilidad en Nicaragua," *La Prensa* (Honduras), November 23, 1996. http://www.laprensahn.com/caarc/9611/c23002.htm.

Angus Reid Group, "Issues and Attitudes in a 1998 Post-Election Quebec." http://www.angusreid.com, December 1, 1998.

Artiga, Alvaro. *La Politica y los Sistemas de Partidos en Centroamérica.* Funda Ungo, San Salvador: 2000.

"A Society Scandalized," *Envio* (Managua), June 2000.

AuCanada. "Bruising Battle Over Tomatoes." Bowling Green, Ohio: Canadian Studies Center, Bowling Green State University, 2002.

Bennahum, David, ed. *In her own words: k.d. lang.* New York: Omnibus, 1995.

Bernard, André. "The Bloc Québécois." In *The Canadian General Election of 2000,* ed. Jon H. Pammett and Christopher Dornan, 139–48. Toronto: The Dundurn Group, 2001.

Bibby, Reginald. *Fragmented Gods: The Poverty and Potential of Religion in Canada.* Toronto: Stodart Publishing, 1993.

Black, Conrad. "The Most Boring Election in History." *Wall Street Journal,* November 30, 2000, A22.

Blais, André, et al. *Anatomy of a Liberal Victory: Making Sense of the Vote in the 2000 Canadian Election.* Peterborough: Broadview Press, 2002.

Bloc Québécois. "Le Québec gagne à voter Bloc." http://www.blocquebecois.org (English version).

Brochu, Édith, and Louis Massicotte. "Élections fédérales de novembre: Coup de loupe sur un scrutin." *Le Devoir,* February 26, 2002, A7.

Brooks, Stephen. "A Tale of Two Elections: What the Leaders' Rhetoric from the 2000 Election Tells Us about Can-Am Political Culture Differences." Paper delivered at the Biennial Meeting of the Canadian Studies in the United States, San Antonio, Tex. November 2001.

Buendía, Jorge. "Incertidumbre y comportamiento electoral en la transición democrática: La elección mexicana de 1988." *Política y Gobierno* VII, no. 2 (1997): 317–52.

Bush, George W. *The Department of Homeland Security*, www.white house.gov/homeland/, 2002a.

_____. *Securing the Homeland and Strengthening the Nation*, www.whitehouse.gov/homeland/, 2002b.

Campbell, James E., and James C. Garand, eds. *Before the Vote: Forecasting American Election Politics*. Thousand Oaks, Calif.: Sage Publications, 2000.

Canada, Chief Electoral Officer. *Official Voting Results*. Thirty-sixth General Election 1997.

_____. *Official Voting Results*. Thirty-seventh General Election 2000.

Canada, House of Commons. *An Act to Give Effect to the Requirement for Clarity as Set Out in the Opinion of the Supreme Court of Canada in the Quebec Secession Reference*. 36th Parliament, 2nd session, 48 Elizabeth II, December 13, 1999.

Canada, House of Commons, Legislative Committee on Bill C-20, *Evidence*, 36th Parliament, 2nd Session, February 23, 2000. http:// www.parl.gc.ca/InfoComDoc/36/2/CLAR/ Meetings/Evidence/ clarev08-e.htm.

"Carnaval Celebrants Grin and Bare it Despite S.F. Fog," *San Francisco Chronicle*, May 27, 2002, B1.

Castañeda, Jorge. "El nuevo activismo internacional mexicano," *Reforma*, September 23, 2001a, Section Enfoque, pp. 15–17.

_____. "Los ejes de la política exterior," *Nexos* 23, no. 288 (December 2001b): 66–74.

_____. "El factor externo y consolidación de la democracia en México," *Reforma*, February 24, 2002, p: 10A.

_____. "Mexico's Circle of Misery." *Foreign Affairs* (July–August 1996): 92–105.

Ceaser, James W., and Andrew E. Busch. *The Perfect Tie.* Lanham, Md.: Rowman & Littlefield, 2001.

"Celine's New Album." *Globe and Mail.* February 7, 2002, R2.

Chenard, Robert E. "Historical Perspective on Waterville's 19C Franco-Americans." http://members.mint.net/frenchcx/frcanwtv/htm.

Chonin, Neva. "Furtado in Control at Warfield." *San Francisco Chronicle,* February 16, 2002, D1.

_____. "Morissette Does Her Own Thing." *San Francisco Chronicle,* May 7, 2002, D3.

Clarke, Harold. *A Polity on the Edge.* Peterborough, Ont.: Broadview Press, 2000.

Clarkson, Stephen. "The Liberal Threepeat: The Multi-System Party in the Multi-Party System." In *The Canadian General Election of 2000,* ed. Jon H. Pammett and Christopher Dornan, 13–57. Toronto: The Dundurn Group, 2001.

"Complicado panorama para elecciones." *Inforpress Centroamericana* (Guatemala), June 22, 2001.

"Contraloría va contra Solórzano." *La Prensa* (Managua), October 11, 2000.

Cooper, Barry. *Sins of Omission: Shaping the News at CBC TV.* Toronto: University of Toronto Press, 1994.

Curiel, Jonathan. "Lack of TV Diversity Hit." *San Francisco Chronicle,* May 15, 2002, A2.

DePalma, Anthony. *Here: A Biography of the New American Continent.* New York: Public Affairs, 2001.

"Desconfianza impera en el ámbito pre-electoral." *Inforpress Centroamericana,* July 28, 2000.

Domínguez, Jorge I., and James A. McCann. "Shaping Mexico's Electoral Arena: Construction of Partisan Cleavages in the 1988 and 1991 National Elections." *American Political Science Review* 89, no. 1 (1995): 34–48.

Durand, Claire. "Electoral Surveys in the 2000 Canadian Campaign: How Did They Really Fare?" http://www.fas.umontreal.ca/socio/durandc/menurecherche.htm.

Ekos Research Associates, Inc. "Fin de siècle: fin de la souveraineté? Quebeckers Think the Unthinkable." http://www.ekos.ca/media. December 14, 1999.

————. "The Political Landscape: Continued Liberal Dominance, Resurgent CA, Conservatives Fading." http://www.ekos.ca/media. May 8, 2000.

————. "The Quebec Political Landscape." http://www.ekos.ca/media. March 5, 1999.

"Encuesta nacional de CINCO: Ningún ganador a la vista," Confidencial, March 18–24, 2001.

"Entre Partidos te veas: Candente ambiente pre electoral." Inforpress Centroamericana (Guatemala), August 18, 2000.

Fair, Ray C. http://fairmodel.econ.yale.edu/. 2002.

Federal Reserve Bank of Cleveland. Economic Trends, May 2002.

Franco, Eliana and Carlos Sojo. Gobierno, empresarios y políticas de adjuste. San José: FLASCO. 1992.

Fry, Earl H., and Jared Bybee. NAFTA 2002: A Cost/Benefit Analysis for the United States, Canada and Mexico. Orono: Canadian-American Center, University of Maine, 2002.

Gibson, Gordon. "Will Separatists Settle for a Half a Loaf?" National Post. http://www.vigile.net/01-1/gibson.html. January 18, 2001.

Gill, Graeme. The Dynamics of Democratization: Elites, Civil Society and the Transition Process. New York: St. Martin's Press, 2000.

Goodman, Tim. "Families, Frisco Formulas for Fall." San Francisco Chronicle, May 27, 2002, D1+.

Graber, Doris. Processing the News: How People Tame the Information Tide. New York: Longman, 1984.

Green, John C., and Rick Farmer. The State of the Parties. 4th ed. Lanham, Md.: Rowman & Littlefield, 2003.

Green, John C., et al. "Murphy Brown Revisited: The Social Issues in the 1992 Election." In Disciples and Democracy: Religious Conservatives and the Future of American Politics, ed. Michael Cromartie, 43–66. Grand Rapids, Mich.: Eerdmans, 1994.

Gzowski, Peter. "Where Do They Stand? How Would We Know?" *Globe and Mail*, November 11, 2000, A13.

Hartley, Thomas, and Josephine Mazzuca. "Fewer Canadians Favour Legalized Abortion under Any Circumstance." *Gallup Poll*. Toronto: Gallup Canada. December 12, 2001.

IDESPO. *La población costarricense del gran area metropolitiana frente a su participación ciudadana y sus valores políticos*. Heredia: IDESPO. May 23, 2001.

INCEP. *Reporte Político/Panorama Centroamericana No. 171: Llegaron las internas partidarias para designación de candidatos*. Guatemala: June 2001.

"Indeciso proceso electoral en marcha." *Inforpress Centroamericana* (Guatemala), April 28, 2000.

Inglehart, Ronald. *Modernization and Postmodernization: Cultural, Economic, and Political Change in 43 Societies*. Princeton: Princeton University Press, 1997.

Inglehart, Ronald, and Wayne E. Baker. "Modernization, Cultural Change, and the Persistence of Traditional Values." *American Sociological Review* 65 (February 2000): 19–51.

"INS Unveils New Plan, Devices for Border," *San Francisco Chronicle*, May 24, 2002, A9.

Iyengar, Shanto, and Donald Kinder. *News That Matters: Television and American Opinion*. Chicago: University of Chicago Press, 1987.

Jones, Randall L., Jr. *Who Will Be in the White House: Predicting Presidential Elections*. New York: Longman, 2002.

Jordan, Mary. "Fewer Migrants Caught on Border." *San Francisco Chronicle*, May 24, 2002, A14.

Kasoff, Mark J., and Christine Drennen, eds. *Canada: A Fractured Political Landscape*. Bowling Green, Ohio: Canadian Studies Center, Bowling Green State University, 1994.

Kitschelt, Herbert. *The Radical Right in Western Europe*. Ann Arbor: University of Michigan Press, 1995.

Kitschelt, Herbert, et al. *Post-Communist Party Systems: Competition, Representation, and Inter-Party Cooperation*. Cambridge: Cambridge University Press, 1999.

Krauze, Enrique. *La Presidencia Imperial: Ascenso y Caída del Sistema Político Mexicano, 1940–1996*. Mexico City: Tusquets Editores, 1997.

L'Hereux, Juliana. "North American French as an Academic Subject." www.happyones.com/franco-american/Julian/North-American-French.htm.

Laxer, James. *Discovering America: Travels in the Land of Guns, God, and Corporate Gurus*. New York: New Press, 2001.

Léger Marketing. "Opinions of Quebeckers toward Provincial Politics and More Particularly the ADQ." May 2002. http://www.leger marketing.com/english/set.html.

_____. "Referendum Voting Intentions." June 2, 2002. http://www.legermarketing.com/english/set.html.

Lehr, Volker G. "Modernización y movilización electoral, 1964–1976: Un estudio ecológico." *Estudios Políticos* 4, no. 1 (1985): 54–61.

"Liberales aceptan inscribir a Maduro." *Inforpress Centroamericana* (Honduras), March 2, 2001.

Lipset, Seymour M. *Revolution and Counterrevolution: Change and Persistence in Social Structures*. New Brunswick, N.J.: Transaction Books, 1988.

_____. *Continental Divide: The Values and Institutions of the United States and Canada*. Washington, D.C.: Canadian-American Committee, 1989.

Lisée, Jean-François. *Sortie de secours*. Montreal: Boréal, 2000.

Lodge, Milton, Marco Steenbergen, and Shawn Brau. "The Responsive Voter: Campaign Information and the Dynamics of Candidate Evaluation." *American Political Science Review* 89, no. 2 (June 1995): 309–26.

Macpherson, Don. "The Evil of Two Lessers: Neither Liberals nor the Bloc Can Hold Heads High as Apathy Ruled in Quebec." *Montreal Gazette*, November 29, 2000.

Magaloni, Beatriz. "From Hegemony to Multipartism: Issue-Voting and the Emergence of Partisan Cleavages in Mexico." Working Paper 2000–03, Department of Political Science, ITAM, 1997.

Magaloni, Beatriz, and Alejandro Moreno. "Catching All Souls: Mexico's Partido Acción Nacional." In *Christian Democracy in Latin America: Electoral Competition and Regime Conflicts*. Scott Mainwaring and Timothy Scully eds., Stanford: Stanford University Press, 2003.

Magaloni, Beatriz, and Alejandro Poiré. "Sincere and Strategic Party Switching in the Course of the Presidential Campaign." In *Mexico's Pivotal Democratic Election: Campaigns, Voting Behavior, and the 2000 Presidential Race*, ed. Jorge I. Domínguez and Chappell Lawson. Stanford: Stanford University Press, 2004.

Martinac, Paula. *k.d. lang*. Philadelphia: Chelsea House, 1997.

Mas, Jorge Rovira. *La democracia de Costa Rica ante el siglo XXI*. San José: FLASCO, 2000.

McCarthy, Shawn. "Shut down Campaign, PM Orders Martin." *Globe and Mail*, May 31, 2002, A1.

McNamee, Tammy. "The Clarity Bill: Examining Liberal Party Hegemony in the Transitional Party System." M.A. Major Research Paper, Wilfrid Laurier University, 2000.

"Milagro Electoral de Enrique Bolaños." Interview with Victor Borge (Borge & Asociados) by Adolfo Pastran. August 9, 2001.

Miljan, Lydia, and Barry Cooper. *Hidden Agendas: How Journalists Influence the News*. Vancouver: University of British Columbia Press, 2003.

"Modelo económico impulsa crecimiento con pobreza." *Inforpress Centroamericana*, December 1, 2000.

Molinar Horcasitas, Juan. *Èl tiempo de la legitimidad: Elecciones, autoritarismo y democracia en México*. Mexico City: Cal y Arena, 1991.

Mollison, Andrew. "Researchers Attack Bush's Education Reforms." *San Francisco Chronicle*, March 16, 2002, A4.

"More People Say That They're Just 'Americans.'" *San Francisco Chronicle*, June 8, 2002, A8.

Moreno, Alejandro. "Party Competition and the Issue of Democracy: Ideological Space in Mexican Elections." In *Governing Mexico: Political Parties and Elections, Macmillan-ILAS Series, Institute of Latin American Studies*, ed. Mónìca Serrano. University of London, 1998.

_____. "Ideología y voto: Dimensiones de competencia política en México en los noventa." *Política y Gobierno* 6, no. 1 (1999): 45–81.

_____. *Political Cleavages: Issues, Parties, and the Consolidation of Democracy*. Series on Latin America in Global Perspective, Boulder, Co.: Westview Press, 1999.

_____. "Mesa 1: Encuestas preelectorales, serie incluyendo últimas encuestas (Estimación de los votantes probables)." In *El Papel de las encuestas en las elecciones federales: Memoria del taller Sumiya 2000*. Federal Elections Institute (IFE), Mexican Association of Research Agencies (AMAI), and Colegio Nacional de Actuarios, 2000.

_____. "The Effects of Negative Campaigns on Mexican Voters." In *Mexico's Pivotal Democratic Election: Campaigns, Voting Behavior, and the 2000 Presidential Race*, Jorge I. Domínguez and Chappell Lawson, ed. Stanford: Stanford University Press, 2004.

Moreno, Alejandro, and Patricia Méndez. "Cómo llegó: La debacle y el triunfo." *Reforma*, December 1, 2001.

Moreno, Alejandro, and Roy Pierce. "The impact of the PRI Primary of November 1999 on the Mexican Presidential Election of July 2000." Unpublished manuscript.

Mutz, Diana, C. "Effects of Horse-Race Coverage on Campaign Coffers: Strategic Contributing in Presidential Primaries." *Journal of Politics* 57, no. 4 (November 1995): 1015–42.

National Post. April 29, 2002; May 5, 2002.

Navarro, Mireya. "Hollywood's Dirty Little Broom Closet." *San Francisco Chronicle*. May 17, 2002, D13.

Nelson, Thomas, and Donald Kinder. "Issue Frames and Group Centrism in American Public Opinion." *Journal of Politics* 58, no. 4 (November 1996): 1055–78.

Nevitte, Neil. *The Decline of Deference: Canadian Value Change in Cross-National Perspective*. Peterborough, Ont.: Broadview Press. 1996.

"No tengo la alternativa ideal." *Confidencial* (Managua) 5, no. 206, August 27–September 2, 2000.

Orozco, Manuel. *International Norms and Mobilization of Democracy*. London: Ashgate. 2002.

"Pactos, descrédito, inestabilidad," *La Nación* (San José), 1995.

Panetta, Alexander. "PQ Strongly Considers Referendum to Ask Ottawa for More Cash: Landry." *Montreal Gazette*, June 4, 2002.

Pastor, Robert. *Toward a North American Community*. Washington, D.C.: Institute for International Economics, 2001.

Peeler, John. *Building Democracy in Latin America*. Boulder, Co.: Lynn Reiner, 1998.

Pomper, Gerald M. "Parliamentary Government in the United States: A New Regime for a New Country." In *The State of the Parties*, ed. John C. Green and Rick Farmer. 4th ed. Lanham, Md.: Rowman & Littlefield, 2003.

Popkin, Samuel. *The Reasoning Voter: Communication and Presidential Campaigns*. Chicago: University of Chicago Press, 1991.

"Presidente Alemán admite desgaste," *La Prensa* (Managua), October 19, 2000.

Québec, Assemblée Nationale. *An Act Respecting the Exercise of the Fundamental Rights and Prerogatives of the Québec People and the Québec State*. 36th legislature, first session, December 15, 1999.

———. Commission des États généraux sur la situation et l'avenir de la langue française au Québec. *Le français, une langue pour tout le monde*. Québec, 2001.

———. Premier ministre. "Allocution à l'occasion de la démission du premier ministre du Québec," January 11, 2001. Available at the website of the *Association internationale des études québécoises*. http://www.aieq.qc.ca/bouchard.htm.

"Renuncian candidates conservadores," *La Prensa*, July 17, 2001.

"Renuncia evidencia lucha por el poder." *Inforpress Centroamericana* (Guatemala), May 26, 2000.

Richler, Mordecai. "More Proof That Pundits Can't Be Trusted." *National Post*, December 2, 2000, A18.

Rodriguez, Richard. *Brown: The Last Discovery of America*. New York: Viking, 2002.

Roy, Roger. "An Analysis of the Assimilation of French-Canadian Language and Culture into American Language and Culture: How French-Canadian Became Franco-American and then Became Invisible." Graduate research essay for EDU 690 Social Context of Higher Education, University of Maine.

Ryden, David K. "Out of the Shadows, but Still in the Dark? The Courts and Political Parties." In *The State of the Parties*, ed. John C. Green and Rick Farmer. 4th ed. Lanham, Md.: Rowman & Littlefield, 2003, 79–94.

Sabato, Larry J. *Overtime*. New York: Longman, 2002.

Sandoval, Consuelo and Nidia Ruiz López. "Solórzano sorprende a politicos." *La Prensa* (Managua), March 17, 2001.

Schneiderman, David, ed. *The Quebec Decision*. Toronto: Lorimer, 1999.

Schultz, Nick. "Canadian Energy Policy and Trade with the United States." In Kasoff and Drennen, 2003.

Secretaría de Relaciones Exteriores (SRE). *Estudio binacional México-Estados Unidos sobre migración*. México, D.F., 1997.

Serrano, Mónica, ed. *Governing Mexico: Political Parties and Elections* Macmillan-ILAS Series, Institute of Latin American Studies. University of London, England, 1998.

Sojo, Eduardo, et al. "Sociedad para la Prosperidad. Reporte a los Presidentes Vicente Fox y George Bush." Monterrey, Mexico, March 22. Electronic copy, 2002.

Statistics Canada. http://www.statcan.ca/.

———. *Television Viewing Fall 2000. The Daily*. Statistics Canada. October 23, 2001.

Stavans, Ilan. "Spanglish: Tickling the Tongue." *World Literature Today* 74, no. 3 (Summer 2000): 555.

Stevenson, Matthew. "Canada's Other Brain Drain: The Continuing Exodus from Quebec." *Political Options/Options Politiques*. October 2000: 63–66. www.irpg.org/po/archive/oct00/stevenso.pdf.

Tanguay, A. Brian. "Sclerosis or a Clean Bill of Health? Diagnosing Quebec's Party System in the 21st Century." In *Quebec: State and Society*, ed. Alain-G. Gagnon. 3rd ed. Peterborough, Ont.: Broadview Press, 2004.

"The Air is Thick with Electoral Fraud," *Envio*. Managua: July 2000.

"Tom, Tom and Julia . . . The Names Say It All," *Globe and Mail*. February 6, 2002, R2.

Toronto Globe and Mail. March 6, 2002; April 25, 2002; April 29, 2002; May 22, 2002.

Torres Rivas, Edelberto. *Costa Rica crisis y desafios*. San José: Departamento Ecuménico de Investigaciones (DEI), 1987.

Tremblay, Michel. "Hydro-Québec and TransÉnergie: Continuity in a Changing Environment." In *Canada: A Fractured Political Landscape*, ed. Mark J. Kasoff and Christine Drennen. Bowling Green, Ohio: Canadian Studies Center, Bowling Green State University, 1994.

United Press International. September 10, 2001.

Villasuso, Juan Manuel, Jenny Díaz, and Laura Chinchilla. *Gobernabilidad democrática y seguiridad ciudadana: El Caso de Costa Rica*. Managua: CRIES, 2000.

Wall Street Journal. April 24, 2002.

Walton, Anthony. Review of *Brown: The Last Discovery of America* by Richard Rodriguez, *New York Times Book Review*, April 7, 2002, 7.

Whitaker, Reginald. *The Government Party*. Toronto: University of Toronto Press, 1977.

White House. Office of the Press Secretary. *Estrategia nacional para la seguridad del territorio nacional. Resumen ejecutivo.* www.white house.gov/news/releases/2002/07/200207-16 es.html, July 16, 2002.

Young, Robert A. *The Struggle for Quebec*. Montreal: McGill-Queen's University Press, 1999.

About the Contributors

Carol L. Beran is professor of English at Saint Mary's College of California. She has published essays on works by many Canadian writers, including Margaret Atwood, Robert Kroetsch, Hugh MacLennan, Alice Munro, Michael Ondaatje, and Aritha Van Herk. Her book *Living over the Abyss* is about Atwood's *Life before Man*.

Stephen Brooks is professor in the department of political science at the University of Windsor and visiting professor in the department of political science at the University of Michigan. His most recent books include *Canadian Democracy* (4th ed.) and *As Others See Us: The Causes and Consequences of Global Perceptions of America*.

Anthony DePalma was bureau chief and correspondent for the *New York Times* in Mexico City and Toronto. He continues to cover the three nations of North America as international business correspondent for the *Times*.

Rick Farmer is director of committee staff at the Oklahoma House of Representatives. He has written and taught about campaigns and elections, political parties, and term limits.

José Luis Garcia-Aguilar is associate professor of international relations in the department of international relations, Universidad de las Americas-Puebla, where he is currently chair. Professor Garcia teaches courses on Canada, American foreign policy, and theories of international relations. He also often comments on several networks about international issues.

John C. Green is the director of the Ray C. Bliss Institute of Applied Politics at the University of Akron, as well as a professor of political science. He has done and written extensive research on American religion and politics, political parties, and campaign finance.

Mark J. Kasoff is director of Canadian studies and professor of economics at Bowling Green State University. His research interests include Canadian direct investment in the United States, Canada-U.S. trade flows and NAFTA, and comparative business costs between Canada and the United States.

Mary K. Kirtz is professor emerita of English and director of Canadian studies at the University of Akron. She has served on the executive council of the Association of Canadian Studies in the United States and as president of the Midwest Association of Canadian Studies. She is an associate editor of the *American Review of Canadian Studies*, has published widely on contemporary Canadian literature and culture, and received the Rufus Z. Smith Prize for an article on Marion Engels. Her most recent work appears in the essay collection, Margaret Atwood's *Textual Assassinations*.

Lydia Miljan is assistant professor of political science at the University of Windsor and director of the National Media Archive at the Fraser Institute. Her analysis of issues ranges from free trade to privatization, from health care to women's issues, and from elections to referendum campaigns.

Isidro Morales is dean of the School of Social Sciences at the Universidad de las Americas-Puebla, in Mexico. He has co-authored two books and published several articles dealing mainly with integration and trade-related topics.

Alejandro Moreno is professor of political science at the Instituto Tecnológico Autónomo de México, ITAM, and head of the department of survey research at *La Reforma*, both in Mexico City. He is the author of *Political Cleavages: Issues, Parties, and the Consolidation of Democracy* (1999), and co-author of *Human Values and Beliefs: A Cross-Cultural Source-Book* (1998).

Manuel Orozco is senior researcher at the Institute for the Study of International Migration at Georgetown University in Washington, D.C.

A. Brian Tanguay is an associate professor in the department of political science at Wilfrid Laurier University. His main areas of interest are Quebec politics, Ontario politics, political parties, and interest groups and social movements. He is the co-editor of two books, *Canadian Parties in Transition* and *Democracy with Justice*.

Index